Kaius Tuori

Ancient Roman Lawyers
and Modern Legal Ideals

Studies on the impact of contemporary concerns
in the interpretation of ancient Roman legal history

Studien zur
europäischen Rechtsgeschichte

Veröffentlichungen des
Max-Planck-Instituts
für europäische Rechtsgeschichte
Frankfurt am Main

Band 220

Vittorio Klostermann
Frankfurt am Main
2007

Kaius Tuori

Ancient Roman Lawyers and Modern Legal Ideals

Studies on the impact of contemporary concerns in the interpretation of ancient Roman legal history

Vittorio Klostermann
Frankfurt am Main
2007

Bibliographische Information der Deutschen Nationalbibliothek
Die Deutsche Nationalbibliothek verzeichnet diese Publikation in der
Deutschen Nationalbibliographie; detaillierte bibliographische Daten
sind im Internet über *http://dnb.d-nb.de* abrufbar.

© Vittorio Klostermann GmbH
Frankfurt am Main 2007

Alle Rechte vorbehalten, insbesondere die des Nachdrucks und der
Übersetzung. Ohne Genehmigung des Verlages ist es nicht gestattet,
dieses Werk oder Teile in einem photomechanischen oder sonstigen
Reproduktionsverfahren oder unter Verwendung elektronischer Systeme
zu verarbeiten, zu vervielfältigen und zu verbreiten.

Druck: Wilhelm & Adam, Heusenstamm
Typographie: Elmar Lixenfeld, Frankfurt am Main

Gedruckt auf alterungsbeständigem Papier ISO 9706

Printed in Germany
ISSN 1610-6040
ISBN 978-3-465-04034-7

ricordando mio padre

Table of contents

Acknowledgements IX

Chapter 1 Introduction 1

Chapter 2 The Birth of Legal Science 21
    Q. Mucius Scaevola Pontifex, the founding father
    of legal science 22
    Science as the ideal of law 36
    The ancient and modern roots of the legal system 52
    Conclusions 67

Chapter 3 In Defence of the Autonomy of Law 71
    The *ius respondendi* and Roman jurisprudence 73
    Sovereign power and the freedom of jurisprudence ... 86
    The independent jurist and the creation of continuity ... 112
    Conclusions 131

Chapter 4 The Disputed Codification of Law 135
    Edictum perpetuum, Salvius Iulianus and the supposed
    codification 136
    The ideals of legal positivism and the transformation
    of the Praetor's edict 144
    Hadrian and the phantom modernity of Rome 160
    Conclusions 176

Chapter 5 Conclusions: Ancient Roman Lawyers
    and Modern Legal Ideals 181

Abbreviations 195
Bibliography 197
Index locorum 217

Acknowledgements

The observation of discrepancies between the Roman sources and the reconstruction of events in historiography, the ideas that later led to this book, were first expressed in the relentless desert heat of a Jordanian summer during my discussions on the curious nature of ancient history with Joonas Sipilä in 1998 while working on excavations on the Mount of Aaron near Petra for the Finnish Jabal Haroun project. It is an act of serendipity that after studies in history, law, and classical archaeology I wound up in Rome in January 2002 to start working on the doctoral project that resulted in this book. During the long path between the initial idea and this study, I have been helped by the extraordinary kindness and generosity of all whom I have encountered along the way. Ideas have been exchanged, drafts read, advice given, libraries made available, coffees offered, grants granted, and much more. It has undoubtedly made the book better, but more importantly it has made it much more fun to write.

My supervisors, professors Jukka Kekkonen of Helsinki and Ditlev Tamm of Copenhagen, have ensured that I have had the financial and factual possibilities needed for the successful completion of this project. The preliminary examiners, docents Antti Arjava and Heikki Pihlajamäki, have with ruthless but polite accuracy given their constructive remarks on the earlier manuscript, resulting in extensive rewriting and an immeasurably improved book. Professor James Q. Whitman has kindly agreed to act as the official opponent. To all of them I offer my sincere gratitude.

Several people were kind enough to read the manuscript at different phases. For this my heartfelt thanks (in alphabetical order) to professor Marie Theres Fögen, Dr Tomasz Giaro, Dr Toomas Kotkas, Dr Douglas Osler, Mr Janne Pölönen, and professor Kaarlo Tuori. Parts of the text and ideas that have been incorporated in it have been discussed with and commented on by professor Giuliano Crifò, Mr Henrik Forshamn, professor Dirk Heirbaut, Mr Samuli Hurri, Dr Neil Jones, Dr Mia Korpiola, director Pia Letto-Vanamo, Ms Stiina Löytömäki, professor Antonio Mantello, professor Dag Michalsen, Dr Paul du Plessis, Mr Jussi Sallila, Dr Jørn Øyrehagen Sunde, Ms Iisa Vepsä, Dr Kaj Sandberg, and professor Laurens Winkel, to name a few.

This book has been largely written in the lively section of legal history in the Faculty of Law at the University of Helsinki. Having an office in the Institute of International Economic Law gave me the opportunity to enjoy the youthful and stimulating atmosphere of a pure research institute with its friendly and efficient staff. During my yearly courses on Roman legal history the gifted students of the Faculty of Law acted as a testing ground for my ideas and offered their apt remarks. My warmest thanks to you all.

As important to my academic life have been the numerous voluntary networks and reading circles, of which I would like to gratefully mention the Urbanus circle of legal philosophy led by professor Panu Minkkinen, the small circle of Finnish enthusiasts of Roman legal history, the students of ancient Roman history, the legal anthropology workshop, the young European legal historians, and the network of young Nordic legal historians (REUNA).

The department of Roman law of the Università degli studi di Roma 'La Sapienza' opened my eyes to a whole new world of Roman law during my postgraduate studies there during the spring semester of 2002. The libraries of the University of Helsinki, the law library, the rare books collection, and the library of the *Institutum classicum*, were all invaluable, as were the Biblioteca Apostolica Vaticana, the library of the Ecole Française in Rome, the Roman law library of 'La Sapienza', the library of the American Academy in Rome, the British Library, and the law libraries of the Universities of Regensburg, Lund, Rotterdam, and Copenhagen. During my innumerable visits to Rome, the *Institutum Romanum Finlandiae* in Villa Lante has been my home and through its courses I have found both Rome and many friends. The *Max-Planck-Institut für europäische Rechtsgeschichte* in Frankfurt am Main provided me with an opportunity to work there during the spring of 2005 and enjoy the inspiring intellectual atmosphere and their magnificent library. My earnest thanks to the directors and staff of all, who have all been kind, efficient, and helpful.

My doctoral studies have been funded by a broad range of institutions and foundations, to which I extend my gratitude. The Finnish Cultural Foundation and the foundation for the *Institutum Romanum Finlandiae* provided most of my wages during the first few years. For the two final years of this project I have been lucky enough to secure a position at the doctoral school OMY, funded by the Academy of Finland. Smaller grants have been given by (in chronological order) the Finnish Lawyers Association, Alfred Kordelin Foundation, Kone Foundation, Finnish-Danish Cultural Foundation, Chancellor of the University of Helsinki, Niilo Helander Foundation, and the Foundations of the University of Helsinki.

What is written below has in many cases been discussed with some audience beforehand, either at international or national conferences and workshops,[1] or in the course of teaching, and parts of this book have been published before.[2]

Ms Laura Nissinen, Mr Ari Saastamoinen, Mr Antti Laitila, and Mr Teemu Immonen have all assisted me during the arduous work of collecting, checking and re-checking of sources. Mr Daniel Blackie took on the demanding task of proof-reading the manuscript. The mistakes that remain are naturally my own.

Finally, on a personal note, I wish to thank my family and friends for their continuing support. My wife Taina has been a wonderful companion both at home and during the innumerable visits to Italy and beyond. This book is dedicated to the memory of my father Tapani Tuori, who had an unfailing interest in my work but sadly did not live to see its completion.

Kaius Tuori
At the *camera rossa* of Villa Lante in Gianicolo, January 2006

After the first, very limited edition was no longer available, the Max-Planck-Institut für europäische Rechtsgeschichte in Frankfurt am Main offered to include a corrected second edition in their series. Numerous, mostly technical corrections and minor additions have been made, but otherwise the argumentation is unaltered. I would like to thank Dr Karl-Heinz Lingens and his staff at MPIeR for efficiently producing a book out of the manuscript.

Kaius Tuori
Helsinki, January 2007

---

[1] Parts of chapter 2 have been presented at the *Forum junger Rechtshistoriker-Innen* held in Budapest 22 May 2003, whereas parts of chapter 3 were presented at the same event at the University of Warsaw a year later (27 May 2004) and at the conference of the *Société Internationale 'Fernand De Visscher' pour l'Histoire des Droits de l'Antiquité* at the Ruhr-Universität Bochum 21 September 2005. The argumentation of chapter 4 was much improved by comments presented in the discussion at the meeting of the *Legal history on the edge of Europe: Nordic law in the European legal community 1000–2000 a.d.* (REUNA) network workshop in Lund, Sweden in 10 September 2004, and the *XIII Finnish Seminar on Late Antiquity*, Tvärminne on 15 October 2004.

[2] Sections of chapter 2 have appeared as articles in the *Tijdschrift voor Rechtsgeschiedenis / Legal History Review* 72 (2004), pp. 243–262 and *Oikeus* 2 (2003), pp. 151–162. Earlier versions of chapter 3 have been published in the *Revue Internationale des droits de l'Antiquité* 51 (2004), pp. 295–337, and *Lakimies* 6/2005, pp. 884–897. An article on the theme of chapter 4 has also been published in *The Journal of Legal History* 27 (2006), pp. 219–237.

Chapter 1

Introduction

On the left wall of the Cappella degli Spagnoli of the Santa Maria Novella in Florence there is a fresco by Andrea da Bonaiuto painted between 1365 and 1367 with the theme 'The triumph of St. Thomas Aquinas'. In the lowest section of the fresco, below the personifications of virtues, characters from the Bible, and the muses of arts and sciences, are a row of figures representing the sciences. On the extreme left, emperor Justinian is seated with his Code in hand, dressed in contemporary garments. The depiction of Justinian and the Code illustrates the presentness of ancient legal learning at the time, its practical usefulness and actuality. But the Justinian it presents is a medieval Justinian introduced in the light in which he was understood by the Dominican commissioners of the fresco, as a Christian emperor and the founder of contemporary civil law.[1]

Justinian may perhaps not be the founder of contemporary civil law, but recent text-books on Roman law and legal history reveal that Roman law was 'highly sophisticated': there was the 'technical superiority of its reasoning' and the 'important role' it played in the 'creation of the idea of a common European culture'.[2] The uses of Roman law presented in the textbooks may be distilled into three notions: that the system of Roman law has scientific value for the contemporary jurist; that there exists a continuity in legal learning from the Roman law tradition; and, finally, that it has an inherent value in itself as a legal classic.[3]

---

1   Daniel Russo, 'Religion civique et art monumental à Florence au XIVe siècle. La décoration peinte de la salle capitulaire à Sainte-Marie-Nouvelle', in A. Vauchez (ed.), *La religion civique à l'époque médiévale et moderne (chrétienté et islam)*, Roma 1995, 279–296.
2   Peter Stein, *Roman law in European History*, Cambridge 1999, 1–2: 'It has indelibly impressed its character on European legal and political thought.' (p. 2).
3   Theo Mayer-Maly, *Römisches Recht*, (2nd ed.), Wien 1999, 1–3: 'Leistung', 'Vorbildlichkeit', 'Chance'. Jop E. Spruit, *Enchiridium*, Deventer 1994, vi: 'De rechtsgeleerde splendeur van de Romeinse juristen en de vormende kracht van het Romeinse rechtsdenken zullen dan ook voor de Europese jurist in de eenentwintigste eeuw niets van hun exemplarische werking verliezen.' Andrew Borkowski, *Textbook on Roman Law*, (2nd ed.), London 1997, ix: 'Roman law provides an invaluable introduction to the understanding of legal concepts

The purpose of this study is to examine three questions regarding the writing of Roman legal history:

1) How did legal scholars from the fifteenth century to the present use Roman legal history and Roman lawyers as a surrogate forum on which to project their contemporary ideals, preconceptions, and controversies?
2) How did the scholarship on Roman law of the nineteenth century adapt the historical narrative of Roman law to the ideals of modern legal science?
3) How have these interpretations continued in the current writing of Roman legal history?

The concept of modern defines the scope of this inquiry in two ways. First it is understood as the period of time and ideological currents starting from the late fifteenth century (*Neuzeit*) and the beginnings of legal history; second it is seen as legal modernity or the development process of modern law. Due to the intimate connection between legal science and legal history, and the particular position of Roman law in Germany, the history of Roman law written in the first half of the nineteenth century by the Historical School of jurisprudence in Germany incorporated several themes relevant to contemporary law at the time. These tendencies were continued in the expansion of historical scholarship during the latter half of the century, in which Roman legal history as an independent discipline was truly formed. These themes were partly a continuation of old and established historical interpretations that had already been formed in the early modern period. Other themes, however, were completely new.

Through these processes I wish to demonstrate how the legal paradigms of the nineteenth century are still present in the current historiography of Roman law. There are three main features of the effect of the Romanistic tradition which have influenced the writing of Roman legal history: the systematising tendency; the idea of continuity from antiquity; and classicism. The issue is of vital importance now, as the same narratives that were used to promote Roman law in the nineteenth century are re-used to advocate its revival in the new European civil law.

The investigation is divided into three cases. These focus on the ideals of science, autonomy, and codification, respectively. The three ideals were

> and a passport to the appreciation of Continental legal systems.' It would nevertheless '... be eminently worthy of study for its own sake. For it is the product of the genius for good order and organised common sense of a remarkable ancient civilisation, and it constitutes a legacy that has had profound influence in subsequent ages.'

chosen to provide vantage points to different discussions in Roman legal history, such as the nature of legal science, its relationship to the power of the state, and the codification of law. The common denominator to all three cases is that the Roman jurists scarcely saw them as meaningful; the very concepts in their present modern meaning were unknown to them, and thus their significance to law is, in general, a later development.

Each of the three main cases is divided into three sections that each focus on different aspects of the main issue. First, the historical case and its current main interpretations are presented, along with the Roman sources that are the foundation of the historical interpretation. Second, the history of interpretations is followed from the fifteenth century to the present. In the analysis of the debate, I intend to show how, in each case, the main differences in the various major interpretations can be traced to matters of legal principle, and the changes of interpretation reflect changes in legal ideals. My aim is to establish how the fundamental issue in each case became a matter of utmost importance for the nineteenth century legal debate. The interpretations are also examined as narratives that were given various meanings from the formation of history to the construction of lawyers' identities. Third, I attempt to generalise, using another example, how the issue was not confined solely to the case in hand.

The first case examines the notion of legal science, a concept that has provoked much debate over issues such as the relationship between ancient and contemporary concepts of science, and the definition of what actually constitutes legal science. The starting-point of this investigation is the belief that Roman jurisprudence is the origin of Western legal science and, specifically, the theory that the Late Republican jurist Quintus Mucius Scaevola Pontifex would be the founding father of the current legal science. The main points of inquiry are:

- The position of Quintus Mucius as the father of Western jurisprudence in the Romanistic tradition and the foundations of this claim in the Roman sources.
- The treatment of the concept of legal science and the biography of Quintus Mucius by legal historians from the sixteenth century onwards, and the gradual association of these two narratives in the foundation myth of legal science in the mid-nineteenth century, leading to the adoption of Quintus Mucius as the founding father of the newly formulated concept of legal science.
- The existence of a systematic Roman legal science and its Greek influences, and the role of systematisation in the scheme of the Historical School and its relationship with legal history.

The second case analyses the importance of the autonomy of law. The relationship of law and the legal profession to political power has been problematic and opinions on whether or not the jurists control law have been numerous. In this case, these discussions are observed through the controversy over the *ius respondendi* of Augustus. The crucial question is whether or not the emperor took control over jurisprudence in the beginning of the Principate. The wider implications of the matter extend well over the Roman period, as the Roman jurists have been used as the figureheads of the autonomy of law. Among the issues:

- The claim that the *ius respondendi* would have been a defining moment in the relationship between the emperors and lawyers and consequently to the concept of the autonomy of jurisprudence and the Roman sources supporting the existence of the institution as traditionally understood by the scholarship.

- The freedom of jurisprudence as the leading theme in the historical interpretation of the *ius respondendi* and the stereotypes of benevolent and malevolent emperors as narrative reflections of changes in the juristic ideology on the relationship between the imperial power and learned lawyers. The changes in modern historiography are examined through the concept of patriotic narrative and the question of why even completely opposite interpretations always seem to be beneficial to jurists.

- The visibility of the patriotic narrative in other themes of Roman legal history and the belief in continuity from the Roman to the modern jurist. The significance of the idea of continuity to the Roman law tradition and its reflections in the writing of Roman legal history.

The third and final case investigates the concept of codification. The codification of law, the collection of legal norms into a single text, is a model with a life span extending from ancient Mesopotamia to modern law. The influence of the idea of codification is examined through the case of the Hadrianic *edictum perpetuum* or the Perpetual Edict. As a modern phenomenon, codification has been linked with legal positivism and the growth of bureaucracy, and these qualities have also emerged in the descriptions of the Roman events. The main problems are:

- The conflicting current interpretations of the *edictum perpetuum* as a rational and systematic codification, a compilation like previous yearly edicts, or a fiction with no historical foundation. The lack of contemporary Roman sources and the fact that the existing Roman sources are from the post-classical period.

– The modern ideals of codification in the depiction of the *edictum perpetuum* in the historiography and the theories of comprehensive systematic codification and limited unsystematic compilation in the debate over legal positivism.
– The reign of Hadrian as a quasi-modernity in historical scholarship and the effects of the idealisation of Hadrian, positive law, and bureaucracy and the changing position of Roman law in the writing of its ancient history.

There are two historiographical hypotheses this study seeks to prove. First, that the stories and characters from the history of Roman law have been used, consciously or unconsciously, as narratives with contemporary significance and implications from the fifteenth century to the present. Second, that these narratives have also had their own internal dynamics and continuities. Stories and examples based on the Roman sources have continued through the centuries in literature, because authors have used them for their own purposes, such as authoritative statements, legitimation, and idealised examples of law and lawyers.[4] It has been established that good stories have both historical lives and afterlives though intellectual recycling, because the same narratives may be used by different authors to convey different meanings without much regard for their strict historical correctness or original context.[5]

The contested claims that the writing of history has always been influenced by its ideological and cultural context[6] and that this applies also to contemporary studies has been presented in legal history earlier.[7] Nevertheless, of the

---

[4] Giuliano Crifò gave an interesting example of how ancient precedents were used in the discussion on the preferred form of administration for the newly unified Italy in the late nineteenth century. Giuliano Crifò, 'Contributo dei giuristi allo studio del mondo antico', in *Soggetti individuali e soggetti collettivi*, Milano 1995, 543–545.

[5] Eco described the success of the transmission of historical falcities: 'And yet each of these stories had a virtue: as narratives, they seemed plausible, more than everyday or historical reality, which is far more complex and less credible. The stories seemed to explain something that was otherwise hard to understand.' Umberto Eco, *Serendipities*, London 1998, 23.

[6] Cf. Otto G. Oexle, 'Das Mittelalter als Waffe', in O. G. Oexle (ed.), *Geschichtswissenschaft im Zeichen des Historismus*, Göttingen 1996, 163–215.

[7] Antonio Mantello, *Per una storia della giurisprudenza romana: Il problema dei 'Miscelliones'*, Milano 1984, 3–6: 'Anche l'esame delle varie forme ideologiche o – se si preferisce – delle varie "letture" storiografiche delle fonti antiche deve servire il più possibile per smuovere acque stagnanti, acquisire nuove consapevolezze, conferma la perfetta relatività e soggettività di ogni elaborazione, pervenire a diverse impostazioni, ma sempre in vista di un'indagine testuale che maggiormente soddisfi l'ideologia e i valori di cui il nuovo interprete è portatore.'

vast amount of material published on Roman law, critical insights about the tradition of legal history itself are rare. Though the scope of this book is mostly uncharted territory, there are studies that have thrown light on some important details, such as the later cultural influence of some themes in Roman legal history,[8] the Pandectistic preconceptions in nineteenth century legal history,[9] the use of Roman law as a precedent in contemporary legal debates,[10] and the ideological connotations of supposed continuity from Roman law to modern law.[11]

In previous studies of Roman law and modernity, the focus has been on the use of Roman law as a historical example and authoritative argument. In the current study, this focus has been reversed to highlight how the modernising of law influenced the history of Roman law. The novelty of this study is that I wish to show how the earlier historical interpretations and with them, elements of modern law, still continue as narrative elements in and behind the contemporary history of Roman law and how the credibility of these interpretations may stem from their compatibility with the ideals of modern law. The patterns of modernising interpretations are among the classical criticisms on the dogmatic approach to Roman law observed by earlier scholars already in the nineteenth century. Rudolf von Jhering accused his contemporaries of planting the thoughts of modern scholars in the minds of Romans, while Axel Hägerström claimed that the modern Roman law scholarship had modernised the superstitions of the Romans.[12]

While the Romanistic scholarship of the nineteenth century has attracted considerable interest, I would like to stress the importance of the earlier, pre-Pandectistic scholarship. Previously certain characteristics were simply labelled as modern influences. What I aim to present is a view of a long duration, providing an insight not simply on the nineteenth century but also

---

8   Marie Theres Fögen, *Römische Rechtsgeschichten*, Göttingen 2002.
9   Tomasz Giaro, 'Romanistische Constructionsplaudereien: Auf den Spuren eines anachronistischen Begriffes', *Rechtshistorisches Journal* 10 (1991), 221; Dario Mantovani, 'L'editto come codice e da altri punti di vista', in L. De Giovanni, A. Mazzacane (eds.), *La codificazione del diritto dall'antico al moderno*, Napoli 1998, 129–178.
10 James Q. Whitman, *The Legacy of Roman Law in the German Romantic Era*, Princeton 1990.
11 Pier G. Monateri, 'Black Gaius: A Quest for the Multicultural Origins of the "Western Legal Tradition"', *Hastings Law Journal* 51 (2000), 479–555.
12 Rudolf von Jhering, *Geist des römischen Rechts*, (10th ed.), Aalen 1993 [1906], vol. III, 323: '... gleich als hätten die ungesunden Spekulationen eines modernen Theoretikers im Kopfe eines alten Römers Platz finden können ...' Axel Hägerström, *Der römische Obligationsbegriff I*, Uppsala 1927, iii.

what earlier influences from the fifteenth century onwards have been transmitted to us via the so called modernity in law.

The intention of this work is to explain an important part of the cultural history of Roman law and the history of the reception of ancient culture, not once more underline the ineptitude of previous scholars. It has been claimed that the importance of a history of science is in the expansion of self-understanding.[13] The history of Roman law cannot be understood without the influence of Roman law to modern law and its use in the development of modern legal science. Within the emerging reception studies of today, reception is seen as a continuous dialogue between the past and present. Lorna Hardwick described the effect of the reception of ancient tradition to its interpretation as threefold: that the intellectual processes involved between the interpreter and the ancient text are always unique; that the private and general context of the interpretation influences its results, and that the interpretation of the classic may function as an authority to legitimate something in the present.[14]

Direct precedents on how contemporary debates have influenced the history of ancient Rome should mostly be searched for from outside the field of legal history.[15] P. J. Rhodes claimed that as much as the Athenian ideal of democracy has influenced us, our modern concept of democracy has influenced our view of Athenian democracy.[16] Richard Hingley discussed a similar process when he noted 'the association that the English have drawn between themselves and the Romans and the influence of this association on the

---

[13] Okko Behrends, 'Das Werk Otto Lenels und die Kontinuität der romanistischen Fragestellungen', *Index* 19 (1991), 169: 'Die Erkenntnis, daß jede Disziplin ihre Wissenschaftsgeschichte pflegen muß, um wirklich zu wissen, was sie getan hat und tut und warum es von ihr getan wurde und wird, gehört gewiß – ich bin sicher, daß jeder Leser dem zustimmen kann – zu den wichtigsten Fortschritten der modernen Wissenschaft.'

[14] Lorna Hardwick, *Reception Studies*, Oxford 2003, 4–5, 10: 'Receptions do in practice affect perceptions of and judgements about the ancient world and therefore need to be analysed.'

[15] An important exception is June Starr, 'The "Invention" of Early Legal Ideas: Sir Henry Maine and the Perpetual Tutelage of Women', in J. Starr, J. Collier (eds.), *History and Power in the Study of Law*, Ithaca 1989, 345–368.

[16] P. J. Rhodes, *Ancient Democracy and Modern Ideology*, London 2003, 70: 'There is nothing new in the colouring of the study of Athenian democracy by the student's own political views, or in the notion that such study may have relevance for the world in which the student lives; nor is there anything new in disagreement resulting from the different views of different students: the opposition to democracy of Mitford, and the different hostile reactions to him of Macaulay and of Grote, provide one clear example.' See also Moses I. Finley, *Democracy Ancient and Modern*, (2nd ed.), London 1985, 3–37.

practice of archaeology'. In Victorian and Edwardian England the classics were used as examples, as a historical stage on which to project current matters such as imperialism. As the Britons used the classics to define themselves as the heirs of Rome, classicism was developed to define the barbaric other as the negation of their civilisation.[17] From the Middle Ages to the Renaissance, the Enlightenment to the French Revolution, the late nineteenth century to Italian Fascism, the political idealisation of Roman Antiquity has translated into various forms of historical scholarship.[18]

Historical interpretations have served distinct functions in their time, having a clear contemporary purpose. Now that Roman legal history is becoming increasingly historical, it is important to remember this. In an age where the review of previous scholarship tends to end with Mommsen, I have sought to demonstrate how the pre-mommsenian roots, namely legal scholarship from the Humanists to the Historical School and its successors, and especially the intellectual environment of the nineteenth century, still has a profound impact on our views of Roman law and jurists.

* * *

As one of the stated aims of the current study is to follow the development of historical interpretations in Roman legal history, I would like to first lay out a brief general outline of the discipline. The purpose of this is to establish lines of continuity and moments of change that have laid the foundations of current interpretations. According to the traditional history of Roman law, Roman law scholarship has three ages: the birth of science in twelfth century Bologna, the elegant jurisprudence of the French and Dutch Humanists, and the Historical School of Savigny and the Pandectists.[19] However, the development of the history of Roman law is not the same thing, though it cannot be completely separated from it. The purpose of this outline is to demonstrate

---

[17] Richard Hingley, *Roman Officers and English Gentlemen*, London 2000, xiii, 7, 10–11. Nationalists later discovered the heroic natives of Roman Britain as their predecessors. Cf. also, Maria Wyke, *Projecting the Past: Ancient Rome, Cinema, and History*, New York 1997, 8: 'Drawing on a whole constellation of nineteenth- and twentieth-century historiographic genres, cinema has long provided its own distinctive historiography of ancient Rome that has vividly resurrected the ancient world and reformulated it in the light of present needs.'

[18] Andrea Giardina, André Vauchez, *Il mito di Roma: Da Carlo Magno a Mussolini*, Roma 2000; Karl Christ, 'Aspekte der Antike-Rezeption in der deutschen Altertumswissenschaft des 19. Jahrhunderts', in K. Christ, A. Momigliano (eds.), *L'Antichità nell'Ottocento in Italia e Germania*, Bologna 1988, 31–37, 21–37.

[19] Franz Wieacker, 'Eclipse et permanence du droit romain', in P. Mesnard (ed.), *Pédagogues et juristes*, Paris 1963, 62.

that the roots of the interpretations lie deeper in the tradition of Roman legal history than the nineteenth century Pandectistic jurisprudence, and that there is a continuity of tradition extending from the fifteenth century, a tradition that is constantly evolving in contact with both the development of historiography and Roman law.

When tracing the development of certain ideas and interpretations, there is always a distinct danger of falling in to the temptation of a mythology of coherence, as described by Quentin Skinner. In it, authors of a certain period or description are stereotyped as representatives of a school of thought and their views are made to coherently reflect the modern reconstruction of what the basic tenets and questions of that school were. Another danger is that of overemphasising what readers see as the sense of a given work or its relationship with other works from their modern vantage point.[20] As one of the stated intentions of the current work is to describe a genealogy of ideas and their relationship with the general intellectual climate, these considerations are of utmost importance. Historical authors are first of all considered as individual actors, not representatives of a given school, and secondly their relationships with each other are deduced from their writings and references in them, and what is known of their intellectual environment.

The inquiry is based on the assumption that a connection can be made between individual historical interpretations and the general intellectual currents of the time. The assumption can itself be contested and contains dangerous elements such as ascribing certain thoughts to certain authors on the basis of supposed similarities. However, though causal connections are difficult to establish, the diffusion of influences should not be overlooked. In the more modern legal history connections can be established with some certainty because of the use of references, whereas in earlier literature these references are rare. The question of whether a link or an influence between two authors or an author and a school of thought can be established if such a link is not obvious from a quotation or openly acknowledged is taken seriously. In addition to making only cautious conclusions, I have also attempted to include a considerable number of authors and to extend the time-span to minimise the effects of small changes in the doctrine. Although the work aims to discuss anachronistic interpretations, I am consciously using contemporary terminology in concepts such as science and legal positivism.

Throughout the development of Roman legal history three major factors have influenced the writing of ancient legal history: the development of legal

---

20 Quentin Skinner, 'Meaning and understanding in the history of ideas', in Q. Skinner, *Visions of Politics I*, Cambridge 2002, 67–79. This article appeared originally in *History and Theory* 8 (1969), 3–53.

science and the role of Roman law in it; the development of historiography; and the general cultural significance of Antiquity, especially the idealisation of ancient Rome.

For most of its history the purpose of legal history has been something more than simply writing history for its own sake: history served to legitimise current policies and acted as a storehouse of examples. After Pomponius' *Enchiridion* was included in the Digest of Justinian, a silence fell on Roman legal history that was to last until the fourteenth century. It was emblematic that most of the text of the *Enchiridion* included in Justinian was gradually omitted from the later Byzantine compilations. Similarly neither the glossators nor the commentators were interested in legal history. For example, Baldus (1327?–1400) did not comment on Pomponius' *Enchiridion* but used words in Pomponius to observe matters of contemporary interest.[21] Such an approach is typical of the early interpretations.[22]

Scholars generally locate the beginnings of legal historiography in the Humanist authors of the late fifteenth century. Savigny used them as precursors to the Historical School while formulating the foundation narrative of the school, naming Aymar Du Rivail (c. 1490–1557) as the first legal historian.[23] Savigny's version of legal history has continued in the standard

---

21   Baldus de Ubaldis, *In primam Digesti Veteris partem Commentaria*, Venezia 1586, 16–17 [ad Dig. 1,2,2]; Lelio Lantella, *Le opere della giurisprudenza romana nella storiografia*, Torino 1979, 101–107.

22   The first treatments of Roman legal history were small treatises on Roman magistrates by Flavio Biondo (1392–1463), *De militia et iurisprudentia* (ed. Otto Lobeck), Dresden 1892, whose contribution to the history of Roman jurisprudence was to equal the glory of Roman jurists to the glory of Roman soldiers (p. x). and Pomponius Laetus (1428–1497), *De magistratibus et sacerdotiis, praeterea de diversis legibus Romano*, Basel 1535. His work consisted of lists: a list of magistrates, a list of priestly offices, and a list of laws. Both Biondo and Laetus followed the traditions of court historiography and made scant references to jurisprudence. See also Giuliano Crifò, *Materiali di storiografia romanistica*, Torino 1998, 11–14, 55.

23   Friedrich C. von Savigny, *Geschichte des römischen Rechts im Mittelalter VI*, Bad Homburg 1950 [1831], 419–421, 449–452 claims that the new scientific school was founded by Alciatus in Italy and France and Zasius in Germany (p. 421). Even though Du Rivail is the first to use the title *Historia* in connection with Roman law, Maffei contends that the contents do not redeem the promise of the title as we would currently understand it. Domenico Maffei, *Gli inizi dell'umanesimo giuridico*, Milano 1956, 82, 138–139. On du Rivail's history, cf. Jean-Louis Ferrary, 'Naissance d'un aspect de la recherche antiquaire. Les premiers travaux sur les lois romaines: de l'*Epistula ad Cornelium* de Filelfo à *Historia iuris civilis* d'Aymar du Rivail', in M. H. Crawford, C. R. Ligota (eds.), *Ancient History and the Antiquarian*, London 1995, 53–72; Crifò 1998, 56–57.

versions of legal historiography. Douglas Osler has called it the *Rechtsgeschichte* narrative of legal history, which highlights the major developments of legal history. These turning points include: the rediscovery of the Digest in the eleventh century Italy; the French Humanists in the fifteenth; the movement of learning to the Netherlands after the eviction of the huguenots, the shift to Germany and the birth of the Historical School.

> For the jurists of the *Historische Schule*, Roman law lay at the heart of the legal history of Europe, and their heroes were the legal humanists, the university professors who had devoted their lives to the historical and philological investigation of the legal system of ancient Rome. And so they envisaged European legal history as a *translatio studii*, in which the *fax iurisprudentiae elegantioris* was handed on from one European nation to another in a single, teleological projectory.[24]

The problem with this interpretation is that it only gives the foundation myth of German legal history as German legal historians want to see it.[25]

The Humanists dramatically expanded the scope and volume of historical research on Roman law. According to Lantella the sixteenth century marks the beginnings of three lines of legal history that extend to the eighteenth century. The first group are the historical commentaries of Pomponius' *Enchiridion* that are separated from the Digest itself, for example Guillaume Budé (1467–1540) and Ulrich Zasius (1461–1535). The second group are the biographies of jurists in the style *de viris illustribus* by Thomas Diplovatatius (1468–1541), Bernard Rutilius (1504–1538) and Guido Panziroli (1523–1599). The third group are the universal legal histories initiated by Laetus that concentrated thematically on magistrates, law and jurists, of which Aymar Du Rivail and Valentinus Forster (1530–1608) are the foremost examples.[26]

One of the main charges of the Humanists against medieval jurists was that they were ignorant of classical civilisation in general and Roman legal history particularly. To the Humanists in general, the classics formed an ideal of civilisation and culture, which they strove to examine through a new critical

---

24 Douglas J. Osler, 'Teramo and the *ius commune*', in P. Campanella, R. Viola (eds.), *Le Cinquecentine della Facoltà di giurisprudenza*, Pescara 2004, xv.
25 Douglas J. Osler, 'Preface', in *Bibliographica iuridica 2*, Ius Commune Sonderheft 131, Frankfurt am Main 2000, vii–xxv; Douglas J. Osler, 'The myth of European Legal History', *Rechtshistorisches Journal* 16 (1997), 393–410. For the traditional view of the development of legal history, see for example Franz Wieacker, *A history of private law in Europe*, Oxford 1995; Stein 1999, 2.
26 Lantella 1979, 110–117; Crifò 1998, 58–62; Julian H. Franklin, *Jean Bodin and the sixteenth-century revolution in the methodology of law and history*, New York 1963, 22.

scholarship of original readings of the ancient texts, including those in Greek.[27] Legal Humanists of the late sixteenth century saw the study of the past not as a pedagogical objective but a practical part of the legal education necessary for the so-called revolution in legal method.[28] The classical ideal is evident in Budé's commentary of the *Enchiridion* with its repeated and quite unnecessary quotations in Greek and references to Aristotle, Plato, and Cicero.[29]

As is often the case, the Humanists have been stereotyped as Lutheran zealots with an interest in Greek. A good example of this stereotyping is the figure of Ulrich Zasius. Zasius did indeed stay in contact with Erasmus, Budé, and Alciatus and even had Erasmus as a guest in Freiburg in the summer of 1529, but he was no admirer of Luther's and knew no Greek. The idea of the Humanistic legal triumvirate of Budé, Alciatus and Zasius is a Renaissance myth, which despite its inaccuracy continues to the present day. Contrary to the popular idea that the Humanists initiated some kind of proto-modern historiography, Zasius' commentary of *de origine iuris* was filled with references to contemporary colleagues and literary figures. He used the words in Pomponius as excuses for forays into other themes, many of which were of a contemporary nature unrelated to the text at hand. Rowan maintained that though Zasius is often counted as an expatriate member of the French Humanist School, he was in fact critical of their legal scholarship and unaware of the legal history of Du Rivail.[30]

27   Guido Kisch, 'Die humanistische Jurisprudenz', in *La storia del diritto nel quadro delle scienze storiche: Atti del primo Congresso internazionale della Società Italiana di Storia del Diritto*, Firenze 1966, 469–490; Franklin 1963, 18–19; Peter Stein, *Regulae Iuris: From Juristic Rules to Legal Maxims*, Edinburgh 1966, 163; Franz Wieacker, *Römische Rechtsgeschichte I*, München 1988, 41. For a critique of this simplistic view, see Osler 2000, viii.

28   Franklin 1963, 3; Donald Kelley, *Foundations of Modern Historical Scholarship: Language, Law, and History in the French Renaissance*, New York and London 1970, 53–148.

29   Gulielmus Budaeus, *Opera tomus III, annotationes in pandectas*, Basel 1557 [reprinted 1969], 25–61 [ad Dig. 1.2].

30   In his later years, Zasius became increasingly hostile to both Luther and the new style of textual scholarship in law. Steven Rowan, *Ulrich Zasius: A Jurist in the German Renaissance 1461–1535*, Frankfurt am Main 1987, xi, 97–104, 108, 151–154, 160–162, 206–207: 'It was Zasius' ill fortune that he would achieve his greatest work at the very moment when fashion was promoting methods which would eventually pick the *Corpus iuris civilis* to bits.' (p. 108). For the traditional view of Zasius the Humanist, see Wieacker 1995, 63, 116, 120, 130–131: '... his works of pure historical scholarship such as the *Lucubrationes* are by the standards of the time and place outstanding for their fluency, clarity, and elegance.' (p. 116). Of the literature, see Roderich Stinzing, *Geschichte der Deutschen Rechtswissenschaft*, München und Leipzig

Within the traditional historiography on Roman legal history, the seventeenth and eighteenth centuries have been usually seen as an intermediary period. However, that period should not be reduced to a dichotomy with the Humanist influence on one side and the Historical School on the other. Preceded by the first history of jurisprudence in Jacques Godefroy's (1587–1652) history of Roman law, Roman legal history as a literary genre began to grow rapidly during the eighteenth century. The appearance of the first external histories of law by Gian V. Gravina (1664–1718), Burkhard G. Struve (1671–1738), Johann Gottlieb Heineccius (1681–1741), and Johannes Augustus Bach (1721–1758) are often described as the beginnings of real legal history.[31]

The common feature of the legal histories of this period is that they compile and describe the ancient sources, striving to provide a concordance of the source materials. The most famous of the eighteenth century German jurists, Johann G. Heineccius, a student of Thomasius, was influential in the fields of natural law, *usus modernus*, and history. His historical writings were immensely influential, not least because they were widely distributed and translated around Europe. While Heineccius's analytical historical method was the culmination of the compilative approach, Bach's easy accessibility made his Roman legal history a popular textbook. The Roman legal history presented by these authors was still dominated by the model given by Pomponius, which was supplemented and strengthened by additional material from the Roman sources. Heineccius' posthumous influence was later diminished by the notables of the Historical School, who denied his considerable influence on them. Koschaker and Wieacker, who replicated these views, call him an unoriginal natural lawyer and an insignificant antiquarian.[32]

A general interest in classical antiquity was awakened during the eighteenth century, partially through the archaeological finds in Herculaneum (1736)

1880, 155–174; Carlo Ghisalberti, 'Il commentario dello Zasio al Dig. 1.2.2', *La Parola del passato* 21 (1966), 81–110; Karl-Heinz Burmeister, 'Ulrich Zasius', in P. G. Schmidt (ed.), *Humanismus im Deutschen Südwesten*, Sigmaringen 1993, 105–124; Hans Thieme, 'L'œuvre juridique de Zasius', in P. Mesnard (ed.), *Pédagogues et juristes*, Paris 1963, 31–38.

31 Lantella 1979, 117–122; Crifò 1998, 62–63.
32 Klaus Luig, 'Johann Gottlieb Heineccius als Kritiker des Naturrechts von Hugo Grotius', in E. Donnert (ed.), *Europa in der Früheren Neuzeit: Festschrift für Günter Mühlpfordt 2*, Weimar 1997, 31; Reinhard Voppel, *Der Einfluß des Naturrechts auf den Usus modernus*, Köln 1996, 159–163; Jan Schröder, *Recht als Wissenschaft: Geschichte der juristischen Methode vom Humanismus bis zur historischen Schule (1500–1850)*, München 2001, 134, 183; Wieacker 1995, 173–174; Paul Koschaker, *Europa und das römische Recht*, (4th ed.), München 1966, 120; Wieacker 1988, 43; Crifò 1998, 62.

and Pompeii (1748). The classical revival was just one of the many 'revivals' that signified a general curiosity in the past. In the foundation myth of scientific history, this was followed by the introduction of the critical method in history espoused by Leopold von Ranke.[33]

> In the early nineteenth century a radical change took place in the Western world generally in the way history was researched, written and taught as it was transformed into a professional discipline.[34]

Only recently has it been recognised that Ranke had been preceded by a rich tradition of late Enlightenment historical scholarship. Nevertheless, during the first half of the nineteenth century in Germany history emerged as a profession of tremendous prestige and academic value.[35]

The advent of the scientific approach to history as a self-described contrast to previous approaches, pejoratively dubbed as antiquities, spread rapidly to legal history. The new way of making legal history was characterised by the systematic historical approach and the use of the vernacular instead of Latin. The first example of this new approach was the Roman legal history of Gustav Hugo (1765–1844), a natural lawyer of the Neohumanistic school of Göttingen. The most novel feature of Hugo's works compared to previous literature was that he began to rationalise the past by analysing sources rather than merely reproducing them. Hugo's history was not really a complete work, but rather a critical preparation for one.[36] These new methodological approaches have been linked with the revival of Romanising Neoclassicism.[37]

---

33 Arnaldo Momigliano, 'Ancient History and the Antiquarian', in *Studies in Historiography*, London 1966, 1–2; Leopold Ranke, *Geschichten der romanischen und germanischen Völker von 1494 bis 1514*, (2nd ed.), Leipzig 1874, Vorrede vii: 'Man hat der Historie das Amt, die Vergangenheit zu richten, die Mitwelt zum Nutzen zukünftiger Jahre zu belehren, beygemessen; so hoher Aemter unterwindet sich gegenwärtiger Versuch nicht; er will bloß sagen, wie es eigentlich gewesen.'

34 Georg Iggers, *Historiography in the Twentieth century*, Hanover 1997, 25.

35 Robert Harrison, Aled Jones and Peter Lambert, 'The institutionalisation and organisation of history', in P. Lambert, P. Schofield (eds.), *Making history: an introduction to the history and practices of a discipline*, London 2004, 10–11: 'Ranke had been masterly in his self-promotion as the inventor of a wholly new approach to history.' (p. 11).

36 Okko Behrends, 'Gustav Hugo: Der Skeptiker als Wegbereiter der vom Geist der Romantik geprägten Historischen Rechtsschule', in E. Gibbon, *Historische Übersicht des Römischen Rechts, übersetzt, eingeleitet und kommentiert von Gustav Hugo*, Göttingen 1996, 172.

37 Lantella 1979, 125–129; Whitman 1990, 82–83; Paolo Cappellini, *Systema Iuris I*, Milano 1984, 173–195

As in the case of Heineccius, Hugo has been given the marginal role of a precursor to the Historical School of jurisprudence by both Wieacker and Koschaker.[38]

One of the ways in which the empirism of Heineccius, Gravina, and other Enlightenment scholars influenced later legal history was through Edward Gibbon's (1737–1794) *Decline and Fall of the Roman Empire*, which Hugo translated into German.[39] Behrends saw the translation of Gibbon as one of the culminative writings of the Historical School.[40]

Though the Historical School of jurisprudence is generally held to be the forerunner of scientific legal history, such a view is problematic, because the purpose of the Historical School was not historical study for its own sake but for the advancement of common German law. Its founder Friedrich Carl von Savigny (1779–1861) held that law had to be based on historical material and systematic in its analysis and organisation of that material. Despite their criticism of the natural lawyers, however, Savigny and his followers still adopted similar methods for analysing and organising law.[41]

---

38 Wieacker 1995, 300–302 calls him inaccessible; Koschaker 1966, 253–254: 'Vorgänger Savignys'. Whitman reminds us of Hugo's crucial and well-known role in the revival of Roman law scholarship, Whitman 1990, 84–85.

39 Patricia Craddock, *Edward Gibbon, luminous historian 1772–1794*, Baltimore and London 1989, 200–201 noted how through Hugo's translation and adaptation Gibbon's influence spread far and wide, but does not note Gibbon's own roots. Joseph Levine, *The autonomy of history: truth and method from Erasmus to Gibbon*, Chicago 1999, 165 attempted to restore Gibbon's reputation as a scientific historian.

40 Behrends 1996, 165.

41 Friedrich C. von Savigny, 'Einleitung zu den Pandekten 1811–1842', in A. Mazzacane (ed.), *Friedrich Carl von Savigny, Vorlesungen über juristische Methodologie 1802–1842*, Frankfurt am Main 1993, 174–216; Friedrich C. von Savigny, *Vom Beruf unserer Zeit für Gesetzgebung und Rechtswisseschaft*, Heidelberg 1814, 11, now in H. Akamatsu, J. Rückert (eds.), Friedrich C. von Savigny, *Politik und Neuere Legislationen*, Frankfurt am Main 2000, 221: '... der eigentliche Sitz des Rechts das gemeinsame Bewußtseyn des Volkes sey.' Friedrich C. von Savigny, *Pandektenvorlesung 1824/25*, Frankfurt am Main 1993, 4; Wieacker 1988, 45; Wieacker 1995, 284–299; Koschaker 1966, 269, 275–291 writes that the similarities between the Historical School and Natural law were that both were *Professorenrecht* and both had Roman law as their main source; Giovanni Pugliese, 'I pandettisti fra tradizione romanistica e moderna scienza del diritto', in *Scritti giuridici scelti III: Diritto romano*, Napoli 1985, 419–423. For the sake of clarity, it should be noted that the methodological thought of Enlightenment scholars such as Thomasius was concerned with an outer presentation, whereas the nineteenth century scholars were preoccupied with an inner system of law. Cf. Jan Schröder, *Christian Thomasius und die Reform der juristischen Methode*, Leipzig 1997, 27.

The original interest of the Historical School on Roman law was based solely on its status as learned law in Germany. Savigny maintained that there would be a time when legal science was so advanced that it would leave Roman law to history.[42] While his main aim was the renewal of legal science,[43] his pupil, Georg Friedrich Puchta (1789–1846) sought to apply Savigny's vision to Roman legal history.[44] Puchta's construction of the Pandects was a classic example of a conceptual balancing-act, which both incorporated and kept separate the tradition of the Historical School and the imports from the rationalistic natural lawyers. He was later labelled the initiator of both Romanistic Pandectism and the jurisprudence of concepts.[45]

Although Pandectism has been described pejoratively as a constructivist movement, Savigny's original idea was not the construction of a rational order, but rather a re-construction of an immanent unity.[46] Haferkamp claimed that the relationship between Puchta and legal history is more complicated than the stereotypical and simplistic, and at times controversial, portrait that later observers like Wieacker and Koschaker have painted of Puchta and his jurisprudence of concepts.[47] Puchta criticised the traditional division of legal history as inner and outer, preferring instead to concentrate on the totality and wholeness of the law, in which different aspects of legal history are integral parts.[48]

Puchta was the last representative of the Historical School in the sense that he attempted to combine historical and normative material. During the latter half of the nineteenth century the Historical School was divided between the Pandectists, recognisable by their tendency to write multi-volumed systematical presentations of law under the title *Pandecten*, and the more strictly historical Romanists. The latter gained great fame with their technical mastery of the sources and their lucid historical presentation. Their prowess

---

42 Savigny 1814, 150; Mario Bretone, *Diritto e tempo nella tradizione europea*, Bari 2004, 80.
43 Franz Wieacker, *Gründer und Bewahrer*, Göttingen 1959, 117 quotes Savigny's friend from childhood v. Leonhardi: 'Sein Plan, ein Reformator der Jurisprudenz, ein Kant in der Rechtswissenschaft zu werden, ist groß …'
44 Whitman 1990, 127.
45 Wieacker 1995, 316–318; Pugliese 1985, 428–430.
46 Lars Björne, *Deutsche Rechtssysteme im 18. und 19. Jahrhundert*, Ebelsbach 1984, 65.
47 Hans-Peter Haferkamp, *Georg Friedrich Puchta und die 'Begriffsjurisprudenz'*, Frankfurt am Main 2004, 5–24.
48 Gothofredus Guillelmus Leibnitz, 'Methodi novae discendae docendaque jurisprudentiae', in *Opera omnia IV*, Geneve 1768, 191: *jurisprudentia historia est vel interna vel externa*. Joachim Bohnert, *Über die Rechtslehre Georg Friedrich Puchtas (1798–1846)*, Karlsruhe 1975, 36–37.

in writing history highlighted the ahistorical nature of Pandectist scholarship. It was quite common for the same scholar to write in a manner reminiscent of both the Pandectist and historical approaches.[49]

One of the greatest changes in classical scholarship in the mid-nineteenth century was the scientification of ancient history. The Roman history of Theodor Mommsen (1817–1903) was a model for the new kind of history. As a result of Mommsen's influence, new source editions like the *Corpus Inscriptionum Latinarum* and the *Thesaurus Linguae Latinae* were published. A number of new journals were founded, and new libraries and seminars were opened.[50]

Rudolf von Jhering (1818–1892) was one of the first to claim that the Pandectists wished to project their own complicated views on the Romans. He unsuccessfully tried to replace the Pandectism of conceptual jurisprudence with a natural historical method, later dubbed as the jurisprudence of interests. Haferkamp claimed that the drastic difference between Jhering and Puchta's jurisprudence of concepts was a reflection of Jhering's self-promotion. The Pandectists never grew fond of Jhering's theories and still prefer the younger Pandectist Jhering over the later critical one. As Coing has pointed out, Jhering was actually closely involved in the process of strengthening the systematic and dogmatic sides of the Historical School and making it the leading scientific method of the time. In the end, legal historians at the end of the nineteenth and beginning of the twentieth centuries like Rudolf Sohm combined the basic propositions of Puchta and Jhering in a way that they recognised both the logical and systematic inner nature of law and the conflicts of interests that were the origins of legal change.[51]

In the 1880s there was a noticeable shift away from dogmatic interpretations as scholars began to focus on political, social, and cultural realities. According to Wieacker, the Romanists had to choose whether they were historians of the past or dogmatic lawyers for the present, a transformation forced on them by the advent of the codification of the private law in Germany. This new historical research in Roman law began with Gradenwitz and Mitteis and ended with the birth of what is now known as modern legal history.[52]

---

49 Wieacker 1995, 331–334; Pugliese 1985, 434.
50 Christ 1988, 27–31.
51 Jhering 1993 [1906], vol. III, 323; Giaro 1991, 220; Helmut Coing, 'Der juristische Systembegriff bei Rudolf von Ihering', in J. Blühdorn, J. Ritter (eds.), *Philosophie und Rechtswissenschaft*, Frankfurt am Main 1969, 151–171; Rudolf Sohm, *Institutionen: Geschichte und System des römischen Privatrechts*, (14th ed.), Leipzig 1911.
52 Wieacker 1988, 46.

The final downfall of the German Pandectist jurisprudence came with the advent of positive law in the form of the *Bürgerliches Gesetzbuch* (BGB). This removed the practical value of Pandectist interpretation. Much has been made of the fact that one of the key figures in the drafting of the BGB was Windscheid, a leading Pandectist.[53] The separation of the heirs of the Historical School was now complete: positive law and legal history emerged from these trends. The historical turn initiated in the 1880s and the voluminous literature on areas like the reconstruction of Roman legal texts, and new studies on the other ancient legal traditions, can be called an 'expansion of the past'.[54] This proved to be crucial to the future of the discipline, as the studies of the following generation were increasingly historical in their method.

The dogmatic branch of Roman law gradually abandoned the Pandectistic construction of contemporary rules of law from the material of Roman law, to the degree that the concept of construction is currently euphemism for making matters too complicated. The final flowering of construction was ironically enough during the interpolation debate that began in the late nineteenth century, in which the material of Roman law was scoured for Late Antique additions that may have altered the classical rules. The quest for historical accuracy in the sources was troubled by the fact that their studies were still based on the systematic conceptual framework of Pandectism.[55]

Despite their disparity, Wieacker maintains that the studies produced in the pioneering age of 1880–1930 had a common agenda: the historification of normative interpretations and the combination of legal and historical knowledge.[56] The crisis of Roman law in the 1930s did not affect the spread of the latest neohumanistic historical scholarship as much as the teaching of Roman law. After the Second World War research on the history of Roman law separated itself farther from its origins in substantive law. This is manifested in the continued interest in archaic law, vulgar law, juristic prosopography,

---

53   Later observers have noted that the presentation of Windscheid as simply a positivist, as done for instance by Wieacker, is stereotypical and misleading. Cf. Ulrich Falk, *Ein Gelehrter wie Windscheid*, Frankfurt am Main 1989, 2–4, 216–218. Erik Wolf, *Große Rechtsdenker der Deutschen Geistesgeschichte*, Tübingen 1951: 'Windscheids Rechtsideal war also ein zugleich historisches und idealistisches, es erwuchs im Zusammenhang mit den Bildungsgütern des Klassizismus und Idealismus.'

54   Wieacker 1995, 333; Reinhard Zimmermann, *Roman law, contemporary law, European law*, Oxford 2000, 22–31.

55   Giaro 1991, 231; Giuliano Crifò, 'Pandettisti e storicisti nel diritto romano oggi', *Diritto romano attuale* 1 (1999), 12–13. The interpolation critique is generally understood as to have began with Gradenwitz's *Interpolationen in den Pandecten* in 1887.

56   Wieacker 1988, 49–51.

and juristic ideology, as well as the advent of the social history of Roman law.[57]

Contemporary relevance is always a vital part of the writing of history and the progress of scholarship, be it the Marxist approach to slavery, the narrative of European unity, or gender studies. The influence of contemporary ideas in the history of Roman law takes many shapes and forms. For example, Tony Honoré, in the new edition of his biography of Ulpian, has added the new subtitle 'Pioneer of Human Rights', and lauds Ulpian as the champion of equality, freedom, and dignity.[58]

---

57 Wieacker 1988, 52–55.
58 Tony Honoré, *Ulpian: Pioneer of Human Rights*, Oxford 2002, ix.

Chapter 2

The Birth of Legal Science

In the modern continental theory of law, if such a generalisation can be made, there is a widespread hypothesis or an assumption that the body of law or legal norms together forms a legal system, which is formulated, studied and perpetuated by legal science.

This preoccupation with science is characteristic of modern law, to the extent that in contemporary parlance, jurisprudence has become nearly synonymous with legal science. Science has become so ingrained within the whole concept of examining law that the distinction between jurisprudence and legal science is fading.

Like most scholarly disciplines or sciences, legal science has been interested in its own past as a science.[1] Whereas most of the natural sciences date their origins to the scientific revolution of the seventeenth century, legal science has traced its beginnings farther back in time, as far back as Antiquity.

The difficulty in seeking a clear point of origin is that traditions lasting a few millennia undergo such profound changes that it is always a matter of debate when such traditions start and when they end. For instance, protagonists of the scientific revolution from the sixteenth century onwards, like Francis Bacon, drew a clear distinction between their contemporary critical thinking and the medieval tradition. The medieval tradition represented backwardness, belief in the authorities and theological dogmas, scholastics and Aristotelianism. The new critical thought of the scientific revolution represented progress, new scientific methods, experimental inquiry and mathematical-geometrical logic. Had the question been presented to people like Newton, they would probably have defined themselves as the initiators of science. The dilemma of the multiple origins of a discipline is whether the true origins can be traced to Herodotos or Ranke, Galenos or Harvey, Theophrastos or Copernicus.[2]

In legal science the question of multiple origins has a peculiar feature in the two roots of Roman legal science. On one hand, Roman law was created by

[1]   Panu Minkkinen, *Thinking Without Desire: A First Philosophy of Law*, Oxford 1999, 30: 'as a modern science, the traditional paradigm of the philosophy of law is neo-Kantian.'
[2]   Donald Kelley, *The Descent of Ideas*, Aldershot 2002, 206–209.

the ancient Romans, on the other, Roman legal science is the product of later Romanistic and Pandectistic scholars. The ever more widely accepted paradox is that Roman jurisprudence was casuistic, whereas the Pandectists of the nineteenth century operated in a closed system that was constructed with the use of abstract concepts and principles. The modern interpretation of the Aristotelian concept of science was applied by the later Romanists to the ancient Roman sources, thus exporting their own concept of science to Rome in a process that is only slowly being undone.[3]

To analyse the development of the debate of the birth of science, I shall begin with the case of Quintus Mucius Scaevola, who is one of the supposed founders of legal science. The value of concentrating on a single person is that even though authors do not necessarily discuss abstract concepts like the birth of legal science, they do debate the ideas and deeds of a well-known person such as Quintus Mucius and raise different issues according to their interests.

Q. Mucius Scaevola Pontifex, the founding father of legal science

In a recent introduction to the history of legal interpretation from Antiquity to the present day, the birth and development of Western legal science is credited to the jurist Quintus Mucius Scaevola Pontifex, Roman consul for the year 95 BC (c. 140–82 BC). We learn that he established Roman jurisprudence as a distinct science and thus caused a revolutionary change in Western jurisprudence. Intellectual rigour, rationalisation, and organisation raised Roman jurists to the level of professional lawyers and gave jurisprudence the status of science.[4]

On closer examination one finds that the author has relied on a selection of well-known Romanists as his sources. Despite the fact that these sources unanimously give Quintus Mucius special credit, they still disagree about the exact nature of his accomplishment. Fritz Schulz praised the dialectical method of Quintus Mucius: '... for Roman jurisprudence it proved to be verily the fire of Prometheus.'[5] Peter Stein said that he was 'The earliest jurist to provide clear evidence of the influence of the Greek methods ...'[6] Alan Watson wrote that 'Quintus Mucius deserves the highest praise for being the

---

3   Pugliese 1985, 446–447. Similarly, Giaro 1991, 221.
4   David J. Bederman, *Classical Canons: Rhetoric, classicism and treaty interpretation*, Aldershot 2001, 73–81.
5   Fritz Schulz, *History of Roman Legal Science*, Oxford 1946, 64, 68, 94.
6   Stein 1966, 36.

first to arrange the civil law *generatim*.'⁷ Bruce Frier informed us that, as the innovator of the hypothetical case, Quintus Mucius is 'the father of Roman legal science and of the Western legal tradition', because he is 'undeniably the earliest jurist to have significant impact on the juristic tradition of Rome' and his 'intensity marked a quantum leap in legal science'.⁸

Something very interesting is going on here. Who is this man and how do we know that he is the father of the Western legal tradition? What is this legal tradition they are talking about? What are the significance of dialectical method, Greek methods, *generatim*, hypothetical case, and quantum leap?

The purpose of this chapter is to analyse the different threads of tradition woven around Quintus Mucius Scaevola Pontifex (hereafter Quintus Mucius), statesman, old Roman hero, leading jurist and the supposed founder of the science of law.

If we are to examine whether a historical person originated a tradition that has continued unto the present day, we should first decide on a matter of definition: what kind of science are we looking for? In our case, there are essentially two options. The first is that we should deduce how the Romans defined legal science as compared to mere jurisprudence, the second proceeds from some external yardsticks such as the modern concept of science.

Distinguishing the Roman concept of legal science can further be divided into two additional questions: how did the Romans themselves define it and how have modern researchers reconstructed the Roman conception? The Roman definition of *iuris scientia* is rather vague in the light of the legal sources and does not contain a clear distinction from *iuris prudentia*.⁹ This has led to an interesting discussion about the possibilities of a modern reconstruction of the Roman concept of legal science. There is an abundance of literature on the matter, in which the focus of the discussion has been on the possibility of finding some objective criteria for legal science.¹⁰

---

7 Alan Watson, *Law making in the later Roman republic*, Oxford 1974, 155.
8 Bruce W. Frier, *The Rise of the Roman Jurists: Studies in Cicero's pro Caecina*, Princeton 1985, 163, 168–171.
9 Dig. 1,1,10,17 (Ulpian) *Iuris prudentia est divinarum atque humanarum rerum notitia, iusti atque iniusti scientia*, see also Paul Dig. 45,1,91,3 *esse enim hanc questionem de bono et aequo: in quo genere plerumque sub auctoritate iuris scientiae perniciose, inquit, erratur.* The famous passage of Celsus in Ulpian's Dig. 1,1,1pr *ius est ars boni et aequi* has brought into the discussion also the possible distinction between *ars* and *scientia*. See also Cic. *top.* 31.
10 Félix Senn, *Les origines de la notion de jurisprudence*, Paris 1926; Giorgio La Pira, 'La genesi del sistema nella giurisprudenza romana', 4 articles, subtitles: 1. 'Problemi generali', in *Studi in onore di F. Virgili*, Siena 1935; 2. 'L'arte sistematrice', BIDR 42 (1934), 336–355; 3. 'Il metodo', SDHI 1 (1935), 319–348; 4. 'Il concetto di scienza', BIDR 44 (1936-37), 131–159; Schulz 1946,

The starting point of the debate was the conviction that Roman legal science was the origin of the current tradition. For many years, this position was almost universally accepted. Giorgio La Pira eloquently described Roman jurisprudence as the foundations of the great scientific building of law.[11] This consensus was, however, shattered by Theodor Viehweg's book in which he questioned whether Roman jurists developed a science in general, by comparing their ideas with Greek theories of science.[12] Mario Bretone pointed out that Viehweg denied the scientific nature of Roman legal science only because it did not fulfil his Aristotelian criteria.[13]

This began a series of debates on the methods of Roman jurists and the possible Greek influences.[14] The nature of logic used by Roman jurists, how it should be categorised, and to what it should be compared with was disputed at length from the late 1960s onwards by Horak, Flume, and Waldstein, among others. Horak strongly criticised the use of anachronistic models of legal science, such as Waldstein's use of Leibniz and Flume's use of Savigny.[15]

There have been questions on whether Roman legal science should be evaluated against some external criterion at all. Even as early as 1955, Hoetink warned of the use of anachronistic models and concepts. He admitted that the Roman legal historians should employ some concepts of modern law, but cautioned against the influence of the systematic tradition in interpretations. More recently, Tomasz Giaro has attacked as anachronistic neopositivism even the concept of science used by Horak, because all attempts at proving the scientific nature of Roman jurisprudence only mirror what the observer deems to be scientific. In a relativist note, Giaro claimed that the Roman jurists could not care less whether their activities could be considered scientific or not.[16]

      64, 68, 94; Johannes Stroux, *Römische Rechtswissenschaft und Rhetorik*, Potsdam 1949; Theodor Viehweg, *Topik und Jurisprudenz*, (3rd ed.), München 1965 [1953], 26–39; Max Kaser, *Zur Methode der römischen Rechtsfindung*, Göttingen 1962, only to name a few.
11   La Pira 1936/1937, 131.
12   Viehweg 1965, 37–39.
13   Mario Bretone, 'La logica dei giuristi di Roma', *Labeo* 1 (1955), 77.
14   Laurens Winkel, 'Le droit romain et la philosophie grecque', TR 65 (1997), 376.
15   Franz Horak, *Rationes decidendi*, Aalen 1969, 9–44, 65–76; Wolfgang Waldstein, 'Konsequenz als Argument klassischer Juristen', ZRG 92 (1975), 26–31. Franz Horak, 'Die römischen Juristen und der "Glanz der Logik"', in D. Medicus, H.H. Seiler (eds.), *Festschrift für Max Kaser zum 70. Geburtstag*, München 1976, 29–38. Already E. Cuq criticised the use of Leibnitz, Edouard Cuq, *Les institutions juridiques des romains II*, Paris 1908, 58.
16   H.R. Hoetink, 'Les notions anachroniques dans l'historiographie du droit', TR 23 (1955), 1–20; Tomasz Giaro, 'Die Illusion der Wissenschaftlichkeit', *Index* 22 (1994), 118–128.

The second option, embracing the modern definition of science as a starting point is supported by the fact that we are looking for the roots of contemporary legal science. The Encyclopaedia Britannica Online defines science as 'any system of knowledge that is concerned with the physical world and its phenomena and that entails unbiased observations and systematic experimentation. In general, a science involves a pursuit of knowledge covering general truths or the operations of fundamental laws.'[17] This is naturally a modern view of science, originating from the natural sciences tradition. However, the origins of the modern definition of legal science are partly within the natural sciences. Its beginnings can, for instance, be traced to Leibnitz's idea of the mathemathisation of jurisprudence with the help of concepts and axioms.[18] A more familiar example is von Savigny, who presented the idea of calculating with concepts (rechnen mit Begriffen) while outlining the method of the new kind of legal science.[19]

To use the modern concept of science would involve the culturally relative definition of modern legal science, and it would also contain the notion that legal development is the process of becoming like us, the modern legal scientists. That would mean that if we define legal science as continental systematic legal dogmatics as developed mainly during the 19th century in Germany,[20] we would run the risk of universalising our own legal culture at the expense of others. The problematic conceptual basis is manifested also in the development of literature on Quintus Mucius.

* * *

Even a comprehensive survey of the ancient sources sheds little light on the scientific nature of Quintus Mucius, because none of his writings have been preserved to us in their original form.[21] All we have left is a collection of

---

17 Science is notoriously hard to define and it could be argued whether law should be included discipline-wise as a science at all. See, Riccardo Orestano, *Introduzione allo studio del diritto romano*, Bologna 1987, 28–29; Paul Koschaker, *Europa und das römische Recht*, (2nd ed.), München 1953, 210: 'Der Terminus "Rechtswissenschaft" ist eine Erfindung der deutschen historischen Schule, ist made in Germany und Quelle von zahlreichen Unklarheiten geworden.'
18 Leibnitz 1768.
19 Savigny 1814, 29. Cf. also Dieter von Stephanitz, *Exakte Wissenschaft und Recht: der Einfluß von Naturwissenschaft und Mathematik auf Rechtsdenken und Rechtswissenschaft in zweieinhalb Jahrtausenden; ein historischer Grundriß*, Berlin 1970.
20 Cf. Walter Wilhelm, *Zur juristischen Methodenlehre im 19. Jahrhundert*, Frankfurt am Main 1958. This would not, of course, apply to lawyers from Common law countries, not to speak of other legal cultures.
21 The closest to the original may be Dig. 50,17,73.

quotations and references in the works of later Roman authors. This has led to considerable difficulties in determining the real meaning of his work.[22]

The main Roman sources to prove Quintus Mucius' scientific innovation are easily summarised: Pomponius informed us that Quintus Mucius Pontifex was the first to arrange the civil law *generatim*, Gaius wrote that Quintus Mucius distinguished five kinds of tutorship, and Paul criticised his *genera possessionis*.[23] The conventional wisdom is that these sources prove that Quintus Mucius organised the law into systematic categories.[24]

However, there is a second contender to the title of 'the father of Roman legal science and of the Western legal tradition': Servius Sulpicius Rufus (consul 51 BC), Cicero's friend and contemporary. Cicero wrote that while Quintus Mucius had great practical knowledge (*usus*) of the law, only Servius treated it as a science (*ars*).[25]

22 The authoritative biography of Q. Mucius with comprehensive references to classical sources is still F. Münzer's and B. Kübler's survey in *Pauly-Wissowa Real-Encyclopädie* 16, 437–446. Considerably more elaborate is Richard A. Bauman, *Lawyers in Roman Republican Politics*, München 1983, 340–421. See also A. Schneider, *Die drei Scaevola Ciceros*, München 1879, 22–50; Salvatore di Marzo, *Saggi critici sui Libri di Pomponio 'Ad Quintum Mucium'*, Palermo 1899; Gabriel Lepointe, *Quintus Mucius Scaevola: Sa vie et son œuvre juridique: Ses doctrines sur le Droit pontifical*, Paris 1926; Aldo Schiavone, *Nascita di giurisprudenza*, (2nd ed.), Bari 1976, 92–101; Okko Behrends, 'Die Wissenschaftslehre im Zivilrecht des Q. Mucius Scaevola pontifex', *Nachrichten der Akademie der Wissenschaften in Göttingen, Philologisch-historische Klasse* 7 (1976), 263–304; Vincenzo Giuffrè, *La traccia di Quinto Mucio*, Napoli 1993. On the position of Q. Mucius in Republican jurisprudence, see Wolfgang Kunkel, *Die Römischen Juristen: Herkunft und soziale Stellung*, (reprint of 2nd edition 1967) Köln 2001, 18, 45–53; Mario Talamanca, 'Développements socio-économiques et jurisprudence romaine à la fin de la république', in *Studi in onore di Cesare Sanfilippo 7*, Milano 1987, 773–791; Dario Mantovani, 'Iuris scientia e honores', in S. Romano (ed.), *Nozione formazione e interpretazione del diritto; Ricerche dedicate al F. Gallo I*, Napoli 1997, 648.
23 Dig. 1,2,2,41; Gaius Inst. 1,188; Dig. 41,2,3,23.
24 Schulz 1946, 64; Behrends 1976, 265–266.
25 Cic. *Brut.* 41,152; Stein 1966, 41–42. Servius' writings have not survived, but he is quoted by others in the Digest. Also Gellius and Festus quote him on a few occasions. Mario Bretone, 'La tecnica del responso serviano', *Labeo* 16 (1970), 7–16; Peter Stein, 'The place of Servius Sulpicius Rufus in the development of Roman legal science', in O. Behrends et al. (eds.), *Festschrift für Franz Wieacker zum 70. Geburtstag*, Göttingen 1978, 175–184; Wolfgang Waldstein, 'Cicero, Servius und die "Neue Jurisprudenz"', *IURA* 44 (1993), 85–147. Cf. also R. Schneider, *Questionum de Servio Sulpicio Rufo*, Leipzig 1834; Federico d'Ippolito, 'Cicerone e i maestri di Servio', in F. Cancelli (ed.), *La giustizia tra i popoli nell'opera e nel pensiero di Cicerone, Atti del convegno*,

The above presented material gives a slightly distorted image of how Quintus Mucius is depicted by Roman authors. Although Quintus Mucius is often evaluated primarily on the basis of Pomponius' short text, in the Roman sources the impression of Quintus Mucius, like that of nearly all late Republican jurists, originates from the numerous writings of Cicero. There are also clear connections between the accounts of Cicero and Pomponius. Bretone even suspects that one of Pomponius' sources was Cicero's lost book on *ius civile*.[26] One of the basic problems of the research on late Republican jurists is the fact that Cicero forms his own cosmos by virtue of being nearly the sole and definitely the most voluminous source available.[27]

The character of Quintus Mucius became a fixture of Cicero's creative imagination ever since he became a student of Quintus Mucius at the age of 18 after the death of Publius Mucius Scaevola. Cicero does not mention how long he followed the teaching of Quintus Mucius, but at the time of his death Cicero was 24 years old. Cicero wrote nothing of the nature of his education in the hands of Q. Mucius, although Behrends speculates on this. In the composition of his Sicilian edict Cicero incorporated many parts of Q. Mucius' Asian edict. Of these, two are mentioned, the *ex fide bona* -clause in contracts, and the legal autonomy of the Greeks, which states that cases between Greeks are to be settled according to Greek law.[28]

Cicero's references to Quintus Mucius fall roughly into three categories: statesman, lawyer, and orator. Cicero presents Quintus Mucius as an idealised figure, an *exemplum* of a virtuous Roman, who sought the glory of his forefathers in the traditional way by emulating them. His father, P. Mucius Scaevola, was *pontifex maximus* and an esteemed lawyer.[29]

Roma (1993), 53–71; Javier Paricio, 'La vocación de Servio Sulpicio Rufo', in M. Schermaier (ed.), *Iurisprudentia universalis: Festschrift für Theo Mayer-Maly zum 70. Geburtstag*, Köln 2002, 549–561.

26 Paul Krüger, *Geschichte der Quellen und Litteratur des Römischen Rechts*, (2nd ed.), München und Leipzig 1912, 64; Behrends 1976, 265–266. Mario Bretone, 'Pomponio lettore di Cicerone', *Labeo* 16 (1970), 177–182.

27 Franz Wieacker, 'Cicero und die Fachjurisprudenz seiner Zeit', *Ciceroniana* 3 (1978), 69–77; Mario Bretone, 'Cicerone e i giuristi del suo tempo', *Ciceroniana* 3 (1978), 47–68.

28 Cic. Lael. 1,1 *Quo mortuo me ad pontificem Scaevolam contuli, quem unum nostrae civitatis et ingenio et iustitia praestantissimum audeo dicere*. Behrends 1976, 268–269. Cic. Att. 6,1,15 ... *ex Q. Muci P. f. Edicto Asiatico, EXTRA QVAM SI ITA NEGOTIVM GESTVM EST, VT EO STARI NON OPORTEAT EX FIDE BONA, multaque sum secutus Scaevolae, in iis illud, in quo sibi libertatem censent Graeci datam, ut Graeci inter se disceptent suis legibus.*

29 Cic. off. 1,32,116 *Quorum vero patres aut maiores aliqua gloria praestiterunt, ii student plerumque eodem in genere laudis excellere, ut Q. Mucius P. f in iure civili, Pauli filius Africanus in re militari.*

Of the career of Quintus Mucius, Cicero mentions four phases on his *cursus honorum*: tribune of the plebs (106 BC),[30] curule edile (103 BC),[31] the consulate in (95 BC)[32] and the pontificate. He shared both the tribune and edile offices with L. Crassus, but nothing is recorded of either of his terms in office. Politically, he was securely optimate, and during 100 BC he took part in the campaign against the demagoque Saturninus.[33] Q. Mucius was also consul in 95 BC with L. Crassus. Regarding Q. Mucius' time in that capacity, Cicero mentions only the law that prevented non-citizens enjoying the privileges of citizens, which paved the way for the catastrophic Social War.[34]

Quintus Mucius was successful and liked as a governor of the province of Asia, although the year is uncertain. Cicero mentions him as an example of a good governor, whose reputation was such that Mithridates did not cancel the games that were held in his honour after having conquered the province of Asia.[35] Cicero gives few details on Quintus Mucius' time as *pontifex maximus*, except when Q. Mucius quotes his father on the necessity of legal knowledge to be a pontiff.[36]

The many virtues of Quintus Mucius, wisdom, intelligence, justice, prudence, moderation and modesty, were outlined and stressed repeatedly by Cicero. On many occasions he mentioned how Quintus Mucius was widely honoured because of his fine character and unblemished reputation.[37] According to Cicero his honesty was beyond doubt. As an example he told how Q. Mucius once bought a farm for a set price. Upon seeing it himself he raised the price by 100 000 sestertii, because he thought that the farm was worth more than the asking price.[38] In the Verrine orations, Cicero referred to Q. Mucius three times as a parable of honesty and authority in contrast to the dishonourable thugs represented by Verres and his like.[39]

---

30   Cic. *Brut.* 43,161.
31   Cic. *Verr.* 4,59,133; Cic. *off.* 2,16,57.
32   Cic. *Brut.* 64,229; Cic. *Verr.* 2,49,122.
33   Cic. *Rab. perd.* 7,21,100.
34   Cic. *off.* 3,11,47.
35   Cic. *Verr.* 3,90,209; Cic. *Verr.* 2,21,51 *Mithridates in Asia, cum eam prouinciam totam occupasset, Mucia non sustulit.*
36   Cic. *leg.* 2,19,47.
37   *Sapientissimus* (*off.* 3,11,47), *excellens ingenium ornatus vir* (*Brut.* 40,147), *praestantissimus et iustitia et ingenio* (*Lael.* 1,1), *prudentissimus homo* (*Caecin.* 18,53), and *omnium hominum moderatissimus* (*off.* 2,16,57).
38   Cic. *off.* 3,15,62 *Q. quidem Scaevola Publi filius, cum postulasset ut sibi fundus, cuius emptor erat, semel indicaretur idque venditor ita fecisset, dixit se pluris aestimare: addidit centum milia. Nemo est qui hoc viri boni fuisse neget; sapientis negant, ut si minoris quam potuisset vendidisset!*
39   Cic. *Verr.* 2,10,27; 2,13,34; 3,90,209.

To Cicero, Quintus Mucius is an ideal character, one of the virtuous ancestors (*maiores*) that attained lasting glory in the service of the Republic. Should one examine it as a narrative, Quintus Mucius also appears as a stock character, stereotypical and without dimension, whose virtue is a literary *topos* of Cicero's. He uses Quintus Mucius to appeal to the idealisation of Old Romans that was widespread during the late Republic. As his student, Cicero may have thought to gain some of the aura of rectitude.[40]

Cicero's references to Quintus Mucius' reputation as a jurist are numerous as are quotations of his legal opinions. Like his father, Quintus Mucius was a lawyer of the highest order, whose authority was based foremost on his distinguished learning in the civil law.[41] The citations of Quintus Mucius' opinions are frequent and at times bordering on irreverent, as in the case of the instructions he gave to Trebatius on how to survive the British winter, written in the form of a legal opinion which mentioned that the famous jurist Quintus Mucius supports the use of blankets.[42] In the *Topica* he gives a lengthy definition of inheritance and finally mentions that Q. Mucius agrees with him: *Hoc fortasse satis est. Nihil enim video Scaevolam pontificem ad hanc definitionem addidisse.* Q. Mucius' use of the term *ex fide bona* (in good faith) and its application and wide terms of reference (guardianships, partnerships, trusts, commissions, buying and selling, hiring and letting) is discussed by Cicero in *de officiis*. In a letter to Trebatius in June 44 BC he discusses a matter of inheritance law, in which Q. Mucius' opinion is given along with a number of others.[43]

The two failures of Quintus Mucius as a speaker are used repeatedly as negative examples of old-fashioned forensic speeches in Cicero's rhetorical works *Brutus* and *De Oratore*. The first speech had a minor role in the unsuccessful defence of P. Rutilius Rufus, Quintus Mucius' friend and legate. The charge against Rutilius was based on his actions as Quintus Mucius' legate in the province of Asia. Cicero mentioned that Rutilius did not employ professional orators, as would have been wise in a case like this, but defended himself with the help of Quintus Mucius. According to Cicero, Q. Mucius'

---

40   Wieacker 1978, 70; Donald Earl, *The Moral and Political Traditions of Rome*, London 1967, 7–33; L.R. Lind, 'Roman moral conservatism', in C. Deroux (ed.), *Studies in Latin Literature and Roman History I*, Bruxelles 1979, 36–40; Juhani Sarsila, *Some aspects of the concept of virtus in Roman literature until Livy*, Jyväskylä 1982. On the inseparability of virtue and law, Cic. *leg.* 1,15,42.–16,43.
41   Generally, *iuris peritissimus* (*leg.* 2,19,47), *disciplina juris civilis eruditissimus* (*de orat.* 1,39,180), and legal authority (*Caecin.* 24,69).
42   Cic. *fam.* 7,10.
43   *Top.* 29; *off.* 3,17,70; *fam.* 7,22.

speech was clear and lucid, simple and polished, but without the fire and fullness which a trial of that kind would have demanded.[44]

The second speech examined by Cicero is Quintus Mucius' duel with L. Crassus in the celebrated *Causa Curiana*. This was a case in the centumviral court in 93 BC about the right of a certain Manius Curius to an inheritance. L. Crassus represented Curius, and made a plea for equity, while Q. Mucius represented the other heir, demanding strict interpretation of the law. Despite all his intelligence and learning in jurisprudence, Quintus Mucius lost the case because of the superior expressiveness of L. Crassus though he did establish a reputation for eloquence for himself. For Cicero the case was a highly symbolic one, because L. Crassus had taught him eloquence and Q. Mucius law.[45] The case has been highly contested also in the debate on the relationship between jurists and orators in Rome.[46]

Quintus Mucius' virtues only highlight the gruesomeness of his murder in front of the statue of Vesta by the supporters of Marius in the riots of 82 BC. He had already been wounded in the riots after the funeral of Marius in 86 BC, but had stood his ground and preferred a virtuous death at the hands of the Marians than fleeing and taking up arms against his country. This Cicero took as an example of virtue and guidance to use during a desperate situation in the civil war in 49 BC. He also used the murder of Q. Mucius later in *De natura deorum* as an example of the mysterious ways of the gods. Why did they allow the virtuous and prudent Q. Mucius to be killed in front of the statue of Vesta?[47]

---

44 *Brut.* 30,115 *Q. Mucius enucleate ille quidem et polite, ut solebat, nequaquam autem ea vi atque, copia quam genus illud iudici et magnitudo causae postulabat*; Cic. *de orat.* 1,53,229 *Dixit item causam illam quadam ex parte Q. Mucius, more suo, nullo apparatu, pure et dilucide*. Jean-Michel David, *Le patronat judiciare au dernier siècle de la république Romaine*, (B.E.F.A.R. 277) École Française de Rome (1992), 716–717.

45 *Brut.* 39,145 *Cum uterque ex contraria parte ius civile defenderet, ut eloquentium iuris peritissimus Crassus, iuris peritorum eloquentissimus Scaevola putaretur*; *de orat.* 1,39,180 *cum Q. Scaevola, aequalis et collega meus homo omnium et disciplina juris civilis eruditissimus, et ingenio prudentiaque acutissimus, et oratione maxime limatus atque subtilis, atque, ut ego soleo dicere; iuris peritorum eloquentissimus, eloquentium iuris peritissimus*; *Caecin.* 18,53.

46 Jan W. Tellegen, 'Oratores, Iurisprudentes and the "Causa Curiana"', RIDA 30 (1983), 293–311; Franz Wieacker, 'The Causa Curiana and contemporary Roman Jurisprudence', *Irish Jurist* 2 (1967), 151; Gian L. Falchi, 'Interpretazione "tipica" nella "Causa Curiana"', SDHI 46 (1980), 383–430; Jan W. Tellegen and Olga E. Tellegen-Couperus, 'Law and Rhetoric in the causa Curiana', *Orbis Iuris Romani* 6 (2000), 171–202.

47 *Att.* 8,3,5–6 *Qua autem aut quo, nihil scimus. At, si restitero, et fuerit nobis in hac parte locus, idem fecero quod in Cinnae dominatione L. Philippus, quod*

Cicero does not mention Quintus Mucius in connection to the systematic presentation of the law. Neither does he say that Quintus Mucius had an interest in Stoic philosophy, whereas Q. Mucius Scaevola Augur is mentioned by Cicero as an enthusiast of Stoic learning.[48]

There are, however, several passages in which Cicero ponders the possibility of legal science that could have been linked to Quintus Mucius, should Cicero have thought it appropriate to do so. Cicero stated, in general, that the dialectic method and civil law were being studied. He also pondered the possibility of dividing civil law according to *species* and *genus*. This division he introduced as the basis of his own presentation of civil law, a project that would divide the law into general classes and subdivisions, all with clear definitions of significance. The result would be an *ars* of civil law, or legal science.[49]

As mentioned before, Cicero assigns the science of law to his friend Servius Sulpicius Rufus in the celebrated passage where he gives Quintus Mucius the credit for making good practical use, *magnus usus*, of the civil law. Servius, on the other hand, made it into an *ars* of *iuris scientia*.[50] As Wieacker says, it is not totally insignificant that Cicero, who knew both jurists and their work well, should say that Q. Mucius did not practise legal science.[51]

The Ciceronian presentation of Quintus Mucius could be summed up as a virtuous old Roman, who excelled as a lawyer and orator. It is clear that

---

L. *Flaccus, quod Q. Mucius, quoquo modo ea res huic quidem cecidit; qui tamen ita dicere solebat, se id fore videre, quod factum est, sed malle quam armatum ad patriae moenia accedere; nat. deor.* 3,32,80.

48 Cic. *de orat.* 1,11,45.

49 Cic. *off.* 1,6,19; *top.* 31; *de orat.* 1,42,190 *primum omne ius civile in genera digerat, quae perpauca sunt; deinde eorum generum quasi quaedam membra dispertiat; tum propriam cuiusque vim definitione declaret; perfectam artem iuris civilis habebitis, magis magnam atque uberem, quam difficilem atque obscuram.*

50 *Brut.* 41,152 *Etiamne Q. Scaevolae Servium nostrum anteponis? Sic enim, inquam, Brute, existimo, iuris civilis magnum usum et apud Scaevolam et apud multos fuisse, artem in hoc uno; quod numquam effecisset ipsius Iuris scientia, nisi eam praeterea didicisset artem quae doceret rem universam tribuere in partis, latentem explicare definiendo, obscuram explanare interpretando, ambigua primum videre, deinde distinguere, postremo habere regulam qua vera et falsa iudicarentur et quae quibus propositis essent quaeque non essent consequentia. Hic enim attulit hanc artem omnium artium maximam quasi lucem ad ea quae confuse ab aliis aut respondebantur aut agebantur.*

51 Franz Wieacker, 'Über das Verhältnis der römischen Fachjurisprudenz zur griechisch-hellenistischen Theorie', *IURA* 20 (1969), 464. Cf. also Ferdinando Bona, 'L'ideale retorico ciceroniano ed il "ius civile in artem redigere"', SDHI 46 (1980), 282–382.

Cicero uses Quintus Mucius as a stereotypical presentation of the respected old Romans, *maiores*.

After Cicero, Roman authors mention Quintus Mucius frequently, as a historical person and a legal author. Varro quotes him on two occasions in *De lingua Latina*;[52] Diodorus Siculus speaks at length of Quintus Mucius' auspicious governorship in Asia and his death, while Velleius Paterculus only reports that Quintus Mucius, *pontifex maximus* and the celebrated author of divine and civil law, was among the victims of the massacre ordered by praetor Damasippus in the Curia Hostilia during the battle of Sacriportus.[53] Asconius' extant comments on Cicero's speeches make reference to Quintus Mucius,[54] and Valerius Maximus hails the temperance of Quintus Mucius when giving a *responsum*.[55] Other authors include the epitome of Livy, Columella and Lucan.[56] Augustine says that Quintus Mucius divided gods into three *genera* (*theologia tripertita*), which is the only non-legal reference to Quintus Mucius and categorisation present in the Roman literature.[57]

52   On the sanctity of the calendar and the *nefas*-day (*ling.* 6,4,30), and on the etymology of the word *pontifex* (*ling.* 5,15,83).
53   Diodorus Siculus 37,5–6; 37,29; 38/39,17; Vell. 2,26,2.
54   He prevented L. Crassus' triumph. Asconius, *Pis.* 62 mentions *lex Licinia Mucia* of the most wise consuls. Ascon. *Corn.* 67,20–23 (Marshall) has a similar theme to Cic. *off.* 3,11,47. The interpretation of *Pis.* 62 has been contested, since it provides the only dating for Q. Mucius' governorship in Asia. The phrase *idem provinciam ... deposuerat ne sumptui esset* has been read to mean both years 100–98 and 94. On the dating, see Lepointe 1926, 23–25; B. A. Marshall, 'The Date of Q. Mucius Scaevola's Governorship of Asia', *Athenaeum* 54 (1976), 117–130.
55   Val. Max. 4,1,11 *Quod animi temperamentum etiam in Q. Scaeuola, excellentissimo viro, adnotatum est. Testis namque in reum productus, cum id respondisset, quod salutem periclitantis magnopere laesurum videbatur, discedens adjecit ita sibi credi oportere, si et alii idem asseverassent; quoniam unius testimonio aliquem cadere pessimi esset exempli. Et religioni igitur suae debitam fidem et communi utilitati salubre consilium reddidit.* He is mentioned as the glorious colleague of L. Crassus, who was hailed by the Senate as a model governor for Asia (8,15–16). Also mentioned is the political nature of the trial of Rutilius (6,4,4).
56   The epitome of Livy faulted the trial of Rutilius on the knights, whose excesses Rutilius had limited in Asia. Liv. *perioch.* 70. Q. Mucius is dubbed proconsul (C. Mucii pro cos.) and his first name is mistaken as Gaius. Q. Mucius was killed *fugiens in vestibulo aedis Vestae* (Liv. *perioch.* 86). Columella gave an example of Q. Mucius' frugality, noting that the *preaestantissimus vir* had built too small buildings for his farm (1,4,6, quoted also by Plin. *nat.* 18,32). Lucanus gave a gruesome account of Q. Mucius' death in *Pharsalia* (2,126–130).
57   *De civitate dei* 4,27. On Q. Mucius' theological dimension, see Bauman 1983, 351–361; Aldo Schiavone, *Giuristi e nobili nella Roma repubblicana*, Bari

The legal sources contain a wide variety of material on Quintus Mucius of which only the above quoted Gaius and Pomponius, and his own passage in Dig. 50,17,73 lend any support to the founding father theory. The earliest legal quotations are from Gaius, who discussed how many kinds (*species*) of guardianship (*tutela*) there are and into how many classes (*genera*) these kinds may be divided as well as how the ancient lawyers did this. Quintus Mucius divided *tutela* into five classes, Servius Sulpicius into three and Labeo into two. Gaius also mentioned a disagreement between Quintus Mucius and Servius on the definition of the nature of partnership (*societas*).[58] Aulus Gellius quoted four legal opinions by Quintus Mucius and two definitions of the meaning of words.[59]

Quintus Mucius is mentioned in the Digest in three different roles: the historical Quintus Mucius of Pomponius' *Enchiridion*, the jurist Quintus Mucius, whose opinion is quoted, and the authority Quintus Mucius, who inspired several works *ad Q. Mucium*.[60]

Pomponius mentioned Quintus Mucius twice in the extant chapters of the *Enchiridion*. The first passage outlines Quintus Mucius' general achievements in the development of the civil law:

> Quintus Mucius, son of Publius and a pontifex maximus, became the first man to produce a general compendium of the civil law by arranging it into eighteen books.[61]

The main difficulty in the translation is *ius civile primus constituit generatim*. The German translation of the same text formulates this as 'ordnete ... das Zivilrecht nach Begriffen ...', which demonstrates how difficult it is to trans-

---

1987, 73–108; Aldo Schiavone, 'Quinto Mucio teologo', *Labeo* 20 (1974), 315–361.

58   Gaius Inst. 1,188 *(Tutelarum) quidam quinque genera esse dixerunt, ut Q. Mucius: alii tria, ut Ser. Sulpicius; alii duo, ut Labeo; alii tot genera esse crediderunt, quot etiam species essent.* On *societas* Gaius Inst. 3,149.

59   The opinions regard the possibility of a woman being liberated from the *tutela* (3,2,12), a formula prepared by Q. Mucius for adoption (5,19,6), the limits of use of a borrowed object (6,15,2) *Itaque Q. Scaevola in librorum quos De Iure Civili composuit XVI, verba haec posuit: 'Quod cui servandum datum est, si id usus est, sive quod utendum accepit, ad aliam rem atque accepit usus est, furti se obligavit.'* and the correct interpretation of *lex Atinia* (17,7).

60   On Quintus Mucius' fundamental role as a part of the prehistory of law in the works of Pomponius in general, see Emanuele Stolfi, *Studi sui 'libri ad edictum' di Pomponio I*, Napoli 2002, 309–314.

61   Dig. 1,2,2,41 *Post hos Quintus Mucius Publii filius pontifex maximus ius civile primus constituit generatim in libros decem et octo redigendo.* Translation by D.N. MacCormick in Mommsen-Krüger-Watson (eds.), *The Digest of Justinian*, Philadelphia 1985.

late technical vocabulary and how much intellectual baggage each translation brings as the whole meaning of the text depends on how *generatim* is understood.[62]

The second passage in the *Enchiridion* is a story about Servius Sulpicius asking for the advice of Quintus Mucius and repeatedly not understanding the reply he was given. For this Quintus Mucius reproached him severely, saying that it was a disgrace for a patrician of a noble family who regularly appeared as an advocate in courts to be ignorant of the law on which his cases relied. This insult supposedly led Servius to the serious study of law.[63]

Quintus Mucius is chronologically the earliest jurist in the Digest, and his opinions are quoted by other jurists 46 times.[64] The vast majority of quota-

---

[62] Okko Behrends et al., *Corpus Iuris Civilis: Text und Übersetzung II*, Heidelberg 1995, 107.

[63] Dig. 1,2,2,43 *Servius autem Sulpicius cum in causis orandis primum locum aut pro certo post Marcum Tullium optineret, traditur ad consulendum Quintum Mucium de re amici sui pervenisse cumque eum sibi respondisse de iure Servius parum intellexisset, iterum quintum interrogasse et a Quinto Mucio responsum esse nec tamen percepisse, et ita obiurgatum esse a Quinto Mucio: namque eum dixisse turpe esse patricio et nobili et causas oranti ius in quo versaretur ignorare. Ea velut contumelia Servius tactus operam dedit iuri civili et plurimum eos, de quibus locuti sumus, audiit, institutus a Balbo Lucilio, instructus autem maxime a Gallo Aquilio ...*

[64] Dig. 7,8,4,1 Ulp. 17 Ad Sab.; Dig. 8,2,7pr Pomp. 26 Ad Q. Muc.; Dig. 8,3,15 Pomp. 31 Ad Q. Muc.; Dig. 9,1,1,11 Ulp. 18 Ad Ed.; Dig. 9,2,31pr Paul. 10 Ad Sab.; Dig. 9,2,39pr Pomp. 17 Ad Q. Muc.; Dig. 13,6,5,3 Ulp. 28 Ad Ed.; Dig. 17,1,48pr Cels. 7 Dig.; Dig. 17,2,11 Ulp. 30 Ad Sab.; Dig. 17,2,30pr Paul. 6 Ad Sab.; Dig. 18,1,59 Cels. 8 Dig.; Dig. 18,1,66,2 Pomp. 31 Ad Q. Muc.; Dig. 18,2,13pr Ulp. 28 Ad Sab.; Dig. 19,1,40 Pomp. 31 Ad Q. Muc.; Dig. 21,2,75 Ven. 16 Stipul.; Dig. 24,1,51pr Pomp. 5 Ad Q. Muc.; Dig. 26,1,3pr Ulp. 37 Ad Sab.; Dig. 28,5,35,3 Ulp. 4 Disp.; Dig. 32,29,1 Lab. 2 Post. A Iav. Epit.; Dig. 32,55pr Ulp. 25 Ad Sab.; Dig. 33,1,7pr Pomp. 8 Ad Q. Muc.; Dig. 33,5,9,2 Iul. 32 Dig.; Dig. 33,9,3pr Ulp. 22 Ad Sab.; Dig. 33,9,3,6 Ulp. 22 Ad Sab.; Dig. 33,9,3,9 Ulp. 22 Ad Sab.; Dig. 34,2,10 Pomp. 5 Ad Q. Muc.; Dig. 34,2,19,9 Ulp. 20 Ad Sab.; Dig. 34,2,27pr Ulp. 44 Ad Sab.; Dig. 34,2,33pr Pomp. 4 Ad Q. Muc.; Dig. 34,2,34pr Pomp. 9 Ad Q. Muc.; Dig. 34,2,34,1 Pomp. 9 Ad Q. Muc.; Dig. 34,2,34,2 Pomp. 9 Ad Q. Muc.; Dig. 39,3,1,3 Ulp. 53 Ad Ed.; Dig. 39,3,1,4 Ulp. 53 Ad Ed.; Dig. 40,7,29,1 Pomp. 18 Ad Q. Muc.; Dig. 40,7,39pr Iav. 4 Ex Post. Lab.; Dig. 40,12,23pr Paul. 50 Ad Ed.; Dig. 41,2,3,23 Paul. 54 Ad Ed.; Dig. 43,24,1,5 Ulp. 71 Ad Ed.; Dig. 43,24,5,8 Ulp. 70 Ad Ed.; Dig. 43,24,5,9. Ulp. 70 Ad Ed.; Dig. 45,1,115,2 Pap. 2 Quaest.; Dig. 47,2,77,1 Pomp. 38 Ad Q. Muc.; Dig. 50,7,18 Pomp. 37 Ad Q. Muc.; Dig. 50,16,25,1 Paul. 21 Ad Ed.; Dig. 50,16,98,1 Cels. 39 Dig. The list in Otto Lenel, *Palingenesia juris civilis*, Leipzig 1889, 758–764, is at times imprecise. It also adds to these Dig. 41,2,25,2 Pomp. 23 Ad Q. Muc. (probably because van de Water read *quasi magis* as an interpolation of *Quintus Mucius*) and Dig. 46,3,81,1 Pomp. 6 Ad Q. Muc., although neither

tions relate to straightforward points of law. Most of the quotations are positive, leaning on his juridical authority, although there is an exception.[65]

Do the extant passages testify to Q. Mucius' eminent standing among later Roman jurists? Yes, they do. If the question we are asking is whether Quintus Mucius established jurisprudence as a distinct science by organising the material of law in a rational manner, the answer is not so clear. We have short, disconnected fragments from other writers' texts. It is, therefore, difficult to reach a conclusion on Quintus Mucius' categorisations and definitions.

However, there are a few extant categorisations and definitions available. Ulpian, who quotes Quintus Mucius most, cites seven definitions, ranging from a distinction between firewood and timber,[66] what is to be included in the legacy of stores, *penus*,[67] the extent of persons involved in *usus sui gratia paratum* or entourage,[68] the correct interpretation of the testamentary clause *quod eius causa emptum paratumque esset*,[69] what is included in a legacy of silver,[70] and how can force, *vis*, be defined.[71]

Pomponius only quoted one opinion by Quintus Mucius relating to categorisation: if a certain senator habitually wears a woman's dinner dress, that dress would not be included in his legacy of women's clothing.[72] Paul quotes two interesting cases. In the first he criticises Quintus Mucius' choice of definition of what is to be included in the category of possessions, *quod inter genera possessionum posuit*. The second is a definition of what constitutes a part.[73]

The most celebrated example of Quintus Mucius' definitions is an excerpt of his sole book on *Horoi* or definitions, that contains five definitions, two on

mention him, and also Dig. 49,15,4, which more probably refers to P. Mucius Scaevola and his controversy with Brutus (see Bauman 1983, 238, n. 97).

[65] As mentioned above, Paul Dig. 41,2,3,23 referred to his opinion as *ineptissimus*.
[66] Dig. 32,55pr.
[67] Dig. 33,9,3pr; Dig. 33,9,3,9.
[68] Dig. 33,9,3,6 ... *Quintus Mucius sic definiebat* ...
[69] Dig. 34,2,10pr.
[70] Dig. 34,2,19,9; Dig. 34,2,27pr *Quintus Mucius libro secundo iuris civilis ita definit argentum factum vas argenteum videri esse*.
[71] Dig. 43,24,1,5.
[72] Dig. 34,2,33pr. Bernardo Albanese, 'Volontà negoziale e forma in una testimonianza di Q. Mucio Scaevola', in Manfred Harder, Georg Thielmann (eds.), *De iustitia et iure, Festschrift für U. von Lübtow*, Berlin (1980), 157–158 wishes to prove that unisex-clothing was widespread in Rome and that the senator was not necessarily a transvestite.
[73] Dig. 41,2,3,23; Dig. 50,16,25,1 *Quintus Mucius ait partis appellatione rem pro indiviso significari: nam quod pro diviso nostrum sit, id non partem, sed totum esse*.

tutory, one each on the interpretation of a will, the definition of *vis* or force, and surety for another.[74]

In addition to these, there are 140 quotes from Pomponius' work *ad Q. Mucium* in the Digest and seven from Modestin's similarly titled work.

The Roman sources portray different aspects of Quintus Mucius, each depending on their own interests. Cicero gives an idealistic account of Quintus Mucius, statesman, lawyer, orator. To Cicero he was an exemplary nobleman and a true old Roman. The variety of historians, grammarians, antiquarians, and poets citing him mainly stress his virtues and martyrdom. To the legal writers, Quintus Mucius is obviously an authority of the highest degree.

As to the main question under consideration, the scientific breakthrough made by Quintus Mucius, the record is patchy at best. Cicero, a verbocious author who knew the man and his works, and who was familiar with the contemporary concept of science in general, does not say anything about it. Neither do the non-legal authors. The Roman jurists say that Quintus Mucius divided some things into categories and defined a lot of concepts. Is this enough to say that he organised law systematically and rationally? There is no definite answer for that question, which is precisely why following the history of interpretations can be so revealing.

Science as the ideal of law

This overview of sources and literature may leave the uninitiated with a hollow feeling. What has been the cause of this great tradition? Not the Roman sources, that is certain. Sometime in the mid-nineteenth century the scientific beginnings of Roman law were discovered, invented, and accepted with gusto. During that period a veritable scientific revolution was recognised in Late Republican jurisprudence and Quintus Mucius was named as its principal character in a process that may be called the invention of tradition.

The Roman narrative tradition on Quintus Mucius contains several discernible strands, which may be divided into those describing Quintus Mucius as the ideal Roman, and those portraying Quintus Mucius as the great lawyer of the old Roman model. The biography of Quintus Mucius, the ideal Roman, begins with a noble pedigree and continues with his service to the state that is rewarded with an advancement through the *cursus honorum*. In sum, it depicts the attainment of lasting honour through a life of virtue. This story is the creation of Cicero, who used Quintus Mucius as an example of the

---

74   Dig. 50,17,73.

virtuous Roman nobleman. Quintus Mucius' martyrdom provides a fitting end to the story, in which the respected elder finds no sanctuary from the statue of Vesta and dies a victim of senseless civil strife. This obviously struck a chord with poets and historians wishing to portray the destruction inflicted upon Rome during the civil wars.

The story of Quintus Mucius the lawyer also has its roots in the works of Cicero, which provide the testimony of legal sources a narrative foundation. The legal authority of Quintus Mucius was an essential part of Cicero's general presentation of him as the ideal Roman. Cicero heaped praise on his learning and authority, while other Roman authors merely note that he was a lawyer. Though legal sources seldom mention someone's reputation, Quintus Mucius' authority is apparent in the sheer volume of quotations and references to his opinions. The only other source describing Quintus Mucius the jurist besides Cicero is Pomponius, who does not tell much besides the 18 books *generatim*.

Thus it is no wonder, that when legal historians began to depict Quintus Mucius' person, they had precious little to draw upon except Cicero. The image of Quintus Mucius was a combination of Quintus Mucius the lawyer and Quintus Mucius the ideal Roman, a mix of professional and human interest in the best tradition of the history of great men.

The earlier scholarship in legal history from the sixteenth century clearly followed Cicero's example, both in how legal science was defined as divisions and definitions and the respective roles of Servius and Quintus Mucius in it. As an example, the celebrated *De claris iuris consultis* of ca. 1511 by Diplovatatius offers a sketch of Quintus Mucius that closely follows the Roman authors, stressing his authority as a jurist and writer, his virtues as provincial governor and his skill in oratory. There is nothing here about legal science outside the *generatim* of Pomponius.[75] The main composition on Quintus Mucius of the time, F. Balduinus's *Commentarius de iurisprudentia muciana*, is chiefly a commentary of the Digest fragments, but contains a long biography, which glosses very briefly over the *generatim*.[76]

A similar tendency runs through the literature from the sixteenth to the eighteenth centuries. Quintus Mucius is lauded as a virtuous man and the organiser of the law, but science is credited to Servius. Budé, Rutilius, François

---

75 Thomas Diplovatatius, *De claris iuris consultis*, (ed. F. Schulz), Berlin und Leipzig 1919, 202–205. This edition is based on the Olivieris Hs. in Pesaro of 1550. Laetus 1535; Valentinus Forster, *De historia iuris romani*, Helmstedt 1609, 443–450 [ch. 33]; Guido Panziroli, *De claris legum interpretibus*, Leipzig 1721, 26–27 [ch. 1.11] does already mention order and *scientia*.
76 Franciscus Balduinus, *Commentarius de iurisprudentia muciana*, Basel 1558, biographical notes p. 95–306, on *generatim* p. 153–154.

Hotman (1524–1590), and others heap praise at Servius for *iuris scientia*, dialectics, *regulae*, definitions, and distribution *in partes* while scarcely noticing Quintus Mucius and the 18 books *generatim*.[77] The accomplishments of Republican jurists in science and organisation are also noted elsewhere. Hubert van Giffen (1534–1612) quoted Socrates in that nothing is as beautiful and useful as order (*ordine, dispositione*), and Servius ranks as one of the great organisers of law along with Justinian and Julian.[78] J. Godefroy praised the Republican jurists for bringing science into law through commentaries and responses. They edited the law according to a reliable scientific method and reduced the immense volume of laws into a few books.[79]

Later, the predominance of the idea of science waned, and many biographers omit the whole theme. For instance, Gerhard Feltmann's (1637–1696) account is typical of the development as he does not mention the whole concept of *ars*. Q. Mucius is briefly mentioned as the one who organised matters in his writings, whereas Servius is given much more space.[80]

During the eighteenth century interest in legal science increased, but Quintus Mucius was still unrecognised. Johann Gottlieb Heineccius's 1728 commentary on Pomponius' text fails to even mention Quintus Mucius in the list of notable early legal writers.[81] Later, Heineccius only briefly mentions Quintus Mucius' life and works, but on several occasions, referred to Servius

77   Budaeus 1557 [1969], 7, 59 [ad Dig. 1,1; 1,2,2,41–43]; Bernard Rutilius, *Iurisconsultorum vitae*, Basel 1537, 111–116, 121–127 [Q. Mucius, Servius]: *primus arte quadam eam scientiam pertractavit* (p. 122); Franciscus Hotomannus, *De iurisconsultorum vitis*, Frankfurt 1587, 162 [Ser. Sulpicius]. Donald Kelley, *The Human Measure: Social Thought in the Western Legal Tradition*, Cambridge 1990, 197: 'They [French jurists of Bourges] also invoked the analogy of mathematics and geometry, especially in connection with "harmonic justice," and they preserved and even extended the connections between law and logic. ... The drift of these analogies was to establish the "scientific" nature of jurisprudence in general, an issue which has dominated social thought down to the present day.'

78   Hubertus Giphanius, *Oeconomia juris sive dispositio methodica*, Strasbourg 1612, 1–2: *Jurisconsulti arte & ordine omnia tractare coeperunt.* (p. 2).

79   Jacobus Gothofredus, *Manuale juris seu parva juris mysteria*, Napoli 1766, 22–23 [ch. 2.6]: *de jure civili in artem & ad certum modum redigendo, & in paucissimos libros ex immesa diffusaque legum copia conferendo.* (p. 23)

80   Gerhardus Feltmannus, *Commentarius ad Digestorum seu Pandectarum lib. I et II.*, Leipzig 1678, 77–79 [ad Dig. 1,2,2,42–43]. Similarly, Wilhelm Grotius, *Vitae Jurisconsultorum*, Leiden 1690, 45 [P. Mucius], 58–61 [Q. Mucius], 74–78 [Servius], mentioned in passing the *libri Horoi*, but mixed his Scaevolas and misplaced Pomponius' *generatim*.

81   Johann Gottlieb Heineccius, *Elementa iuris civilis secundum ordinem Pandectarum*, Amsterdam 1728, 25 [ad Dig. 1,2,2].

and the concept of *ars*, and that many lawyers were Stoics. The contribution of Stoic learning to jurisprudence he divided into the derivation of names, definitions, and divisions (such as *corporales* and *incorporales*).[82]

The rise in Quintus Mucius' fortunes may be linked with Johannes Augustus Bach's *Historia Jurisprudentiae Romanae*, which stressed the virtues of Quintus Mucius in Ciceronian tones and his stature as the greatest jurist of his time. However, according to Bach it was Servius, the greatest of *all* jurists, who gave jurisprudence the strong exactness of science.[83]

A complete reversal on these grounds was made by the Spanish polymath Gregorio Mayáns y Siscar or Gregorius Maiansius (1697–1781) who first raised the issue of science in connection with Quintus Mucius in his extended biography. Maiansius wrote that Quintus Mucius was the first to collect rules of law under the influence of scientific reason in order to construct the civil law on the foundation provided by P. Mucius, Brutus, and Manilius. He recounts Quintus Mucius' life, career, virtues (*prudentia, integritas, fortitudo*, p. 175), and cruel death, even the fact that Cicero is partial to Servius.[84] To Maiansius, science was the collection and application of legal rules, *regulae iuris*. The creativity of Quintus Mucius is emphasised: '*Hoc certum est. Q. Mucium Scaevolam ex Jurisconsultis primum fuisse Regularum collectorem, & ut erat acutissimo ingenio, fortasse etiam inventorem.*'[85]

The new interpretation of Maiansius was not picked up by his contemporaries. Scholarship in general was more curious with regard to science and began to elaborate on its definition. In the influential chapter 44 of the *Decline and Fall of the Roman Empire* (1788), Edward Gibbon stressed the

---

82   Johann Gottlieb Heineccius, *Historia Iuris Civilis Romani et Germanici*, Strasbourg 1751, 226–228 [ch. 144–145], 233 [ch. 150]; Johann Gottlieb Heineccius, *Antiquitatum Romanarum Iurisprudentiam Illustrantium Syntagma secundum ordinem Institutionum*, Geneve 1747, 29–30 [ad Inst. Iust. 1,1,4], 300–301 [ad Inst. Iust. 2,2].
83   Johannes Augustus Bach, *Historia Jurisprudentiae Romanae*, Lucca 1762, 136–138 [ch. 2.2.4.39–40, 44]. Similarly, Antoine Terrasson, *Histoire de la jurisprudence romaine*, Paris 1750, 229.
84   Gregorius Maiansius, *Ad triginta jurisconsultorum omnia fragmenta quae exstant in juris civilis corpore commentarii*, Geneve 1764, 169–185: *Didicimus etiam, patrem eius P. Mucium una cum Bruto &Manilio fundavisse Jus Civile. Ergo hi veluti caementa Juris Civilis posuerunt: Q. autem Mucius Jus Civile construxit. Illi videntur casus & responsa proposuisse: Hic Juris argumenta distribuisse, singola tractans generatim, hoc est, definitionibus, sive regulis: qua ratione Scientia tradi debet, & nominatim Jurisprudentia, uti docuit L. Crassus apud Ciceronem, de orat 42, Atque hoc modo Jus Civile in libros decem & octo redegit.* (p. 178–9). Maiansius describes organisation and order as the tasks of jurisprudence (p. i-v).
85   Maiansius 1764, 183.

great advantage to jurisprudence of the alliance with 'Grecian philosophy'. The logic of Aristotle and the Stoics allowed for the reduction of particular cases to general principles, and 'diffused over the shapeless mass the light of order and eloquence.' However, Gibbon followed Cicero on the matter of science and gave credit to Servius Sulpicius for this achievement.[86]

In Hugo's Roman legal history, itself the first to claim to be scientific, the transformation of Roman law into science occurred in Cicero's time. Behind this change was the wide diffusion of Greek learning among jurists, who cite Homer, Hippocrates, Plato, Demosthenes, and Chrysippos, and were conversant in philosophy, especially in austere Stoicism. Hugo's definition of legal science is evident in his references to Leibniz and Kant. He agreed with Leibniz that the Roman jurists were like mathematicians in their rigorous development of legal definitions. For the importance of method in jurisprudence and the use of trichotomies and dichotomies he compared Kant to the Roman jurists. Hugo called Quintus Mucius the first didactic legal author, because he interpreted the word *generatim* as meaning something different than casuistry. The mantle of 'the first' is given to Servius, because it is 'very probable' that methodical order began in this period and it is impossible to bestow it on someone else.[87]

The Quintus Mucius versus Servius controversy is quite visible in Haubold's Roman law textbook from 1826. Haubold tersely noted that the *regulae iuris*[88] are credited to both Quintus Mucius and Servius Sulpicius, who used Stoic philosophy and were otherwise familiar with Greek literature.[89]

A few years later, Friedrich D. Sanio wrote a small thesis on the *regulae iuris*, where he noted the dispute between Quintus Mucius and Servius, and placed emphasis on the evidence given by Pomponius on Quintus Mucius' primacy. He later reformulated his argument so that the beginning of Roman legal science depended on the creation of the *regulae iuris*, which he attributed to Quintus Mucius.[90]

---

86   Edward Gibbon, *The Decline and Fall of the Roman Empire IV*, London 1977 [1788], 390–392.
87   Gustav Hugo, *Lehrbuch der Geschichte des Römischen Rechts*, (Lehrbuch eines civilistischen Cursus 3, 3rd ed.), Berlin 1806, 341–342, 352–354.
88   There is no real equivalent for *regulae iuris* in the English language, the terms legal rules or canons come closest. For the etymological debate, see Stein 1966, 49–53.
89   C.G. Haubold, *Institutionum iuris romani privati historico dogmaticarum lineamenta*, Leipzig 1826, 211–212.
90   Friedrich D. Sanio, *De Antiquis Regulis Iuris*, Königsberg 1833, 5, 22–24; Friedrich D. Sanio, 'Beiträge zur Geschichte der Regulae Juris', in *Rechtshistorische Abhandlungen und Studien*, Königsberg 1845, 136–152.

The combination of the rise in interest to Quintus Mucius and science formed a sound intellectual basis for the discovery of his scientific breakthrough. Georg F. Puchta is the earliest author to explicitly identify Quintus Mucius as the first to compose a scientific presentation of the law. According to Puchta, before Quintus Mucius there was no real science of law, just the *iuris prudentes* with their pre-scientific arguments. Quintus Mucius, encouraged by the tempestuous scientific spirit of the age, then established the real science of law with his systematic presentation and his knowledge of principles. Puchta emphasised that it was only the high grade of Roman jurisprudence that enabled Quintus Mucius to take this step, and thereby make Roman law a schoolmaster for all times.[91] Puchta is the first to openly claim the revolutionary nature of that change by emphasising the element of progress in contrasting the situations before and after. He added the *Eureka* factor to the narrative.

Sanio later wrote in his tentative introduction to the history of Roman legal science (1858) about the new era that began with Quintus Mucius in Roman jurisprudence. Sanio was not as pompous as Puchta, but recounts basically the same arguments, i.e. that the origins of systematisation were firmly rooted in the old Roman tradition, the casuistic material that Quintus Mucius collected and organised. According to Sanio, Quintus Mucius' great original significance was lost on later jurists, as his systematising work was not adequately appreciated and systematisation did not become the method of choise among jurists. This was the first in a long line of excuses. Sanio deftly blames the paucity of sources attesting to Quintus Mucius' great systematic work for the lack of understanding by later writers. The scientific idea was born, but due to the ignorance of contemporaries and later authors it fell into disuse.[92]

During the next decades up to the 1890s the foundational narrative was elaborated in greater detail by numerous authors. Q. Mucius' innovation is also given different contextualisations: Roman and Greek. Voigt and others, such as Jörs, wanted to prove that Quintus Mucius' system was an example from a long line of purely Roman legal systems beginning from Sextus Aelius. The supporters of the Greek option stressed that Quintus Mucius applied Greek learning to convert jurisprudence into legal science. This began from Heineccius, Gibbon, and Hugo and continued through Krüger and Lepointe to Schulz.

---

91   Georg F. Puchta, 'Geschichte des Rechts bei dem römischen Volk', in *Cursus der Institutionen I*, (8th ed.), Leipzig 1875, 174–175, 244–249.
92   Friedrich D. Sanio, *Zur Geschichte der römischen Rechtswissenschaft*, Napoli 1981 [1858], 39–42. It is noteworthy that Sanio dubs Quintus Mucius' *definitiones* as 'Formulirung *(sic)* von Rechtsregeln' or formulating legal rules.

Moritz Voigt wanted to present the great line of advancement in the system of Roman law that began from Sextus Aelius' *Tripertita* c. 200 BC, continued with Quintus Mucius' 18 books, the *libri Pithanon* of Labeo and Cassius' 10 books, and finally to the system of Sabinus. Voigt did not rule out Greek influences, but gave them a minor role. Quintus Mucius' innovation was the application of new Greek philosophical models to purely Roman legal material. The result was a systematic and rational organisation of private law into a uniform and closed system, which was completely independent from Aelius. Voigt also (re)constructed the system of Quintus Mucius, as well as those of other Roman legal authors.[93]

Paul Jörs created a lasting distinction in legal science: the division between cautelary and regular jurisprudence in the first and only part of his history of Roman legal science. Cautelary jurisprudence meant the practical legal work aimed at solving individual cases, regular jurisprudence or *Regularjurisprudenz* sought to construct abstract rules under which individual cases could be subsumed. Jörs presented Cato the younger as the initiator of this new type of jurisprudence, mainly on the basis of the Catonian Rule[94] and a quote from Paul.[95] There are indications that Jörs had planned to continue this division of jurisprudence at least with a third step, systematic jurisprudence, which he would have assigned to Quintus Mucius.[96] Jörs did not belittle Quintus Mucius' worth. Due to his creative power, Jörs described Quintus Mucius as perhaps the greatest of Roman jurists.[97] Sadly, Jörs's project never got beyond the first part, and in a later text he defines Quintus Mucius' works as an attempt to distinguish *genera* and *species*, and to define various legal concepts.[98]

---

93 Moritz Voigt, 'Über das Aelius- und Sabinus-System, wie über einige verwandte Rechts-Systeme', *Abhandlungen der Philologisch-historischen Klasse der Königlich sächsischen Gesellschaft der Wissenschaften* 7 (1879), 337–344. The only source for the *Tripertita* is Pomponius Dig. 1,2,2,38. Voigt was followed by Paul Girard, *Manuel élémentaire de droit romain*, Paris 1911, 46, 65.
94 Dig. 34,7.
95 Dig. 45,1,4,1.
96 Paul Jörs, *Römische Rechtswissenschaft zur Zeit der Republik I: Bis auf die Catonen*, Berlin 1888, 311, note 1: 'Dass die systematische Jurisprudenz noch andere Voraussetzungen hatte als Regularjurisprudenz wird später in der Biographie des Quintus Scaevola zu zeigen sein.'
97 Jörs 1888, 7: '... vielleicht der grösste römische Jurist ...'
98 Paul Jörs, 'Geschichte und System des römischen Privatrechts', in Kohlrausch, Kaskel (eds.), *Enzyklopädie des Rechts- und Staatswissenschaft, Abteilung Rechtswissenschaft II*, Berlin 1927, 18.

Jörs generally failed to convince with his theory of Cato being the first legal scientist,[99] but his idea of regular jurisprudence or *Regularjurisprudenz* did catch on.[100] Because of the improbability of the Catonian option, the next in line, Quintus Mucius, became the initiator of regular jurisprudence and the science of law.

The Greek model of science was resurrected by Paul Krüger in 1888. Krüger gave Quintus Mucius the title 'Gründer der Rechtswissenschaft', the founder of legal science. He stressed the systematic nature of Quintus Mucius' *ius civile*, which made it so important to the development of legal science. He also took into account Voigt's claims about the possibility of earlier systematic presentations, which may have contributed to Quintus Mucius' systematics. Krüger again raised the matter of Greek learning that had been overlooked by both Sanio and Jörs, but criticised Quintus Mucius for being too abstract.[101] Quite soon interpretations grew bolder and connected Quintus Mucius' *genera* directly to the logic of Aristotle.[102]

At this stage, the development of the scientific narrative of Quintus Mucius began to stagnate. When, in 1926, Gabriel Lepointe published the only monograph devoted exclusively to Quintus Mucius, he basically echoed the sentiments of earlier writers. Among Roman legal authors Quintus Mucius was the first to rise above casuistry with his systematic categories. Through his work the science of law was created at the moment when synthesis is affected with what Lepointe termed the *esprit scientifique*.[103]

Lepointe's work is symptomatic of the confusion surrounding the exact nature of the Greek ideas that would have influenced Quintus Mucius: the Stoics, Aristotle, or rhetorics are all given some weight. According to Lepointe, the idea of systematisation was born out of practical legal life, but he credited also the influence of Stoic philosophy in the development of a logical system and the presentation of legal material in a systematic order. Greek rhetorical ideas were also seen as influential, as too was Aristotelian logic, which Lepointe thought inspired Q. Mucius to divide things into classes and parts.[104]

---

99 Stein 1966, 31–33.
100 The term Regulär=Jurisprudenz was already used by Sanio (1833), on the history of the *Regulae Iuris*, see Stein 1966.
101 Paul Krüger, *Geschichte der Quellen und Litteratur des Römischen Rechts*, Leipzig 1888, 59–62. Krüger refers to Voigt 1879. Krüger is generally followed by F. P. Bremer, *Iurisprudentiae Antehadrianae quae supersunt I*, Leipzig 1896, 58–59.
102 Cuq 1908, 40.
103 Lepointe 1926, 43–44.
104 Lepointe 1926, 45–47.

The current reputation and status of Quintus Mucius as the founding father can without doubt be credited to, or blamed on, Fritz Schulz. Schulz gave Quintus Mucius a prominent role in the evolution of Roman legal science. In his 1934 *Prinzipien des römischen Rechts* Schulz recognised Quintus Mucius as the founder of the systematisation of law and rejected as unfounded all claims of earlier systems of Roman law. Following La Pira, he later singled out dialectics as the theoretical foundation of Quintus Mucius' system. Quintus Mucius was truly original in inspiring this great advance from unsystematic collections of opinions and cases to the systematic dialectical presentation of the whole body of law, which laid the foundations not merely of Roman, but of European, jurisprudence. Schulz was dismissive of Cicero and had no trouble disqualifying his opinion and identifying Quintus Mucius as the first scientific lawyer.[105] The tradition of elevating Servius was not forgotten either, as Stroux sought to prove how Quintus Mucius was, despite his Stoic background, a representative of the old school and that it was only Servius who brought theoretical constructions with the help of Greek theory to jurisprudence.[106]

Peter Stein's 1966 *Regulae iuris* sought to trace the origin and development of the scientific revolution in Roman law by exploring the different Roman and Greek influences that had contributed to the creation of the scientific method. His version of Greek method is Aristotelian, relying on axioms, definitions, and hypotheses as foundations for the systematic organisation of *genera* and *species*. Although Stein elaborated on the different arguments and produced a picture of a long developmental process, he also viewed Quintus Mucius as the initiator of the science of law.[107] Bruce W. Frier continued on the path of Schulz and Stein, with his fundamental idea based on Schulz but with a more nuanced historical perspective. For Frier, Quintus Mucius' innovation was the creation of analytical jurisprudence, which was a methodological revolution from within.[108]

---

105 Fritz Schulz, *Prinzipien des Römischen Rechts*, Berlin 1934, 33, 36–37; Schulz 1946, 64, 94. Schulz 1946, 62 refers to La Pira's articles in 1934–36. Schulz evidently had no qualms about the fact that La Pira's version of dialectics is a Ciceronian interpretation of the Aristotle/Plato original.
106 Stroux 1949, 106.
107 Stein 1966, 34–36.
108 Frier 1985, 159–163. This transformation was accomplished by using legal definitions and new canons of interpretation. Definitions: Cic. *top.* 29, *off.* 3,17,70; Varro *ling.* 7,105; Gell. 4,1,17; Gaius Inst. 1,188, 3,149; Dig. 9,2,31 Paul. 10 Ad Sab.; Dig. 17,2,30 Paul. 6 Ad Sab.; Dig. 33,9,3,9 Ulp. 22 Ad Sab.; Dig. 34,2,19,9 Ulp. 20 Ad Sab.; Dig. 34,2,27pr Ulp. 44 Ad Sab.; Dig. 41,2,3,23 Paul. 54 Ad Ed. Interpretations: Gell. 17,7,1–3; Dig. 18,1,59 Cels. 8 Dig.; Dig. 18,1,66,2 Pomp. 31 Ad Q. Muc.; Dig. 28,5,35,3 Ulp. 4 Disp.; Dig. 21,2,75pr

In a reaction to Stein's book sceptical voices began to make themselves heard. Franz Wieacker was one of the first to take a serious critical look at what the Greek science that Quintus Mucius and Servius are supposed to be applying meant. He claimed that there was an anachronistic synthesis visible. Aristotle's classification principles were often seen to have been influences on Cicero, along with those of Plato and Kant. Wieacker questioned whether this systematic scientific model was really behind Quintus Mucius' work. Emphasising the fact that Pomponius was keen to use the word *primus*, the first, in a dramatising and stereotypical manner, Wieacker made a new evaluation of the sources available. His conclusion was that neither Quintus Mucius nor Servius could have built a systematic presentation of the civil law, because they were still hampered by the confusion that the XII Tables had brought to the systematisation of the law. Thus, for Wieacker, Schulz's Promethean fire never burned, and Stein's Scientific Revolution never took place.[109]

At the core of the Quintus Mucius tradition had been the conviction that *genera* were dialectic concepts similar to those employed by Aristotle or Cicero. Bruno Schmidlin examined the *regulae* in the writings of Roman jurists, dividing them into three types: the normative rule, the casuistic rule and the defining rule. Schmidlin's conclusion was that Roman jurisprudence was never transformed into a systematic conceptual system, not even into the *ars* that Cicero envisioned. The *regulae* were integral parts of the casuistic law-finding, but nothing more. Schmidlin judged Quintus Mucius' *liber horon* while bearing in mind Chrysippos' *Horoi*, and concluding that it operates on the Stoic logic of propositions or claims, not the logic of definitions.[110] Further undermining the foundations of the tradition were Martini and Carcaterra, who claimed that *definitio* was not a tool for generalisation and the formulation of abstract rules for Roman jurists.[111]

Reflecting the general historification of Roman legal history, Okko Behrends, a pupil of Wieacker, sought to solve the battle over the title of the first

---

Ven. 16 Stipul.; Dig. 34,2,33pr Pomp. 4 Ad Q. Muc.; Dig. 34,2,34,1 Pomp. 9 Ad Q. Muc.; Dig. 34,2,34,2 Pomp. 9 Ad Q. Muc.; Dig. 43,24,5,8 Ulp. 70 Ad Ed; Dig. 50,17,73,4 Q. Mucius.

[109] Wieacker 1969, 460–469.

[110] Bruno Schmidlin, *Die römischen Rechtsregeln*, Köln 1970; Bruno Schmidlin, 'Horoi, pithana und regulae', in ANRW II. 15 (1976), 106–111. Schmidlin's views did not go uncontested, see Dieter Nörr, 'Spruchregel und Generalisierung', ZRG 89 (1972) 18–93; Dieter Nörr, *Divisio und partitio. Bemerkungen zur römischen Rechtsquellenlehre und zur antiken Wissenschaftstheorie*, Berlin 1972, 31–38.

[111] Remo Martini, *Le definizioni dei giuristi romani*, Milano 1966; Antonio Carcaterra, *Le definizioni dei giuristi romani*, Napoli 1966.

scientific jurist by comparing the scientific methods of Quintus Mucius and Servius. He concluded, like Stroux, that Quintus Mucius and Servius were both scientific, but in totally different ways. Quintus Mucius' method was legal reflection and the inductive contemplation of content, based on the Stoic method of thought. Servius, on the other hand, was building a formal system in the true sense of the word. Thus, the *genera* of Quintus Mucius were not a real system of classification and Cicero was right.[112] Whether such far-reaching conclusions should be drawn from a comparison of fragments and circumstantial evidence is debatable and further studies on the matter would be desirable.

Regardless of the voices of doubt, the belief in the foundational role of Quintus Mucius has continued, but not in the sense of him being viewed as the founder of a rigid system. Now, he tends to be seen more as the founding father of a scientific method and explanation of the law than anything else.[113] In a similar fashion, the exclusive claims linking Quintus Mucius to the Stoics have been replaced by a more balanced assessment of possible Greek influences in particular cases.[114]

* * *

It is strange to see how much a single discovery or invention can change the story. The Pomponian passage is transformed from an obscure sub-plot to the central argument and Cicero's opinion is brushed aside. Legal science grows from a few definitions and division into a closed system. How did this situation arise?

Instead of the Romans, it might be better to look at the Romanists. It is an established fact that Roman legal history was by no means irrelevant to the value of Roman law as contemporary legal material. As Giaro has pointed out, if current existing law is traced from the past, then a distinction between a legal normative discourse and a contemplative historical discourse is impossible. The 'historical legal dogmatics' of the nineteenth century had to preserve, manipulate and legitimise Roman law, all at the same time.[115] For

---

[112] Behrends 1976, 287–290. Similarly, Schiavone 1976, 95–110,132–133.
[113] Aldo Schiavone, 'Forme normative e generi letterari. La cristallizzazione del *ius civile* e dell'editto fra tarda repubblica e primo principato', in L. De Giovanni, A. Mazzacane (eds.), *La codificazione del diritto dall'antico al moderno*, Napoli 1998, 59.
[114] Laurens Winkel, 'Quintus Mucius Scaevola once again', in R. van den Bergh (ed.), *Ex iusta causa traditum, Essays in honour of Eric H. Pool*, (Fundamina, Editio specialis), Pretoria 2005, 425–433.
[115] Puchta 1875, 60–61; Tomasz Giaro, 'Geltung und Fortgeltung des römischen Juristenrechts', ZRG III (1994b), 70, 89–91. Cf. also Riccardo Orestano,

the Historical School of jurisprudence, legal history was an auxiliary helper of legal dogmatics and a political legitimator.[116]

It is also an established fact that 'science' was one of the most cherished ideals of the Historical School of jurisprudence. According to Puchta, scientific veracity provided the legitimisation of Roman law and the reason for its continued use. Only its truthfulness made Roman law the global role model of law.[117] Behind this conviction were two developments that had deeply altered the position of Roman law in Germany: first, the disbandment of the Holy Roman Empire and the Reichskammergericht in 1806; second, the simultaneous rise of legal science and the status of jurists, and the nationalistic idea of 'national spirit'. Both were a danger to Roman law in that the first took away the old use of Roman law of the *usus modernus*, while the second provided ammunition to the Germanists of the Historical School to call for the complete abolition of Roman law in Germany. The survival strategy used by the Romanists of the Historical School was to underline how good, scientifically valid, and well-suited to the general culture of the people the content of Roman law was compared with the primitive law advanced by the Germanists. Puchta likened the meeting of Roman law and old German law to the meeting of savage Indians and civilised Europeans in North America.[118]

Puchta envisioned legal science, as part of jurists' law, as the third source of law in addition to legislation and the 'conviction of the people'. Puchta's Quintus Mucius was strongly bound by Puchta's idea of the connection between theory and practice. For him, the roots of Roman legal science lie in the legal controversies of the ancient jurists, the *disputatio fori*. In these debates, the inner characteristics of law were exposed and this provided a deep knowledge of the law that was necessary for the formulation of a science. Puchta emphasised the natural talent of the Romans for law, and

---

'Diritto romano, tradizione romanistica e studio storico del diritto', RISG 87 (1950), 156–264.

[116] Marcel Senn, *Rechtshistorisches Selbstverständnis im Wandel*, Zürich 1982, 31–34.

[117] Georg F. Puchta, *Pandekten*, (12th ed.), Leipzig 1877, 29; Puchta 1875, 60–61. Earlier in 1828 Puchta bound legal correctness to two criteria, its incontroversiality with the *Volksgeist* and its scientific truthfulness. Haferkamp 2004, 176–183, 188–194, 466.

[118] Peter Bender, *Die Rezeption des römischen Rechts im Urteil der deutschen Rechtswissenschaft*, Frankfurt am Main 1979, 54–69; Puchta 1877, 12. Of the Romanist-Germanist debate, cf. Klaus Luig, 'Römische und germanische Rechtsanschauung, individualistische und soziale Ordnung', in J. Rückert, D. Willoweit (eds.), *Die Deutsche Rechtsgeschichte in der NS-Zeit*, Tübingen 1995, 95–137.

how lawyers felt they were the representatives of the Roman nation in law, as the theory of the Historical School claimed they should be. The law lived in the lawyers' consciousness as it had lived in the consciousness of the whole nation (*Volk*). Because lawyers were not judges and judges were not jurists, Roman jurisprudence avoided the unhealthy confrontation between faulty practice and unsound theory that Puchta saw as the problem of modern law. The freedom of Roman law and lawyers gave them the tools to navigate between the twin rocks of unpractical theory and mechanical application of the law. Roman law was an evolving, practical science that shunned both the impractical theory and the unscientific practice.[119]

The evolution of Quintus Mucius' story is strongly linked to the debate on the nature of legal science that began in the early 19th century when jurisprudence as a concept gave way to legal science. This process began with the writers of the Historical School. The concept of science was a useful legitimising component in the Pandectist interpretation of legal dogmatics as an autonomous and self-guiding science dominating the whole of legal life. As the Historical School gradually gave up on the idea of jurisprudence being just the expression of the spirit of the people interpreted by the jurists, legal science emerged as a noble and wondrous pursuit, in which the scientific jurist transforms jurisprudence into a scientific discipline.[120]

According to Wieacker, Puchta's legal system was a pyramid of concepts, where every legal concept could be derived from another concept higher in the system, hence the designation 'jurisprudence of concepts'. The closed nature of the system ensured its autonomy.[121] This dogmatic construction naturally needed a historical dimension or roots, which evolved around the great jurists of the past.

Quintus Mucius became the starting point for the scientific jurists' law tradition from Puchta onwards and this conception was strengthened in the

---

[119] Puchta 1875, 18, 22, 176, 244–247; Georg F. Puchta, 'Die Quellen des römischen Rechts' (1843), in *Kleine zivilistische Schriften*, Aalen 1970c [1851], 618–619. On Savigny, Puchta and legal science, cf. Horst H. Jakobs, *Die Begründung der geschichtlichen Rechtswissenschaft*, Paderborn 1992, 31–51. On Gerber and the attempts at forming a unified legal science and legal system for Germany, cf. Maurizio Fioravanti, *Giuristi e costituzione politica nell'ottocento tedesco*, Milano 1979, 124–126. The idea of the jurist as a representative of the people was presented already by Savigny 1814, 12: 'Das Recht bildet sich nunmehr in der Sprache aus, es nimmt eine wissenschaftliche Richtung, und wie es vorher im Bewußtseyn des gesammten Volkes lebte, so fällt es jetzt dem Bewußtseyn der Juristen anheim, von welchen das Volk nunmehr in dieser Function repräsentirt wird.'

[120] Puchta 1875, 59–61; Giaro 1994, 109–111.

[121] Wieacker 1995, 316–318.

latter half of the nineteenth century. In this they were in good company, as the traditional historiography often presented a 'history of great men' that focused on a few major figures and their lives and times. In the history of science this took the form of discovering the 'fathers' of various disciplines. These stories may tell of distant, venerable and sage-like figures such as Herodotos, Galenos, Aristotle, or Archimedes, of whom only anecdotal information remains and whose status is based largely on the later reception and influence of their studies. Another archetype is that of the persistent fighter, who makes a discovery, faces prejudice and formidable obstacles but overcomes them with the strength of his conviction, thereby changing the course of science, like Leonardo, Galileo, Darwin, or Einstein.[122] In the case of the modern history of science, we may have sufficient information about the previous situation, the discovery, and subsequent transformation, but when the roots of a bimillenial tradition are sought from the earliest times, from the proverbial dawn of history, things are different. We simply do not know.

It is evident from the development of the foundational narrative of Quintus Mucius that the mantle of the founder would rest on the earliest jurist who shows even the slightest sign of what observers could interpret as being scientific. Jörs saw this in Cato, but the contest has primarily been between Quintus Mucius and Servius. Before he discovered Quintus Mucius, Puchta even bestowed the title upon Labeo.[123]

It is also possible that one of the reasons for the longevity of Quintus Mucius' reputation as the founding father is the age and breadth of the tradition itself. The theme of invented tradition has been examined in other fields for some time now. Bernard Lewis claimed that there are two social purposes for remembering the past, one is to explain and justify the present, the other is to control the future. For both of these purposes, there is a rich tradition of invention to embellish, correct, and censor the image of the past in both popular and academic history.[124] In a popular essay, Eric Hobsbawn wrote that traditions that appear or claim to be ancient are often quite recent in origin and sometimes invented. The use of ancient materials to construct invented traditions of a novel type for novel purposes is well documented in historical examples. Historic continuity could be established by creating an ancient past beyond effective historical continuity, sometimes with the use of semifiction or even forgery. The range of invented traditions is as peculiar as it

---

122 Kelley 2002, 209.
123 Puchta 1970c [1851], 618, 632: 'Im 7. Jahrhundert fing die Jurisprudenz an, einen ganz andern, einen wissenschaftlichen Character anzunehmen.'
124 Bernard Lewis, *History: Remembered, Recovered, Invented*, Princeton 1975, 54–59.

is wide, but examples are mostly linked with the rise of nationalism. In the field of historical distortions prehistory is especially fecund, as whole empires have been imagined on the basis of a few nicely placed stones. In addition to nationalism, the use of invented traditions has spread to cultures outside Europe. In the guise of utopic authenticity and spiritual purity, the strangest fabrications are marketed to Western consumers as ancient native beliefs and rituals.[125]

Is the scientific nature of Roman jurists' law an invented tradition? Perhaps the question should be rephrased: has the story of Quintus Mucius and the birth of legal science gained such importance because it was necessary for giving Roman jurists' law an air of science, a great historic past that establishes the continuity of the present with the past?

A foundation myth is a story that locates the beginnings of an entity to time immemorial, to a mythical past instead of historical time. These myths are woven around a heroic figure whose actions single-handedly changed the course of history. Walter Ong wrote that narratives in oral memory work best with 'heavy' characters, persons whose deeds are monumental and memorable, which naturally creates outsized, heroic figures.[126] Also historical figures often gain a mythical dimension as they are able to excite the popular imagination in a process of mythogenesis, which is still inadequately understood.[127] As recent studies have shown, many have also carefully striven to construct their own historical image through far-reaching propaganda using literature and iconography.[128] Quintus Mucius has, from the time of Puchta onwards, served the role of a founding father larger than life, whose work marked the beginning of a new era. As with traditional narratives, the tradition of Quintus Mucius has incorporated information gleaned from different sources.

125 Eric Hobsbawm, 'Introduction: Inventing Traditions', in E. Hobsbawm, T. Ranger (eds.), *The Invention of Tradition*, Cambridge 1983, 1–7; Michael F. Brown, 'Can Culture be Copyrighted?', *Current Anthropology* 39 (1998), 195, 201; Monateri 2000, 508. Cf. Noël Carroll, 'Interpretation, history and narrative', in G. Roberts (ed.), *The History and Narrative Reader*, London 2001, 251: 'The notion of invention here is a bit tricky and open to equivocation. In one sense, historical narratives are inventions, viz. in the sense that they are made by historians; but it is not clear that it follows from this that they are *made-up* (and are, therefore, fictional).'
126 Walter J. Ong, *Orality and Literacy*, London 1982, 70; Lewis 1975, 59–60; Jan Vansina, *Oral Tradition as History*, London 1985; Stephen Caunce, *Oral History and the Local Historian*, London 1994, 143–165.
127 Cf. Peter Burke, *Varieties of Cultural History*, Cambridge 1997, 51–52.
128 Paul Zanker, *The Power of Images in the Age of Augustus*, Ann Arbor 1990; Peter Burke, *The Fabrication of Louis XIV*, New Haven 1992.

Laurens Winkel was not convinced by my original presentation of the foundation myth of Quintus Mucius as an invented tradition and attempted to prove with Roman material that there was a lively Roman tradition of science with regard to systematisation through *genus* and *species*, divisions and definitions.[129] Winkel's learned insights, however, are not incompatible with my theory. It is obvious from the sources that there was a Roman discussion of divisions and definitions. How much this affected the content of law and what the intellectual origins of those developments were is an interesting question but not the issue here. My point is that these sources were used to present theories, which were not based on Roman sources.

This theory can be further illustrated by the first instance when Quintus Mucius was named the founder of legal science. Why and how did Maiansius make such a change in the interpretation? Why was his theory forgotten for nearly a century? Maiansius was a true universal genius, if the title may be used. His published works include works on topics as diverse as a biography of Cervantes, a study of the origins of the Spanish language, an elegy to chocolate, historical studies on different subjects, treatises on moral philosophy, Latin grammar, rhetoric, and law. It might be tempting to say that his diverse interests gave him an opportunity to transcend the previous tradition, but without knowing his thoughts this would be too speculative. The example of Maiansius demonstrates how impossible it is to make categorical judgements in intellectual history, because his working life was so long that naming him as a representative of one or another 'school' would not be helpful. We know that he received a classical education based on reading Aristotle, Cicero and Pliny. During his studies in Roman and Canonical law, Maiansius read books by Cujas, Donellus and Fabro. As professor of law, he lectured on natural law scholars such as Heineccius, Pufendorf, Locke, and Ramos del Manzano. As an intellectual of international renown, he communicated with other luminaries of the Enlightenment, such as Meerman, Cramer, Tourner, Keene, Strodtmann, Muratori, Plüer, Voltaire, Pereira, Villasboas, Grasset and others.[130] As Maiansius did not reveal the source of his inspiration, we cannot know whether his novel reformulation of the Quintus Mucius tradition demonstrates his genius, a distinct ability to recombine old materials in a new order and the flexibility or inexistence of scientific boundaries, or that he borrowed the idea from someone else.

129 Winkel 2005, 425–433.
130 Maiansius 1764, ii–vii; A. Beuchot, 'Mayans y Siscar, Grégoire', in *Biographie universelle, ancienne et moderne XXVII*, Paris 1820, 610–612. For more comprehensive information, see the site of the 'Gregorio Mayans y Siscar digital' project of the Biblioteca Valenciana at http://193.144.125.24/mayans/principal.htm.

The fact that Maiansius' interpretation of Quintus Mucius as the father of legal science was to resurface after nearly a century of oblivion is a noteworthy example of the curious workings of intellectual tradition in a literary environment. Only in a special kind of culture can the writings of a Spaniard, published in Geneva, be found and used for a different purpose by a scholar in Königsberg the following century.[131] What Maiansius meant by *scientia iuris* was probably different than the meaning it was later given by Sanio and Puchta, but the words of the text were primary. What the interpretation of Maiansius lacked, in comparison to Sanio and Puchta, was an intellectual context, which gave the writings of the latter two authors resonance beyond simple intellectual history. This resonance was according to my theory a result of its role as the foundation myth of the Historical School.

But can we use theories formed mainly on the basis of 'undeveloped' oral cultures to explain the theories of rational Western scientists? Is there not some distinction to be drawn between savages and scientists? Perhaps not. We are, as is evident from the unequal relation between Roman sources and later interpretations, dealing with a matter of belief.

The ancient and modern roots of the legal system

The whole concept of finding the Roman origins of modern legal science contains several hidden assumptions. The foremost, and the most controversial, are the claims that Roman jurisprudence utilised Greek scientific theories, and that the systematisation of law was originally a Roman pursuit.

The common assumption among Romanist scholars who have written about Quintus Mucius is that the roots of legal science lie in Roman Antiquity. This view has in itself been contested. Harold J. Berman has famously located the beginnings of the Western concept of science to medieval jurisprudence, in accordance with an established tradition.[132] Berman argued that while Cicero proposed a systematisation of the law based on Greek models of definitions and abstract rules, these proposals met with no enthusiasm among jurists and the matter came to nothing. The Greek dialectic method was first applied by the European jurists of the eleventh and twelfth centuries to form a systematic body of law by forming abstract principles out of the rules of Roman law and then integrating these together. It was their use of the Roman

---

131 Sanio 1981 [1858], 40 referred to Maiansius.
132 Stephan Kuttner, 'The Scientific Investigation of Medieval Canon Law: The Need and the Opportunity', *Speculum* 24 (1949), now in *Gratian and the schools of law, 1140–1234*, London 1983, vol. I, 497–498.

sources, not the Roman sources themselves, which had marked the beginnings of legal science.[133]

Berman goes as far as to claim that scholastic jurisprudence created a prototype of Western science in general. He defined modern Western science as

> 1. an integrated body of knowledge, 2. in which particular occurrences of phenomena are systematically explained, 3. in terms of general principles or truths 'laws', 4. knowledge of which ... has been obtained by a combination of observation, hypothesis, verification, and to the greatest extent possible, experimentation. However, 5. the scientific method of investigation and systematization, despite these common characteristics, is not the same for all sciences but must be specifically adapted to the particular kinds of occurrences of phenomena under investigation by each particular science.[134]

Based on this, he concluded that the scholarly work of Western European jurists 'constitutes a science of law'[135] beginning from the eleventh century. Their originality was in their construction of general principles that were consistent with the evidence provided by the legal material, and that they empirically tested their theories against the evidence and used those theories to explain the evidence. Berman's founding fathers are jurists like Gratian and the scholarly community he and the other doctors formed.[136]

While Berman defended his choice of jurisprudence as the foundation of all science against the more or less prevailing view that modern science was initiated by the pioneers of empirical natural sciences like Galileo,[137] there again arises the question of where the origins of legal science should be located. Should it be ancient Rome, the Middle Ages or somewhere else? I would also like to ask whether this question is wholly relevant.

The whole exercise of delving into the past to discover the roots of our conception of legal science proceeded from the idea that legal science has had two influences deriving from classical Antiquity: Roman legal material from the Digest and the Greek theory of science stemming from Plato and Aristotle.

Coing claimed that the link between Roman law and Aristotelian philosophy was made only by the Glossators, who were groomed in the scolastic tradition based on Aristotle. The traces of influence found in Roman law lead more in the direction of Stoicism, although Aristotle's influence can be seen in

---

133 Harold J. Berman, *Law and Revolution*, Cambridge 1983, 139.
134 Berman 1983, 152–153.
135 Berman 1983, 152–153.
136 Berman 1983, 152–164.
137 Berman 1983, 155; Kelley 2002, 208.

the legal method and the use of concepts, the formulation of general legal theory and the connection between law and ethics.[138]

Coing's interpretation resembles Berman's theory. Berman claimed that the starting point of the science of law should be located in the eleventh century AD, not the first century BC. In fact, we have two competing theories; the first is that of a unilinear development, the second is one of parallel developments. The supporters of both Q. Mucius and Servius saw the birth of legal science as a single line that began with Plato and Aristotle formulating the scientific method that was then taken up as dialectics by Roman jurists. The combination of Roman law and Greek theory marked the beginnings of Western legal science, which was later fruitfully rediscovered by the medieval jurists.[139] The parallel lines theory envisioned the Greeks developing scientific theory and the Romans developing law independently of each other and without interaction. Only the medieval scholastic jurists, who knew Aristotle and began to work on the Roman sources, had the opportunity of combining the teachings of both of these authorities, and thereby make the perceived scientific revolution in law.

The unilinear theory of Roman jurists being the founders of legal science operated on the assumption that the Romans developed a legal system, either by adopting Greek scientific models or independently. There are two opposite positions with regard to the Roman legal sources that have been passed down to us. The first is that the Romans built and operated a coherent legal system, the second is that they were practically oriented casuists. In the sources, Gaius' Institutes is the most cogent argument supporting the idea of a legal system. It clearly follows a systematic arrangement (the famous *personae, res, actiones*), and has distinctions into *genus* and *species*, such as the division of *res* into *corporales* and *incorporales*. On the side of casuism we have the Digest, which is clearly an unsystematic compilation of case material collected together. In the literature, there is a strong tendency to see the Roman jurists as practical and casuistic interpreters of law, who sought to find the best solution to every individual case but had no interest in formulating abstract principles. Kaser's theory is that Roman legal science and literature was first and foremost practical, but that there was a didactic current aimed at teaching students the law, which followed a systematic order (Gaius). On the whole, the conventional wisdom was that Roman jurists were familiar with Greek philosophy, but abstained from impractical theoretical constructions.[140]

---

138 Helmut Coing, 'Zum Einfluß der Philosophie des Aristoteles auf die Entwicklung des römischen Rechts', ZRG 69 (1952), 29–30, 57–59.
139 Stein 1966.
140 Fritz Pringsheim, 'Höhe und Ende der römischen Jurisprudenz', in *Gesammelte Abhandlungen I*, Heidelberg 1961, 54; Max Kaser, *Das römische Privatrecht I*,

The assumption that the Roman jurists were familiar with Greek philosophy tempted scholars into making a connection between the systematisation of Roman law and Greek models. This is also one of the reasons why the story of Quintus Mucius gained such popularity, as Pomponius' *generatim* struck an immediate chord with their similarity to Aristotelian categories. Since Greek philosophy and its Kantian interpretation formed the basis of Western scientific thought, and Roman law formed the basis of Western legal tradition, it was only natural that Greek philosophy should form the basis of the systematisation of Roman law. As a result, Quintus Mucius had to be a devotee of Greek philosophy. Questions of what kind of Greek philosophy, and what science was involved, were only seriously asked later on.[141]

This deficiency was later corrected, as the connection between Greek philosophy and Roman law attracted considerable attention after the 1930s. However, scholars remained highly divided on the matter. Franz Wieacker divided scholars into two groups. On the one hand there were the Romanists, who saw Roman law as a purely Roman and practical matter. On the other there were the philologists and Romanists, who envisioned Roman jurists and Roman law as the products of a general Greco-Roman cultural tradition in which Greek theoretical elements contributed clearly to the development of Roman jurisprudence. In the latter group he included Riccobono, La Pira, Schulz, Villey, and Stein. Wieacker's view was that the discussion was not only about the movement of influences, but was also about the role of the Greek and Roman heritages in the Western legal tradition.[142]

In Wieacker's division, the main themes of the discussion about Greek influences were simply: 1) whether Roman jurisprudence developed from a practical knowledge into a systematic legal science under the influence of the Platonian-Aristotelian categorising doctrine of the formation of concepts and a system (*Dialektik*), and 2) whether Greek rhetorical ideals brought the ethical concept of equity or *aequitas* into Roman legal interpretation?[143] To this inquiry the first question was of more importance. It had been answered positively but with great ambiguity in the older textbooks. For instance, Krüger mentioned that Republican jurists were for the main part Stoics, but

    München 1955, 3; similarly Krüger 1912, 140; Franz Wieacker, *Vom römischen Recht*, (2nd ed.), Stuttgart 1961, 9; Ulrich von Lübtow, 'De iustitia et iure', ZRG 66 (1948), 460–461; J. A. Ankum, 'Utilitas causa receptum. On the pragmatical methods of the Roman lawyers', in Ankum et al. (eds.), *Symbolae iuridicae et historicae Martino David dedicatae I*, Leiden 1968, 1–6.
141 Wieacker 1969, 463–469; Schmidlin 1976, 106–111; Behrends 1976.
142 Wieacker 1969, 448–452. On earlier literature on the Greek philosophical influences on Roman law in general, see Stroux 1949.
143 Wieacker 1969, 451.

this had no influence on the content of the law nor on its systematisation. Goudy claimed that the ubiquitous use of tripartition or trichotomy by the Roman jurists was the result of numerical symbolism that had little to do with the material of the law itself and was therefore an unfortunate contamination from the Greek sources. Schulz saw a more direct influence and formulated the dialectical method as a way of thinking through distinction and synthesis in addition to the formulation of general principles, which was common to nearly all schools of Greek philosophy, from the Academia to Aristotelian and Stoic schools.[144]

This idea of an intellectual synthesis, a general Greek concept of science that spanned both time and disciplines was presented influentially by Giorgio La Pira, but has since been heavily criticised for being so general as to leave historical development and profound systematic differences unnoticed. Hans J. Mette stated that all previous Roman authors lack the pervasive system demonstrated by Gaius. In contrast to the attempts of Quintus Mucius, Servius, Sabinus, and Cassius Longinus, Gaius demonstrated a conscious use of the methodical principles of Greek scientific thought, especially Stoicism. Gaius' composition of the whole of private law into a system using Greek scientific theories was only possible after the *edictum perpetuum* of Salvius Julianus.[145] Legal science could only develop into a system after the collection of legal norms into a whole by the sovereign.

The general interpretation of the links between Roman law and Greek philosophy was summed up by Gibbon, who wrote that among the Greek influences were Plato, Aristotle and the Stoics, of which 'the armour of the Stoics was found to be of the firmest temper'.[146] Cicero's affinity to the Stoics has led more recent scholars to look for a more direct link between Republican jurisprudence and Stoic doctrine, but the results have been contingent because of the meagre sources we have on the Stoics in general.[147]

---

144 Krüger 1912, 50–51; Henry Goudy, *Trichotomy in Roman Law*, Oxford 1910, 20–22, 72–77; Schulz 1946, 62–63. Schiavone 1976, 96 wrote that Schulz erred in supposing the basic unity of development of the dialectic method. On the multiplicity of the theories surrounding Greek philosophical precedents, the schools of jurisprudence and such, see Tomasz Giaro, 'Von der Genealogie der Begriffe zur Genealogie der Juristen. De Sabinianis et Proculianis fabulae', *Rechtshistorisches Journal* 11 (1992), 508–511, 519, 530, 544 et passim.

145 Hans J. Mette, *Ius civile in artem redactum*, Göttingen 1954, 19, 50, 63–64.

146 Gibbon 1977 [1788], 391. The link to the Stoics presented already Franciscus Balduinus, *Institutione historiae universae et eis cum iurisprudentiae ... vol. II*, Halle 1726, 222, and more directly in Gian V. Gravina, *De ortu et progressu juris civilis*, Leipzig 1704, 97 [ch. 44].

147 Juan Miquel, 'Stoische Logik und römische Jurisprudenz', ZRG 87 (1970), 85–122; Behrends 1976; Schmidlin 1976; Elmar Bund, 'Rahmenerwägungen

The Aristotelian connection has been even less fruitful, even though there have been claims of similarities between the writings of Roman jurists and Aristotle that go beyond the work of Gaius. Still, the preponderance of the Gaian evidence has been seen as an indication that systematisation served the Roman jurists only as an educational tool, as indeed it served Aristotle himself according to Wieacker.[148] The now repudiated theory presented by Sokolowski that the schools of jurisprudence would also have been divided by philosophical affiliation and that the Sabinians would have been Stoics and the Proculians Aristotelians, is more of an indication of how strong the need to find Greek precedents was than a serious argument.[149] Nörr has further pointed out that, since the transmission of learning between the Aristotelian and Stoic tradition was significant, it is difficult to know the exact origins of certain doctrines.[150]

Researchers have attempted to understand the entity that, ever since Gibbon, has been labelled as 'Greek philosophy'. The spread and specialisation of the debate from the 1960s onwards is evident in Winkel's recent survey of the Greek influences on the Roman law debate. According to Winkel, separate discussions have developed on the philosophical orientation of Roman jurists,[151] the concept of law,[152] the *regulae iuris*,[153] the use of logic,[154] and the Greek roots of the system of Institutes,[155] to name a few.[156]

  zu einem Nachweis stoischer Gedanken in der römischen Jurisprudenz', in Manfred Harder, Georg Thielmann (eds.), *De iustitia et iure: Festschrift für U. von Lübtow*, Berlin 1980, 127–145. Cf. bibliography in Schmidlin 1976, 128–130.
148 Mario Talamanca, 'Lo Schema "Genus-Species" nelle sistematiche dei giuristi romani', in *La Filosofia Greca e il Diritto Romano II*, Roma 1977, 289; Wieacker 1969, 467.
149 Paul Sokolowski, *Die Philosophie im Privatrecht I*, Halle 1907, 77; Hägerström 1927, 246–247; Coing 1952, 57. Sokolowski was not original in his theory, as Gottfried Mascov had already presented the idea that Sabinians were Platonians and Proculians Stoics. Gotfrid Mascovius, *De sectis Sabinianorum et Proculianorum in jure civili diatriba*, Leipzig 1728, praef.
150 Nörr 1972, 31–32.
151 Behrends 1976.
152 Michèle Ducos, *Les Romains et la loi. Recherches sur les rapports de la philosophie grecque et la tradition romaine à la fin de la République*, Paris 1984.
153 Martini 1966; Carcaterra 1966; Stein 1966; Schmidlin 1970; Nörr 1972; Schmidlin 1976.
154 Michel Villey, 'Logique d'Aristote et droit romain', RHDFE 29 (1951), 309–328; Coing 1952; Talamanca 1976; Miquel 1970; Nörr 1972.
155 Franz Wieacker, 'Griechische Wurzeln des Institutionen-Systems', ZRG 70 (1953), 93–126.
156 Winkel's list of specialist debates extends to imputability and causality, the

Okko Behrends has, along with others, criticised how Schulz called Quintus Mucius an adherent of the Platonic dialectic method. Behrends himself interpreted Quintus Mucius as a Stoic, while making Servius an adherent of the New Academy, the philosophical arch-rival of the Stoics. For Stoics, the concept of *genus*, according to Behrends, is roughly the same thing as a concept, which is based on an observation. Alan Watson for his part criticised Schulz for overemphasising the Greek connection in general.[157] As of late, this tendency has been followed by a more cautious approach to making wide generalisations on the Greek influences and an interest in more detailed case studies.[158] Generally, one is tempted to agree with Schmidlin. There are too few methodological statements by the Roman jurists and even less evidence for the Ciceronian Hellenistic dialectis to say anything conclusive about the Greek influence on how Roman jurists operated.[159] However, there is a distinct danger that the otherwise important studies of Greek influences on Roman law overshadow a fundamental deficiency in the whole foundational debate. This deficiency is simply its relevance.

It may be said that the whole idea of seeking a point of origin has been an exercise in presentism, that is, the evaluation of the past according to modern criteria. The question of when and how the two lines of development that are seen as the foundations of modern legal science, Greek philosophy and Roman law, were connected, during Antiquity, in the Middle Ages, or in the nineteenth century, is in retrospect moot, because they all are essential parts of the foundations of contemporary law. The difficulties scholars have had in defining the essence of the Greek philosophy that contributed to the foundation of legal science are in part the result of the fact that the Greek roots of the modern Western concept of science are the outcome of a selective reading of Greek sources in the first place.

* * *

The importance of the systematic question in the foundational debate should not, therefore, be looked for in Classical Antiquity but in modern legal developments. The question of how systematising was brought into Roman law has been answered with two opposite theories, which we may again call the unilinear theory and the parallel lines theory. The unilinear theory claims that Roman law was systematised by the Romans, and even though

---

    influence of the philosophy of nature, the definition of law and justice, and the role of custom. Winkel 1997, 376.
157 Behrends 1976, 281–292; Watson 1974, 193–195.
158 Winkel 2005.
159 Schmidlin 1976, 92.

the Digest, a Byzantine collection of Roman law, does not reflect this, the systematic order is immanent in Roman law. Savigny claimed that the task of the Historical School was the reconstruction of this immanent order,[160] which was then carried out during the first half of the nineteenth century. In contrast, the parallel lines theory maintains that modern scientific systematisation was introduced to general legal scholarship during the sixteenth century and was influenced by the general scientific theories of that time. For a long time, systematisation had the strongest effect in the development of rational natural law, while Roman law was bound to the system of the *Corpus Iuris*. It was only from the systematic theories of natural law that the ideal of systematisation was introduced to Roman law by Savigny at the beginning of the nineteenth century.

The question of whether Roman law was a systematic or casuistic legal order runs through most of what has been written on Roman law and jurisprudence during the last five centuries. Pugliese has argued that the discrepancy in interpretations arises from the fact that while Roman jurisprudence was casuistic, based on the deliberation on single cases, sometimes with a topical-dialectical method, the Pandectistic jurisprudence of the nineteenth century worked in a closed system that operated on the vertical relationship between concepts, principles and other factors developed on an Aristotelian basis by German eighteenth and nineteenth century philosophers.[161] In the cases examined in this study, it is basically the question behind both Q. Mucius' founding of the Western legal science and the possibility of the *edictum perpetuum* being a codification.

The unilinear systematic argument, which was elaborated on the basis of supposed Greek precedents, the few postulations of Cicero and Quintus Mucius, and the techniques of Sabinus, assumed the existence of a system that the Roman jurists had developed for centuries and then manifested itself in the order presented by Gaius.[162] When the Gaius-manuscript was found in

---

160 Friedrich Carl von Savigny, *System des heutigen Römischen Rechts I*, Berlin 1849, xxiv–xxv; Wieacker 1959, 139.
161 Pugliese 1985, 446–447. Similarly, Giaro 1991, 221.
162 Giuseppe Grosso, *Problemi sistematici nel diritto romano, cose – contratti*, Torino 1974, 4: 'Gaio representerebbe dunque il perfezionamento e il coronamento di un processo storico di formazione di un sistema del *ius civile*, che si sarebbe svolto attraverso miglioramenti e razionalizzazioni ...' Behrends 1976, 266–268 credited Schulz for establishing the current reputation of Q. Mucius as the starting point of the tradition leading to Gaius, but stated that the conceptual pyramids of Gaius were more or less worthless despite their apparent systematic nature. According to Schiavone 1998, 59 the 'civilistic system' was more a method and a process of legal development than an immutable system. Of Gaius in the general context of systematic didactic

1816, the Romanists of the Historical School of jurisprudence felt that it was as if the real system of Roman law had finally been revealed after years of searching.[163] Whether the system of Gaius was a symptom of a larger trend in systematic legal thinking or quite simply a didactic tool for the presentation of the material of law is presently unclear. What is clear is that Gaius was the star witness of the unilinear theory.

The parallel lines theory, which may be said to reflect the current majority opinion of legal historians, traces the roots of the modern systematic ideal in the mid-sixteenth century and the inclusion of the Humanist principles of rhetoric and logic and the concepts of *ars* and system to legal science. The French Humanists such as Budé drew from Cicero's *ius in artem redigere* their ideal for the development of jurisprudence. Roman law was for them an unsystematised mass of otherwise serviceable material that could be used as a basis for future legal science.[164] As Troje has pointed out, the system of law and legal science existed as inseparable duality, in which jurisprudence becomes a system through science and can only be a system when it is a science. Both dialectics and method were fashionable words in the seventeenth century jurisprudence.[165]

The idea of an extensive legal system was founded on the theories of natural lawyers. The systematic tendencies of Romanism were influenced by the rationalist natural lawyers such as Samuel Pufendorff (1634–1694) and Christian Wolff (1679–1754), and their systematic thought. Important factors were the codifications produced under their influence during the eighteenth and early nineteenth centuries. The founders of the modern Pandectist system of organisation, like Hugo, were influenced both by the old idea of Roman law as *ratio scripta* and the emphasis on the systematic and scientific nature of law. In contrast to the natural lawyers, for Hugo the system of law was a

---

presentations in Antiquity, cf. Manfred Fuhrmann, *Das systematische Lehrbuch*, Göttingen 1960, 104–121.

163 Cristina Vano, '*Il nostro autentico Gaio*': *Strategie della scuola storica alle origini della romanistica moderna*, Napoli 2000, 51.

164 Franklin 1963, 27, 29; Budaeus 1557 [1969], 7 [ad Dig. 1,1]. Vinzenzo Piano Mortari, 'La sistematica come ideale umanistico dell'opera di Francesco Connano', in *La storia del diritto nel quadro delle scienze storiche: Atti del primo Congresso internazionale della Società Italiana di Storia del Diritto*, Firenze 1966, 529–531; Riccardo Orestano, 'Diritto e storia nel pensiero giuridico del secolo XVI', in *La storia del diritto nel quadro delle scienze storiche: Atti del primo Congresso internazionale della Società Italiana di Storia del Diritto*, Firenze 1966, 394–395; Orestano 1987, 228–232.

165 Hans Erich Troje, 'Wissenschaftlichkeit und System in der Jurisprudenz des 16. Jahrhunderts', in J. Blühdorn, J. Ritter (eds.), *Philosophie und Rechtswissenschaft*, Frankfurt am Main 1969, 63, 77.

system of positive law.[166] The systematisation of law was so popular from the last decades of the eighteenth century through the first half of the nineteenth century that Björne's survey of the period lists nearly thirty different attempts at systematising the field of law in Germany.[167]

Though the systematic tendency and achievements of the Historical School are often credited solely to Savigny, Hugo's programme was much too complicated to be reduced to a mere precursor of Savigny. He desired to be the Montesquieau of the spirit of private law, at the same time a systematiser, a historian, and a philosopher. The fact that Hugo treated systematisation and history separately, system as a part of natural law and history as a critical inquiry, distinguishes him from Savigny and the rest of the Historical School, who attempted to combine these approaches.[168]

For the reason why this happened, explanations must be sought in the nature and purpose of the Historical School. First of all, it must be remembered that their main aim was to develop a contemporary legal system based on Roman law. Secondly, history was used both in the development of dogmatics and as an instrument for legitimation for this purpose. The combination of these two factors led to the projection of systematic thought to Roman legal history.

In his 1824/25 lectures, Savigny distinguished between three elements of legal science, the systematic, the historical, and the exegetical. The systematic deals with the organisation of principles; the historical examines the development of law as an object of history; and the exegetical is used in the interpretation of obscure laws.[169] According to Giaro, Savigny actually followed the Roman method of interpretative adaptation to simultaneously conserve and manipulate Roman law. The historiography of the Historical School was therefore geared to the reception and reuse of Roman law.[170] The ahistorical nature of Roman law to the Historical School was necessitated by the dilemma mentioned earlier when discussing the uses of Quintus Mucius, namely the fact that if current law is derived directly from the past, then the past cannot be subjected to criticism that could question its validity. The dogmatic and contemplative interpretations cannot exist simultaneously.[171]

---

166 Andreas B. Schwarz, 'Zur Entstehung des modernen Pandectensystems', ZRG 42 (1921), 581, 583–585; Pugliese 1985, 434–445; Björne 1984, 14–15, 38–39.
167 Björne 1984, 18–105.
168 Cappellini 1984, 194–195. Apparently, also Jhering's *Der Geist des römischen Rechtes* was inspired by Montesquieu. Wieacker 1959, 204.
169 Savigny 1993, 4.
170 Giaro 1994b, 89–90.
171 This dilemma has been frequently observed in Common Law countries, where legal history as a discipline developed relatively late, cf. Mathias Reimann,

Traditionally, the Historical School has been divided into two camps: the dogmatic and the philological. Systematisation was the field of the dogmatic wing of the Historical School, commonly referred to as Pandectists, after the second title of Justinian's Digest, and later also after the Pandectist system of five books. The Pandectists wanted to construct a logically coherent and perfect system based on the Roman (or German or Canonical) sources, a system built, maintained and supplemented by the jurists, a system that was so perfect that for every question there would be an answer within its machinery. Even the process of interpretation would retain its purity within this system, it would be axiomatically and deductively clean, free of values, politically and socially neutral, because all extra-legal matters would be excluded.[172] Even though they would not eagerly admit it, the systematic tendencies of the Historical School had their origins in earlier systematisers of law such as Donellus. Pugliese claimed that the creativity of the Historical School's Pandectists has been exaggerated by the fact that they did not admit the debt they owed to the natural law school for concepts such as subjective right.[173]

If the dogmatic wing of the Historical School progressed during the first half of the nineteenth century, so too did the historical or, more precisely, the philological wing. Originally, the main aim of the investigations into the sources was to provide material for the Pandectistic reconstruction. Savigny himself was interested in historical sources and investigating them. For instance, he was instrumental in the feverish search for manuscripts that produced its most famous result in the discovery of the Gaius-manuscript in 1816 in Verona.[174] His followers continued this trend and began to publish numerous treatises on subjects such as archaic Rome that had little to do with contemporary law. For the first time there began to appear contradictions between the philological results of the historical inquiries and the aims of the school.[175]

The critical evaluation of Roman legal history began with Hugo. While he claimed that he had added very little to his translation, Hugo apparently

---

'Rechtsgeschichte im Common Law', in P. Caroni, G. Dilcher (eds.), *Norm und Tradition*, Köln 1998, 209–229.

[172] Hans-Peter Haferkamp, 'Recht als System bei Georg Friedrich Puchta', *Forum historiae iuris* 19.11.2003; Wieacker 1995, 315–318; Pugliese 1985, 452.
[173] Koschaker 1966, 282; Pugliese 1985, 448–449.
[174] Wieacker 1959, 129: 'passionierter Antiquar'. On the discovery of Gaius, see Vano 2000.
[175] The most famous representatives of the so called historical wing were Bluhme, Mais, Dirksen, the Heimbachs, and Zachariae von Lingenthal; Wieacker 1995, 330–331; Pugliese 1985, 432–423.

could not resist adding periodisation and some dates to Gibbon's text.[176] Of his own writings, the most remarkable novelty in his historical approach is the critical relationship he had with the ancient sources and the previous narratives formed by the scholarship. He also had serious questions about the nature of Roman legal science. In all these cases, he has moved from a descriptive to a critical examination of the sources and questioned the authority of preceding scholarship.

The influence of the ideal of systematisation on the writing of history was evident in Puchta's small essay on legal systems. He wrote that he had no doubt that the classical Roman jurists had developed a system of such perfection that went beyond contemporary law. This perfect system was manifest in Gaius. According to Puchta a system had a dual purpose. The first was outer classification, which is the division and organisation of material, while the other was to achieve an understanding of the inner connections within it, not just as parts, but as members of a living, organic whole.[177] The second part, understanding the system as a rigorous systematic structure with an inner coherence is the clearest development that separated Puchta and the Historical School from the earlier rationalist natural lawyers.[178]

At times, Puchta used Roman precedents unscrupulously as instruments of persuasion in modern debates, at others he delved deeply into the historical details and exposed fictitious constructions made by earlier scholars. It is as if there were two sides of Puchta in legal history or two sides of Rome for Puchta: the lawyer's Rome of applied Roman law of the Pandects and the instrumental use of Roman historical precedents, and the historian's Rome of cultural significance and the historical value of contemplation. As Marcel Senn has maintained, the Historical School had by the second half of the nineteenth century adopted in principle Rankean historism, but still tried to maintain a productive co-operative relationship with legal science.[179]

---

176 Edward Gibbon, *Historische Übersicht des Römischen Rechts, übersetzt, eingeleitet und kommentiert von Gustav Hugo*, Göttingen 1996 [1789], 45.
177 Georg F. Puchta, 'Betrachtungen über alte und neue Rechtssysteme' [1829], in *Kleine zivilistische Schriften*, Aalen 1970 [1851], 221, 233.
178 Bohnert 1975, 124–147: 'Das Recht ist System.' (p. 125); Haferkamp 2004, 257–308, 443–447; Björne 1984, 87–93, 213–220. Puchta actually had several different co-existing systematic structures, which were developed along with a general system. To counter the difficulties this complexity posed, simplifications such as the oft-mentioned pyramid of concepts were presented as early as the late nineteenth century. Cf. Björne 1984, 218; Haferkamp 2004, 94–100.
179 Senn 1982, 34–39.

Puchta's treatment of Quintus Mucius is a good example of his approach to history. He took an old and neglected theory of Maiansius and gave it a new meaning. This new interpretation stressed the important role of Quintus Mucius in the birth of legal science. The legal science that had emerged after Quintus Mucius was a distinctly systematic activity in the way envisioned by Savigny and Puchta himself. This laid, according to Puchta, the foundations of the Historical School. In both cases old, existing legal material was transformed by systematic inquiry and the abstraction of legal principles by the scientific pursuit of lawyers.

Systematic legal thinking spread from the Pandectist system throughout law and far outside the German-speaking world. The jurisprudence of concepts and legal positivism gained more influence as its followers took the ordered and rigorous system of concepts to fields previously little affected by the Romanistic tradition: to public law through Gerber, Laband, and Jellinek; to procedural law, and to legal theory.[180] Within Roman law studies, there were also voices of caution, warning of the dangers of exaggerations.[181] Through the conceptual framework of contemporary law, this systematic thought still affects legal history. On the one hand scholars of every historical denomination have long warned about the dangers of using misleading modern concepts, on the other they have affirmed that history without some reference to contemporary concepts is impossible, as historians must be able to translate ancient concepts into a form understood by their contemporaries.[182]

The systematising tendency has been an integral part of the scholarship of Roman jurisprudence. It has dominated the field to such an extent that Kunkel claimed that only after its eradication could the true nature of ancient Roman law be studied historically.[183] Chronologically speaking, things have

---

180 Cf. Wilhelm 1958; Pugliese 1985, 460.
181 Gino Segrè, *Di alcune pericolose tendenze nello studio sistematico del diritto romano*, Cagliari 1892, 11.
182 Of the difficulty of translating Greek tragedies and their words of specific culturally and historically bound meanings, cf. Jean-Pierre Vernant, 'Greek Tragedy: Problems of Interpretation', in E. Macksey, E. Donato (eds.), *The Structuralist Controversy*, Baltimore 1970, 275. Of the older discussion in legal history, see Hoetink 1955, 10–20.
183 Wolfgang Kunkel, *An Introduction to Roman Legal and Constitutional History* (translated by J.M. Kelly), Oxford 1972, 83: 'The abstract system of Roman law principles which modern science, in particular the theoretical German jurisprudence of the nineteenth century, has distilled from the Roman sources shows, it is true, hardly anything of this peculiar structure of ancient Roman law. In it the historical strata of Roman law are forced into a timeless and rationalizing system and thus their significance is not infrequently dis-

not always been seen so simple. Von Lübtow, a staunch opponent of unpractical theoreticisation, accused Cicero of reverting back to the old jurisprudence of concepts of the nineteenth century in his *de iure civili in artem redigendo*.[184] Giaro has presented classical Roman jurisprudence and German Pandectist jurisprudence as opposites that have a victimological relationship, in which the latter wrongs the former by misrepresenting it according to a logic totally alien to it.[185]

It is often a question of a matter of opinion whether a certain phenomenon is ascribed to the general systematising tendencies of the nineteenth century historical scholarship or to a bias particular to the Historical School. The systematising and monumentalising tendencies of the late nineteenth century scholarship have also been the target of a general historical criticism. Scholars have gradually uncovered anachronistic interpretations and fictitious constructions by comparing the historical reconstructions made in the nineteenth century with what is now known of Roman sources. A good example is the transformation of our view of Republican comitial legislation. Traditionally the Romans named laws after the *gentilicia* of their proposers, and scholars later referred to laws according to these names. However, a recent study by Sandberg has shown that most of the names of the laws used in the scholarly literature are in fact later fabrications made on the basis of scant references in Roman literature sometimes centuries after the supposed event. Laws that had no names in Roman sources were given one by scholars based on the assumption that there was a rigid system in which only the consuls could propose laws and therefore all laws must have been named after the consuls of the year.[186] This was a reflection of the tendency in the nineteenth century historical scholarship to assume the existence of a coherent system and to interpret the sources accordingly.

>torted. Modern research is concerned to free itself from this unhistorical way of looking at the matter, which means not only that our historical knowledge is being made more accurate, but also that an essential contribution is being made to the study of the system of civil law and of the body of concepts in the modern codifications which rests upon it.'

184 Ulrich von Lübtow, 'Cicero und die Methode der römischen Jurisprudenz', in P. Koschaker (ed.), *Festschrift für Leopold Wenger zu seinem 70. Geburtstag*, München 1944, 232–234.

185 Giaro 1991, 209. Already in the 1950s, Artur Steinwenter, 'Römisches Recht und Begriffsjurisprudenz, in *Recht und Kultur. Aufsätze und Vorträge eines österreichischen Rechtshistorikers*, Graz 1958, 52–56 underlined the deep structural division between Roman law and conceptual jurisprudence.

186 Kaj Sandberg, *Magistrates and Assemblies: A Study of Legislative Practice in Republican Rome*, Acta Instituti Romani Finlandiae 24, Rome 2001. The traditional reconstruction is Giovanni Rotondi, *Leges publicae populi romani*, Hildesheim 1962 [1912].

The importance of Roman law to the Historical School was a product of several different factors. The two most important ones were, of course, the wide-spread use of Roman law in Germany and the cultural idea of Rome that influenced the nineteenth century. What made Roman law so practical for the purposes of the Historical School was that Roman law was understood as jurists' law, that is, law created through the actions and interactions of jurists, not through the will of a legislator or the ruling of a judge. Roman jurists' law was interpreted as a kind of precedent for the professorial law-making in Germany. The fact that Roman law seemed to develop and grow organically by itself, without the need for conscious legislation fascinated the Historical School and their followers until the present day, though the anticodificationalist idea was gradually forgotten after 1848.[187] In a similar way, the fact that the Historical School used the Roman legal sources and history meant that it manufactured its own past to create the appearance of a continuing reception of Roman law.[188]

The interest of the Historical School in Roman jurists' law was partly based on the fact that the Romanistic brand of the Historical School itself supported and promoted jurists' law.[189] The Roman precedent was used as a legitimating instrument, in a way that Giaro has called utilising the continuing authority of the Romans. This position led to the identification of contemporaries with the Romans, and in turn to the transportation of contemporary elements of law into the past in order to legitimise them.[190]

The beginnings of systematisation are, in retrospect, as much a display of presentism as the dispute over the combination of Roman law and Greek theory. Scholars of the nineteenth century like Puchta saw in Rome the seeds of their contemporary legal system and projected their ideals and aspirations there.

---

187 Giaro 1994b, 69; Whitman 1990, 126–128, 186, 209.
188 Johannes E. Kuntze, *Das Jus respondendi in unserer Zeit: Ideen über die moderne Rechtsfortbildung*, Leipzig 1858, 6–8 described the Historical School as the highest level of the 600 years of Reception.
189 Koschaker 1966, 180 has noted that the Historical School was not so much in favour of jurists' law as against legislation because of the concept of *Volksgeist*. In contrast, the Germanistic denomination of the Historical School was critical of jurists' law, cf. James Q. Whitman, 'Long Live the Hatred of Roman Law!', *Rechtsgeschichte* 3 (2003), 40.
190 Giaro 1994b, 70–71.

Conclusions

There is a strong tradition in Roman legal history in interpreting Quintus Mucius as the founder of Roman legal science or even the whole Western legal tradition. However, there is no consensus on how to define this Roman legal science he is supposed to have founded, whether by comparison with the present or by a definition of an independent concept of Roman legal science. A further dilemma is presented by the possible Greek theoretical roots of legal science.

The question of whether Quintus Mucius Scaevola Pontifex initiated the science of law remains unanswered even after a thorough investigation of the Roman sources. The sources do tell us a number of things. Cicero lauds Quintus Mucius as the exemplary nobleman and virtuous jurist. To others, he is the famous lawyer and the martyr of the Republic. To legal writers like Gaius and the authors of the Digest, Quintus Mucius is the legal authority whose opinions and definitions are cited frequently.

The Roman sources are less than consistent when it comes to the issue of science. Cicero, a pupil and a friend of Quintus Mucius, referred to him constantly, stressing his virtues and achievements. Cicero did in fact also speak of legal science as having Greek precedents. For this he gave credit to Servius, another friend. The legal sources do contain a number of categorisations and definitions, which have been seen as the characteristics of scientific inquiry. However, the foundations of the tradition are Pomponius and his *generatim composuisse*. The *generatim* of Pomponius and the project of *ars* of definitions and division mentioned by Cicero formed the basis of the concepts of Roman legal science.

The Roman sources provided the budding discipline of legal history with two narratives, Quintus Mucius the ideal Roman, and Quintus Mucius the lawyer. Until the mid-eighteenth century the idea of legal science, produced by importing Greek learning with definitions and divisions, was already existent, but historians followed Cicero in what science was and whom we should thank for it.

This tradition remained unaltered and the passage of Pomponius concerning 18 books organized *generatim* remained a mere number of books written until Maiansius determined that this organisation may have been scientific. The full implications of this discovery were not realised until Sanio and Puchta wrote that Quintus Mucius single-handedly established a new era of Roman jurisprudence, the era of the systematic science of law.

Maiansius was the first to shift the title of founder from Servius to Quintus Mucius, but otherwise left the tradition intact. The significance of scientific method and Greek Stoic learning was strengthened by Gibbon and Hugo. In the early nineteenth century, both Servius and Quintus Mucius were considered as founders of legal science. This interpretation changed in the 1840s when Sanio and Puchta elevated Quintus Mucius to the status of sole founder. From the 1870s to the 1890s more details were added and the story was reinforced by Jörs and Krüger, but debates over the exact nature of the Greek influence continued. Based on this background, Schulz labelled Quintus Mucius as the founder of the whole Western legal tradition. Later supporters of the systematic theory developed the idea of a scientific revolution. From the 1960s onwards, doubts concerning whether the Romans ever developed a legal science as a science were raised. Critics, pointing to the meagre historical data, dismissed the whole idea of looking for the beginnings of science in a single person or discovery as foolish. There were also attempts to return to the old debate and rehabilitating the founding father status to Servius.

The rise in the significance of the story in the 1840s is explained by the general rise of interest in legal science at the same time. The Historical School relied on scientific truthfulness and advancement as the rationale behind the contemporary use of Roman law. Quintus Mucius served as a founding father because a historical precedent was needed. It is fair to call it an invented tradition because its significance and value was a later innovation intended to meet later needs, though based on Roman sources.

The foundation theory of Quintus Mucius was not universally accepted, especially by some medievalists, who believe Gratian deserves the title of the founder of Western science. In the general debate over the foundations of legal science, there seemed to be an understanding that legal science as a modern concept demanded two ancient components: Roman substantive law and Greek scientific theory. To prove the scientific credentials of Roman law, Romanists strove to find evidence of the influence of Greek scientific theories in Roman law. In effect, there appears to be two competing genealogies of Western legal science. The first was proposed by medievalists who claimed that Roman law and Greek theory were combined only by the scholastics of the twelfth century, and the second was suggested by the Romanists, who insisted that this combination already existed in Antiquity.

It is evident that the vital question is not whether or not Quintus Mucius or Servius founded legal science, but why do we search for the father of Roman legal science? Historians of Roman jurisprudence only found science in the form of definitions and *regulae* in the late 18th century. The beginnings of the systematic model of Roman legal science can be traced to Hugo's introduction of Leibniz and Kant as the models of science. The later Romanist obsession with science and system was an inheritance from the Historical School of jurisprudence, in this case mostly from Puchta. The fact that they systematised Roman legal science in addition to their own is explained by their curious relationship with history. The main objective of the Historical School was a systematised legal science. Because they used history to aid legal dogmatics in finding material and as a legitimating instrument to establish precedents, they also ended up systematising Roman legal science.

What then was the meaning of the story? It provided legitimisation for the Romanists and the continuing relevance of Roman law in the form of an invented tradition, which stressed a founding myth. The very nature of the story of the 'founding father' involves a measure of delusion about the possibility of historical continuity. As the founding father is forever located at the dawn of history, his context disappears as do his predecessors. Discoveries are therefore supposed to have been made in a vacuum.

Chapter 3

In Defence of the Autonomy of Law

The autonomy of law is an ambiguous concept historically speaking,[1] with distinct modern connotations.[2] Its ambiguity is increased by its variety. The concept may be divided into the autonomy of law as legal norms or the machinery of law with regard to other forms of social coercion, the autonomy of legal science with regard to other sciences; or the autonomy of jurists or the legal norms with regard to political, economic and social power.

In the literature on Roman law, autonomy has been a major concept ever since Fritz Schulz devoted a whole chapter to *Isolierung,* or isolation, in his *Prinzipien des römischen Rechts.*[3] Before that the issue was not prominent, which reflected the fact that the autonomy of law as a concept was of no interest to ancient Roman jurists. An attempt was made in the 1960s to find out whether or not the autonomy of law was apparent in the writings of Roman jurists. This only managed to prove that there was nothing further to be gained from examining the technical texts of Roman jurists. The jurists made few references to arguments outside of the field of law, to equity, utility, politics, economy, or culture. Nor were they interested in the matter theoretically or from a philosophical or historical perspective.[4]

---

[1] The origins of the ideal of the autonomy of law are unclear. John Finnis, for instance, links autonomy with positive law in the works of Aquinas. John Finnis, 'The Truth in Legal Positivism' in R. P. George (ed.), *The Autonomy of Law: Essays on Legal Positivism,* Oxford 1996, 195.

[2] On the concept of the autonomy of law in a modern context being linked with legal positivism, cf. Gerald J. Postema, 'Law's autonomy and public practical reason', in R. P. George (ed.), *The Autonomy of Law: Essays on Legal Positivism,* Oxford 1996, 79–118; Gunther Teubner, *Recht als autopoietisches System,* Frankfurt am Main 1989, 37 et passim.

[3] Schulz 1934, 13–26. Contra, Bruno Paradisi, 'La storia del diritto della storiografia contemporanea', in *La storia del diritto nel quadro delle scienze storiche: Atti del primo Congresso internazionale della Società Italiana di Storia del Diritto,* Firenze 1966, xx.

[4] Giovanni Pugliese, 'L'autonomia del diritto rispetto agli altri fenomeni e valori sociali nella giurisprudenza romana', in *La storia del diritto nel quadro delle scienze storiche: Atti del primo Congresso internazionale della Società Italiana di Storia del Diritto,* Firenze 1966, 161–191.

In current Romanistic literature there is a general consensus regarding the basic autonomy of Roman legal science.[5] What this autonomy means and the implications that this has for the study of Roman law have been studied less. What are the effects of the modern theoretical ideal of legal autonomy and what kind of reflections are caused by the reception of Roman law as legal texts detached from its social context?[6]

In order to explore how the concept of autonomy emerged in Roman legal history, it is best to start with a concrete example. The most viable option would be to proceed from a period of change, a turning point in the history of Roman law, which would elicit contemplations about the relationship between law and extralegal influences. The most obvious point of departure would be the relationship between law and political power.

The most iconic of the turning points in Roman legal history is what Ronald Syme has called the Roman revolution; the gradual change from Republic to the Principate through the reforms of Augustus.[7] The formation of the Principate is a fruitful object of investigation, as its significance has been recognised for a long time. The underlying conviction ever since Antiquity has been that something fundamental changed in the nature of Rome when Augustus assumed power. It has even been claimed that the reign of Augustus signified the end of the freedom of jurisprudence.[8] What is more significant for the purpose of this study is the scholarly response that this perceived change brought forth.

In this chapter, this response is examined through the prism of the debates on the *ius respondendi*, the contested institution that supposedly gave certain jurists the right to offer legal opinions that would have been binding on judges, in effect giving the emperor a direct way of controlling Roman jurists' law through proxies. The *ius respondendi* is a particularly fruitful example as it has had a continuing presence in the literature from the sixteenth century onwards and has occupied a central position in the relationship between the emperors and jurists.

---

[5] Bruce Frier, 'Law, Roman, sociology of', in *The Oxford Classical Dictionary*, (3rd, rev. ed.), Oxford 2003, 824: '… the most historically significant contributions of Roman law probably depended less on the specific content of its rules than on its emergence as a more or less autonomous discipline that was insulated by its professionalism from directly contending social pressures.' Alan Watson, *The Evolution of Law*, Oxford 1985, 69: 'It is to some extent autonomous, and exists and operates within its own sphere.'

[6] For an example see Bretone 2004, 155–170.

[7] Ronald Syme, *The Roman revolution*, Oxford 1939.

[8] Alvaro d'Ors, 'La signification de l'œuvre d'Hadrien dans l'histoire du droit romain', in Piganiol et al. (eds.), *Les empereurs romains d'Espagne*, Paris 1965, 155: 'Avant Auguste la jurisprudence était libre.'

The *ius respondendi* and Roman jurisprudence

The significance and even the very existence of the *ius respondendi* supposedly established by Augustus is one of the many unsolved puzzles of Roman legal history. This is certainly not due to the lack of effort – there is a rich modern literature that spans from the 1930s to the present.[9] Richard A. Bauman wrote that there are few problems so beset by controversy and doubt as the *ius respondendi*, with prospects of a *communis opinio* so remote that one's first inclination is to set the matter aside and forget about it.[10] That would be a loss, since the issue is of vital importance to the history of law in the Early Principate.

The common assumption is that Augustus gave select jurists the right to create law by making their opinions binding on judges, which would have had important effects throughout the field of law. However, scholars are highly divided on the consequences of the event. Some claim that with the *ius respondendi* Augustus created a superior class of jurists at the request of the same jurists lobbying for his support.[11] Others assert that the proud jurists repulsed the encroachment of Augustus into their hallowed territory, thereby

---

[9] Ferdinand de Visscher, 'Le "ius publice respondendi"', RHDFE 15 (1936), 615–650; Heinrich Siber, 'Der Ausgangspunkt des "ius respondendi"', ZRG 61 (1941), 397–402; Schulz 1946, 112–118; Wolfgang Kunkel, 'Das Wesen des ius respondendi', ZRG 66 (1948), 423–457; Antonio Guarino, 'Il "ius publice respondendi"', RIDA 1.2 (1949), 401–419; André Magdelain, 'Ius respondendi', RHDFE 29 (1950), 1–22; David Daube, 'Hadrian's rescript to some ex-praetors', ZRG 67 (1950), 511–518; Ernst Schönbauer, 'Die Entwicklung des "ius publice respondendi"', IURA 1 (1950), 288; Ernst Schönbauer, 'Zur Entwicklung des "ius publice respondendi"', IURA 4 (1953), 224–227; Giuseppe Provera, 'Ancora sul "ius respondendi"', SDHI 28 (1962), 342–360; Ulrich von Lübtow, 'Miscellanea', in M. Lauria (ed.), *Studi in onore di Vincenzo Arangio-Ruiz II*, Napoli 1953, 377–378; Marijan Horvat, 'Note intorno allo "ius respondendi"', in A. Guarino, L. Labruna (eds.), *Synteleia Vincenzo Arangio-Ruiz 2*, Napoli 1964, 710–716; Kunkel 2001 [1967], 272–299 et passim; Franz Wieacker, 'Augustus und die Juristen seiner Zeit', TR 37 (1969b), 331–349; Mario Bretone, *Techniche e ideologie dei giuristi romani*, (2nd ed.), Napoli 1982, 241–254; Franz Wieacker, 'Respondere ex auctoritate principis', in J. A. Ankum et alii (eds.), *Satura Roberto Feenstra oblata*, Fribourg 1985, 71–94; Filippo Cancelli, 'Il presunto "ius respondendi" istituito da Augusto', BIDR 90 (1987), 543–568; Richard A. Bauman, *Lawyers and Politics in the Early Roman Empire*, München 1989; Javier Paricio, 'El *ius publice respondendi ex auctoritate principis*', in J. Paricio (ed.), *Poder político y derecho en la Roma Clásica*, Madrid 1996, 85–105; Fögen 2002, 199–206.

[10] Bauman 1989, xxvii.

[11] Most recently Bauman 1989.

maintaining the freedom of jurisprudence.[12] Between these extremes mainstream authors have suggested certain compromises with varying degrees of scepticism.[13]

The purpose of this investigation is not to solve the traditional problem of Augustus and the *ius respondendi* at all, but rather to take a fresh look at the historiography of the attempts to solve it as indicators of the changing opinions on the autonomy of law and jurisprudence in the Roman world. As an unsolved puzzle, the *ius respondendi* offers a viewpoint on the evolution of thought.

In this way, I wish to present a genealogy of the tradition surrounding the *ius respondendi*, with a special emphasis on the ideological background and narrative elements they contain. The main theme under scrutiny is the supposed freedom of Republican jurisprudence and the repercussions that this idealised past has had for the history of Roman law.

* * *

As is often the case in Roman legal history, the roots of the enigma lie in Pomponius' introduction to legal history. The passage about the *ius respondendi* in particular is one the most difficult to fathom.

> Massurius Sabinus was of equestrian rank, and was the first person to give state-certificated opinions (*publice respondere*). For after this privilege (*beneficium*) came to be granted, it was conceded to him by Tiberius Caesar. 49. To clarify the point in passing: before the time of Augustus the right of stating opinions at large was not granted by emperors, but the practice was that opinions were given by people who had confidence in their own studies. Nor did they always issue opinions under seal, but most commonly wrote themselves to the judges, or gave the testimony of a direct answer to those who consulted them. It was the deified Augustus who, in order to enhance the authority of the law, first established that opinions might be given under his authority. And from that time this began to be sought as a favor. As a consequence of this, our most excellent emperor Hadrian issued a rescript on an occasion when some men of praetorian rank were petitioning him for permission to grant opinions; he said that this was by custom not merely begged for but earned and that he [the emperor] would accordingly be delighted if whoever had faith in himself would prepare himself for giving opinions to the people at large. 50. Anyway, to Sabinus the concession was granted by Tiberius Caesar that he might give opinions to the people at large. He was admitted to the equestrian rank when already of mature years and almost fifty. (Dig. 1,2,2,48–50)[14]

---

12   Cf. *inter alia* Fögen 2002, 205–206.
13   See, for instance, Olivia F. Robinson, *The Sources of Roman Law*, London 1997, 11–13.
14   *Massurius Sabinus in equestri ordine fuit et publice primus respondit: posteaque hoc coepit beneficium dari, a Tiberio Caesare hoc tamen illi concessum*

74   Chapter 3

The evaluation of Pomponius' text has followed roughly two paths: the text critical path has sought to uncover the true uncorrupted form of the text, while the source critical path has examined Pomponius' position and his reliability as an historical source.

The interest in text critical studies of this passage arose from the evident fact that the text has a number of contradictions and irregularities, such as whether Augustus or Tiberius was the first to grant the *ius respondendi*. These have naturally prompted scholars to correct and amend the text.[15] The modern editors of the Digest, for example Mommsen and Bonfante, attempted to rectify the text by punctuating it differently and adding some words.[16]

The interpolation phase of text criticism began in the late nineteenth century but reached its peak in the 1930s. The hunt for interpolations meant removing parts of the text which were deemed unclassical repetitions on the part of Late Antique jurists who knew nothing of the original situation. Siber eliminated and removed parts of the text that he thought were unnecessary repetitions, Schulz recognised four different hands that had worked on the

> erat. Et, ut obiter sciamus, ante tempora Augusti publice respondendi ius non a principibus dabatur, sed qui fiduciam studiorum suorum habebant, consulentibus respondebant: neque responsa utique signata dabant, sed plerumque iudicibus ipsi scribebant, aut testabantur qui illos consulebant. Primus divus Augustus, ut maior iuris auctoritas haberetur, constituit, ut ex auctoritate eius responderent: et ex illo tempore peti hoc pro beneficio coepit. Et ideo optimus princeps Hadrianus, cum ab eo viri praetorii peterent, ut sibi liceret respondere, rescripsit eis hoc non peti, sed praestari solere et ideo, si quis fiduciam sui haberet, delectari se <si> populo ad respondendum se praepararet (praestaret, praeberet – Mo.). Ergo Sabino concessum est a Tiberio Caesare, ut populo responderet: qui in equestri ordine iam grandis natu et fere annorum quinquaginta receptus est. (Dig. 1,2,2,48–50, Mommsen-Krüger) Translation by D. N. MacCormick in Mommsen-Krüger-Watson (eds.), *The Digest of Justinian*, Philadelphia 1985. The Behrends et al. 1995, 110 German translation is also noteworthy here, but the discrepancies do not affect the points dealt with here.

15   Already U. Zasius lambasted the text: *'Hic textus in omnibus quos vidimus libris, ita fuit corrupte scriptus, ut non solum nulla sermonis elegantia, sed nec ullus vel sensus, vel intellectus, quin poti monstrosa barbaries nostro Iureconsulto minime digna consciperetur.'* Ulrich Zasius, 'In iuris civilis originem scholia, quibus l. II. ff. de orig. iuris elucidatur', in *Singularia responsa sive intellectus juris singulares*, Basel 1541, 283 [ad Dig. 1,2,2,48]. For modern opinions, cf. de Visscher 1936, 619; Siber 1941, 401; Kunkel 1948, 429; Horvat 1964, 712–713; Bauman 1989, 3. Generally on Pomponius' *Enchiridion*, see Bretone 1982, 211–254; Dieter Nörr, 'Pomponius oder zum Geschichtsverständnis der römischen Juristen', ANRW II. 15 (1976), 512–539; Crifò 1998, 69–72.

16   de Visscher 1936, 616–617; Siber 1941, 397–399.

text, some of them post-classical, and additional glosses in various parts of the text.[17]

Kunkel, and later Wieacker, professed their scepticism about the credibility of such extensive changes in the text. They claimed that the text should be analysed as a whole and urged not to use unfounded textual criticism merely to solve problems by removing inconvenient parts of the text as later interpolations. This view has since become dominant, although opinions vary on how much the Pomponius-text was corrupted.[18]

Source criticism has revolved around two questions: how much Pomponius actually knew about the *ius respondendi* and how much of that has been transmitted to us. The difference is significant, as it determines how much of the text (and the errors) can be ascribed to Pomponius himself. Pomponius' credibility as a source was defended by Wieacker, who claimed that Pomponius is stylistically poor, but tolerably well informed, and later by Bauman, who thought that Pomponius is rather accurate.[19]

---

[17] Siber 1941, 399–401, followed by Guarino 1949, 404–409. In the proposal by Schulz 1946, 115–60, the sequence of the hands is: 1st hand (classical, with glosses): *Et ita Ateio…* 2nd hand (post-classical addition): Massurius Sabinus… 3rd hand (classical, with glosses): 49. *Et ut obiter…* 4th hand (post-classical addition): *[Et ideo] optimus princeps…* 1st hand (classical, with glosses): *Sabino concessum…*

[18] According to Kunkel, interpretations such as Schulz's are despite their ingeniousness extremely improbable. Although the text does contain inaccuracies from different manuscripts, the compilators of the Digest should not be accused of alterations without cause, since there was hardly any motive to change history. Kunkel 1948, 432–436. See also Wieacker 1969b, 337–340; Bauman 1989, 3–4; Paricio 1996, 89–95. Schönbauer 1950, 288 tried to restore the text to its original form by adding material he felt had been omitted. Wieacker generally dismissed text critical solutions and conjectures as elegant but worthless guesswork: 'Soweit sich die Kritiker nicht nur von sachlogischen Kriterien leiten ließen, sondern auch von ihren jeweiligen Vorstellungen über das ius respondendi, veranschaulichen ihre Rekonstruktionen nur ihre eigenen Thesen, wie besonders die von Schönbauer oder F. Schulz' "vier Hände". Auch Konjekturen, die sich durch Eleganz oder Ökonomie zu empfehlen scheinen, haben bei einem so uneleganten Autor geringere Überzeugungskraft.' Wieacker 1969b, 340.

[19] Wieacker 1969b, 340; Bauman 1989, 287–288. Bauman 1989, 293 stated that Pomponius is accurate with regard to historical details. He rejected the common assertion (perpetuated for instance in Fögen 2002, 203) that Pomponius was an ignoramus because he supposedly did not know that before Augustus there were no *principes* by pointing out that Pomponius might have also meant the *principes civitatis* of the Republic. In the Behrends et al. (1995, 110) translation they even added a footnote: 'Vor Augustus gab es keine Kaiser.'

Opinions have also differed about the transmission of the text; Schulz was probably the most vocal in condemning the present state of the text, which he calls apocryphal, post-classical and corrupted.[20] Later scholars have offered more balanced judgements. The prevailing view is that the text in the Digest is actually a poorly preserved abridgement of the original, but it contains more or less what Pomponius wrote. Some, especially Bauman, are more optimistic and think that we have in essence what Pomponius wrote.[21]

Traditionally, the second main source of the *ius respondendi* is a passus of Gaius explaining the sources of the law.

> Juristic answers are the opinions and advice of those entrusted with the task of building up the law. If the opinions of all of them agree on a point, what they thus hold has the status of an act; if, however, they disagree, a judge may follow which opinion he wishes. This is made known in a written reply of the Emperor Hadrian. (Gaius Inst. 1,7)[22]

Gaius' passage on the *responsa prudentium* has been frequently seen as a confirmation of Pomponius' account of the *ius respondendi*, particularly the passage about *permissum est*.[23] Indeed, Gaius seems to confirm that there was a group of people licensed to give *responsa*, and that their opinions, if unanimous, had the force of law. Sceptics have nevertheless emerged. Krüger claimed that Gaius probably meant a simple *communis opinio* of the jurists, not the *ius respondendi*. Schulz condemned also this text as post-classical, only to be rebuked again by Kunkel.[24] Provera agreed that Gaius confirmed the *ius respondendi*, though only on account of judicial *responsa*. Wieacker

---

20   Schulz 1946, 116 and passim.
21   Wieacker 1969b, 338–340; Bretone 1982, 211–223; Bauman 1989, 287–288.
22   *Responsa prudentium sunt sententiae et opiniones eorum, quibus permissum est iura condere. quorum omnium si in unum sententiae concurrunt, id quod ita sentiunt, legis vicem optinet; si vero dissentiunt, iudici licet quam velit sententiam sequi; idque rescripto divi Hadriani significatur.* (Gaius Inst. 1,7) Translation by W. M. Gordon and O. F. Robinson, *The Institutes of Gaius*, New York 1988. During the interpolation debate even Gaius was suspected of having post-classical glosses. Siro Solazzi, 'Glosse a Gaio', in *Studi in onore di Salvatore Riccobono*, Palermo 1936, 95 claimed that the phrases *et opiniones* and *si vero ... sequi* are both glosses. This view was not shared by later scholars. Quadrato read *iura condere* as 'to create law', cf. Renato Quadrato, 'Iuris conditor', *Index* 22 (1994), 87–106.
23   Kunkel 1948, 442–443; A. M. Honoré, *Gaius*, Oxford 1962, 121–122; Bauman 1989, 1.
24   Krüger 1912, 124; Schulz 1946, 115: 'The fact that Gaius, unlike Pomponius, puts the *responsa prudentium* among the sources is in itself suspicious, but more than this, the whole section reflects post-classical ideas so completely that it cannot be genuine.' Kunkel 1948, 442–443. To von Lübtow 1953, 377, it is a post-classical Pseudo-Gaius.

found the whole passage awkward, beginning from the meaning of *sententia et opiniones*. Rather than understanding the *ius respondendi* as every utterance of the licensed jurist, Wieacker saw it as jurists' law in its written form, which at Gaius' time was beginning to be included among the sources of law.[25] Similarly, Cancelli and others have challenged the whole link between Gaius Inst. 1,7 and the *ius respondendi* by saying that Gaius does not refer to any specific licence but to the actions of lawyers in general.[26]

However, an analogous passage appears in the Institutes of Justinian that seems to refer to the *ius respondendi* more directly.

> The answers of those learned in the law are the opinions and views of persons authorized to determine and expound the law; for it was of old provided that certain persons should publicly interpret the laws, who were called jurisconsults, and whom the Emperor privileged to give formal answers. If they were unanimous the judge was forbidden by imperial constitution to depart from their opinion, so great was its authority. (Inst. Iust. 1,2,8)[27]

The fact that the reference to *responsa* is conveniently in the past tense, *permissum erat*, has not escaped scholars.[28] Though it has been seen as a necessary confirmation of the *ius respondendi*, the value of the text has often been questioned on the basis of its post-classical date.[29] Schulz said that the

---

25 Provera 1962, 349–350; Wieacker 1985, 75–80 thought that, as Sabinians, Gaius and Pomponius had a special interest in the privilege, which was first given to the head of their school. Bauman 1989, 288 questioned the common assertion that Pomponius was a Sabinian.

26 Cancelli 1987, 545–549. Cancelli noted that the passage may be an interpolated reference to the Law of Citations. Cf. von Lübtow 1953, 377–378. Cancelli's interpretations of Gaius Inst. 1,7 are: 1) *responsa* refers to juristic activity in general, 2) *sententiae* and *opiniones* are modes of *responsa*, 3) *eorum* is a paraphrase of jurists without distinctions, 4) *permissum est* is a reference to those who habitually exercise it, i.e. the jurists. 5) *condere iura* refers to those with an ability to do so, i.e. the jurists, 6) Hadrian merely wrote that in conflict situations the judge should have freedom of choice. Nicola Palazzolo, 'Il princeps, i giuristi, l'editto. Mutamento istituzionale e strumenti di trasformazione del diritto privato da Augusto ad Adriano', in F. Milazzo (ed.), *Res publica e princeps*, Napoli 1996, 321, claims that there is no link between the *ius respondendi* and Gaius Inst. 1,7.

27 *Responsa prudentium sunt sententiae et opiniones eorum, quibus permissum erat iura condere. nam antiquitus institutum erat, ut essent qui iura publice interpretarentur, quibus a Caesare ius respondendi datum est, qui iuriconsulti appellabantur. quorum omnium sententiae et opiniones eam auctoritatem tenent, ut iudici recedere a responso eorum non liceat, ut est constitutum.* (Inst. Iust. 1,2,8) Translation by J. B. Moyle, in J. B. Moyle, *The Institutes of Justinian*, (5th ed.), Oxford 1955.

28 Puchta 1875, 324; Guarino 1949, 401–402.

29 Magdelain 1950, 4; Wieacker 1985, 76, 80–83 wrote that Inst. Iust. 1,2,8 is the only direct evidence available.

post-classical authors did not understand the meaning of the *ius respondendi* and thus interpreted it as a right to make law.[30] Cancelli claimed that Theophilus, the likely compiler of this text, merely interpreted Gaius as he himself understood it at the time when all law emanated from the emperor.[31] Besides the relativisation caused by the late origin, few have challenged the reliability of the text.[32]

Despite their disparity, the main Roman sources, Pomponius, Gaius and the Institutes of Justinian, give an authoritative basis for the *ius respondendi*. However, the criticism levelled against these sources, that Pomponius was confused and incoherent; that Gaius was talking about something else, and that the Institutes are simply a reflection of the Late Antique understanding of the sources of law, makes the sceptical observer wish for some corroboration from other sources.

* * *

In order to examine systematically the historical background of the *ius respondendi*, we should also delve into the question of other contemporary sources that might attest to the privilege. If the *ius respondendi* was a privilege given by the emperor to individual lawyers, as the traditional view claims, one might expect to find some mention of it in other sources, such as contemporary literature and inscriptions.

This is by no means a new observation in itself. The fact that the legal sources give us such a meagre quantity of material on the *ius respondendi* proper has led historians of Roman law to search for sources that could attest once and for all that some jurist had the *ius respondendi* and that he had used it to give *responsa* on the authority of the emperor.

The most straightforward method is to find out whether the words *ius respondendi* are mentioned in the literature. Helssig found three occurrences of *ius publice respondere* in the literature by Gellius, Ulpian and Pliny, but this led to no concrete proof of the existence of the institution. Gellius writes that Labeo gave advice publicly to those who consulted him on legal questions, Ulpian states that Nerva the Younger was said to have given opinions on law

---

30   Schulz 1946, 114: 'In post-classical times there was no clear conception of the Augustan system of authorization of responsa, nor was it known which of the jurists had been authorized and which not. The pre-conceptions of a bureaucratic age led to the belief that Augustus and his successors had empowered the jurists *iura condere*, and all the jurists of the Principate whose writings had survived were assumed to have been so empowered.'
31   Cancelli 1987, 560–562. The underlying logic is that the codification is full of references to emperors who mention juristic *responsa*.
32   Paricio 1996, 99.

in public, while Pliny describes an amusing scene in a poetry recitation session involving Iavolenus Priscus, who despite his questionable sanity responded publicly in law. As is evident, it is difficult to establish whether *publice* means simply 'to the general public' or 'with a special authorisation'.[33]

One of the texts frequently discussed is a passage in Eunapius' (346–414 AD) *Lives of the Sophists*. In his biography of his master Chrysanthius, Eunapius mentioned Chrysanthius' grandfather Innocentius. Innocentius achieved fame and fortune, and finally received the task of compiling legal statutes both in Latin and Greek from the emperor. However, Eunapius makes no mention of whether Innocentius was given the *ius respondendi* or simply the task of making a compilation of legal material.[34] Schulz expressed his doubt that Eunapius' text really refers to the *ius respondendi* with the words 'uncertain and improbable', whereas Bauman considered it 'possible'.[35]

A more popular line of argument proceeded from Inst. Iust. 1,2,8, according to which those with the *ius respondendi* were called *iuris consulti* (*quibus a Caesare ius respondendi datum est, qui iurisconsulti appellabantur*). This led Kipp and Krüger to believe that only privileged jurists had the title of *iuris consultus* as a sign of the *ius respondendi*.[36]

---

33 R. Helssig, 'Die römische Rechtswissenschaft im Zeitalter des Augustus', in V. Gardthausen (ed.), *Augustus und seine Zeit* 1.3, Leipzig 1891, 901; Gell. 13,10 *Labeo Antistius iuris quidem civilis disciplinam principali studio exercuit et consulentibus de iure publice responsitavit*; Ulpian Dig. 3,1,1,3 *qua aetate aut paulo maiore fertur Nerva filius et publice de iure responsitasse*; Plin. epist. 6,1,5,3 *Est omnino Priscus dubiae sanitatis, interest tamen officiis, adhibetur consiliis atque etiam ius civile publice respondet* ... Cancelli 1987, 554 said that *publice* actually means just publicly or to the state, in contrast to 'privately', to friends and clients.

34 Eunapius, *Vitae sophistarum* (ed. Ioseph Giangrande), Roma 1954, *Chrysanthius*, 91; J.F. Boissonade, *Eunapii vitae sophistarum*, Paris 1849, 500. The passus was taken up already by Jacobus Gothofredus, *Codex Theodosianus cum perpetuis commentariis*, Lyon 1665, 32 [ch. 1.4].

35 Schulz 1946, 114; Bauman 1989, 2. The division is possibly the result of Bauman's translation of Eunapius' words ὅς γε νομοθετικὴν εἶχε δύναμιν παρὰ τῶν τότε βασιλευόντων ἐπιτετραμμένος as *cui iura condere ab imperatoribus permissum erat*. In contrast, Boissonade 1849, 500 translates this as *et cui condendarum legum arbitrium et auctoritas imperatorum consensu commissa erat*. In W.C. Wright, *Philostratus and Eunapius: the lives of the sophists*, London 1912, p. 541 the English translation reads '... inasmuch as the emperors who reigned at that time entrusted to him the task of compiling the legal statutes.'

36 Theodor Kipp, *Geschichte der Quellen des Römischen Rechts*, Leipzig 1909, 111: 'Juris consulti war die offizielle Bezeichnung der autorisierten Juristen, und man geht im allgemeinen wenigstens nicht fehl, wenn man annimmt, daß, wo Juristen als Autoritäten mit den Ausdrücken prudentes, iuris auctores, auctores

Schulz rejected the connection between *iuris consultus* and *ius respondendi*, because *iuris consultus* was according to him simply a reference to a responding jurist. The *ius respondendi* was at odds with the imperial council, which is why no reference to the privilege can be found in the epigraphic material such as the honorary inscription of Salvius Iulianus.[37]

Magdelain responded to Schulz's disbelief by attempting to provide indisputable historical evidence of the connection between *iuris consultus* and *ius respondendi*. The fact that evidence is scarce Magdelain ascribed to the nature of the privilege as a *beneficium*, which was not a part of the official *cursus honorum*. Magdelain claimed that he could prove that the jurists Capito, Nerva, Cassius Longinus, Celsus, Julian, Neratius, Pactumeius Clemens, Maecianus, Scaevola, Ulpian and Modestin were recipients of the *ius respondendi*. According to Magdelain, their professional authority, political position and their status in the Digest shows beyond any doubt that they had the privilege.[38] As Magdelain's collection of evidence from legal, literary and epigraphic sources seems to have convinced at least one researcher,[39] it is necessary to take a closer look at it.

If we take a general view of the evidence provided by the proponents of this view, it is remarkably clear that they provide a good argument that *iuris consultus* and the other legal titles were labels used in a professional sense.[40] However, no evidence (besides Inst. Iust. 1,2,8) clearly and indisputably links *iuris consultus* with the *ius respondendi*.

The term *iuris consultus* is cited in the Digest in connection with Papinian and Nerva by Paul.[41] In the Codex, Ulpian is referred to as *praefectus annonae, iuris consultus* and *amicus*, whereas Modestin is just *iuris con-*

---

u. ä. genannt werden, jetzt nur die Autorisierten gemeint sind.'; Krüger 1912, 125.

37   Schulz 1946, 114; CIL VIII, 24094
38   Magdelain 1950, 4–5, 18 wrote that in late classical usage, the term *iurisconsultus* no longer meant the *ius respondendi*, but referred to classical jurists in general.
39   Paricio 1996, 99.
40   The other titles used by jurists in the legal sources are *iuris auctores* (Dig. 22,1,32pr; Dig. 37,14,17pr; Dig. 44,4,4,14; Cod. Iust. 7,18,1,1; Cod. Iust. 7,7,1pr, Cod. Iust. 7,1,1b etc.), *legum auctores* (Cod. Iust. 6,26,10pr), *legis latores* (Cod. Iust. 1,14,12,4; Cod. Iust.1,17,2,20; Cod. Iust. 4,5,11pr; Cod. Iust. 4,18,2,1a; Cod. Iust. 8,47,10,5), *legum conditores* (Cod. Iust. 6,37,26pr), and *iuris peritus* (Dig. 27,1,30pr). See also Kipp 1909, 111; Krüger 1912, 125.
41   Paul, Dig. 20,2,9 *et derisus Nerva iuris consultus, qui per fenestram monstraverat servos detentos ob pensionem liberari posse;* Paul, Dig. 12,1,40pr *Lecta est in auditorio Aemilii Papiniani praefecti praetorio jurisconsulti cautio huiusmodi.*

sultus.⁴² The Codex Theodosianus mentioned Scaevola as *prudentissimus iuris consultus*.⁴³ In the non-legal literature, the title of *iuris consultus* is used in connection with Ateius Capito, Cassius Longinus, Juventius Celsus, Julian and Neratius Priscus in the works of Suetonius and Spartianus.⁴⁴ However, none of these few references imply that the title of *iuris consultus* is anything other than a simple professional title.

An argument for the link between *iuris consultus* and *ius respondendi* could be provided if it could be proved that these titles were used exclusively and consistently by jurists who had the *ius respondendi*. Because it has been clearly shown that both in the Digest and the Codex jurists were called by several different titles, not just *iuris consultus*, evidence from elsewhere is needed.⁴⁵

For this purpose a list of juristic titles used in epigraphic material was compiled. In no way is this list comprehensive, though it covers roughly 90% of the published material.⁴⁶ This coverage is extensive enough to indicate if this title was generally used in a specific way. Therefore if a title is used exclusively as a professional title, it should be clearly reflected in the data.

The term *iuris consultus* was found in 15 instances.⁴⁷ Of those, four were mentioned by Magdelain: the honorary inscriptions to Pactumeius Clemens,

---

42   Cod. Iust. 8,37,4 (Alexander Severus) *Secundum responsum Domitii Ulpiani praefecti annonae iuris consulti amici mei ea ...*; Cod. Iust. 3,42,5 (Gordian) *merito tibi a non contemnendae auctoritatis iuris consulto Modestino responsum est.*

43   Cod. Theod. 4,4,3,3 *Nec si quid ex munificentia morientis fuerint consecuti, infructuosum subscribentes facient testamentum, cum hoc auctorem prudentissimum iurisconsultorum non sit ambiguum Scaevolam comprobasse. dat. xii. kal. april. Arcadio iv. et Honorio iii. aa. coss.*

44   Suet. gramm. 10,2 *hunc Capito Ateius, notus iuris consultus*; Suet. Nero 37,1 *Cassio Longino iurisconsulto ac luminibus orbato*; Hist. Aug. (Spartianus), Hadr. 18 *Cum judicaret, in consilio habuit non amicos suos aut comites solum sed iuris consultos et praecipue Juventium Celsum, Salvium Julianum, Neratium Priscum aliosque, quos tamen senatus omnis probasset.*

45   In Dig. 37,14,17pr Ulpian described Proculus as *iuris auctor* and Maecianus as *iuris peritus*; in Dig. 27,1,30pr Papinian mentioned *iuris periti* of the imperial *consilium*: *in consilium principum adsumptos.*

46   This is a rough estimate. The survey included the indexes of the Corpus Inscriptionum Latinarum (CIL) and L'Année épigraphique (AE), and the Epigraphische Datenbank Heidelberg.

47   The raw material was the bulk of index references to the term *iuris consultus*: CIL VI, 1422; *CIL VI, 1534; CIL VI, 10229; CIL VI, 10525; CIL VI, 12133 (= ILS 8365); CIL VI, 33865; CIL VI, 41294 (= 1628 = ILS 1456); *CIL VIII, 2220 (cf. 17614, 17714); CIL VIII, 7059 (= ILAlg. 2, 645 = ILS 1067); CIL VIII, 7060 (= ILAlg. 2, 646); CIL VIII, 7061 (= ILAlg. 2, 647); CIL VIII, 10490 (= *CIL VIII, 11045); CIL X, 4919 (= ILS 7750); *CIL XIV, 175add.; *CIL

which have *iurisconsulto* in the list of titles,[48] and the honorary inscription to Maecianus, which is only a fragment, containing the letters VLTO.[49] The complete picture is, however, more varied. We have an honorary inscription from Tyre in honour of Ulpian, which includes *iurisconsultus* in the list of his titles.[50] There are also four honorary or funerary inscriptions of *iuris consulti*. The first is an honorary inscription to Annius Namptoius, *iuris consultus* and *magister studiorum*, erected by the senate of Thuburbo Maius in 361 AD.[51] The second is a funerary inscription from Rome dated to 348 AD with the title of *iuris consultor*.[52] The third is a fragment of an equestrian titulature in an honorary or a funerary inscription with the letters IS CONSU, which has been interpreted as *iuris consultus*.[53] The fourth and last is a modest and grammatically challenged funerary inscription from Gigthi for a certain Iunius Urbanus, *carissimus filius* and *ius consultum*.[54] There is also a testament that has been ascribed to L. Dasumius Tuscus, which contains among its legataries a *[Pro]culo iurisconsulto*.[55] The term *iuris consultus* is also mentioned without referring to a certain person in three inscriptions. The first points out that the will has been written without a jurist,[56] while the two funerary inscriptions express a wish that bad will and lawyers stay away.[57] The final five inscriptions do not contain the words *iuris consultus*, and their inclusion in the indexes appears to be based on conjecture.[58]

It is difficult to establish how the interconnection between *ius respondendi* and the title *iuris consultus* could be proven or rejected, even if the material was more extensive. Does proving Magdelain's theory right require that all those mentioned as *iuris consulti* be credible recipients of the *ius respondendi*? If it does, then the varied occurrences of the term make it most likely that *iuris*

XIV, 5348; AE 1963, 73; AE 1988, 1051; ILAfr. 273 (ILPBardo 357 = AE 1916, 20bis = AE 1916, 87 = AE 1916, 88). Fragmentary or otherwise uncertain texts are marked with an asterisk.

48   *CIL* VIII, 7059 (= ILAlg. 2, 645 = *ILS* 1067); *CIL* VIII, 7060 (= ILAlg. 2, 646); *CIL* VIII, 7061 (= ILAlg. 2, 647). The first is the most complete and has the whole title. Magdelain 1950, 4–5.
49   *CIL* XIV, 5348.
50   AE 1988, 1051.
51   ILAfr. 273 (ILPBardo 357 = AE 1916, 20bis = AE 1916, 87 = AE 1916, 88).
52   *CIL* VI, 33865.
53   *CIL* VI, 41294 (= 1628 = *ILS* 1456).
54   *CIL* VIII, 10490 (= *CIL* VIII, 11045).
55   *CIL* VI, 10229. Even if the conjecture is correct, this is not the Proculus in the Digest, see also Kunkel 2001 [1967], 126.
56   *CIL* X, 4919 (= *ILS* 7750).
57   *CIL* VI, 10525; *CIL* VI, 12133 (= *ILS* 8365).
58   *CIL* VI, 1422; *CIL* VI, 1534; *CIL* VIII, 2220 (cf. 17614, 17714); *CIL* XIV, 175add.; AE 1963, 73 (probably a fake).

consultus was simply a general term for a lawyer, alongside *iuris magister, iuris peritus, iuris prudens, iuris studiosus,* and others.⁵⁹ Magdelain remarks that the rarity of the title *iuris consultus* is explained by the fact that the *ius respondendi* was just a *beneficium*, and not a part of the *cursus honorum*.⁶⁰ Nevertheless, if we accept that the linkage existed only in official use and that the term was merely misused by lower classes and provincials who lacked expertise in legal terminology, we make a premiss that supports only the outcome we are looking for and gives us free rein in selecting our evidence. Therefore, we must conclude that the credibility of the theory cannot be proven with epigraphic material.

The efforts Magdelain and others have put into proving the existence of the *ius respondendi* through the connection with the term *iuris consultus* have not elicited much comment from recent authors. Wieacker noted that, besides Pomponius and Gaius, there are no sources that could be linked to the *ius respondendi*. He was convinced that the link between the *ius respondendi* and *iuris consultus* was established only during Late Antique jurisprudence.⁶¹ Likewise, Cancelli wondered why not a single source, besides Pomponius and the Institutes, mentioned the *ius respondendi*. It is unlikely that it would have been so regular or so uninteresting that nobody would mention it. The fact that a number of Roman authors, like Vitruvius, Tacitus, Quintilian, and Gellius, described the lives and careers of Roman jurists and their relationship with the emperors means that there were numerous possibilities for such a statement. Cancelli saw this silence as evidence for the non-existence of the *ius respondendi*.⁶²

The *responsa* or legal opinions of jurists were described on numerous occasions in various literary contexts. Vitruvius mentioned how it was necessary for an architect to be familiar in nearly all fields, including the opinions of the jurists.⁶³ Seneca said that the opinions of a jurist were valid

---

59 *Iuris magister: CIL* VI, 1602 (= X, 8387 = *ILS* 7748); *CIL* VIII, 12418. *Iuris peritus: CIL* V, 1026add. (= Inscr.Aq. 705); *CIL* VI, 1621; *CIL* VI, 9487 (= *ILS* 7743); *CIL* VI, 33867; *CIL* VI, 41307; *CIL* VIII, 8489a; *CIL* VIII, 20164 (= 10899); *CIL* VIII, 27505; *CIL* X, 6662 (= *ILS* 1455 cf. 3163); *CIL* XIV, 2916; AE 1975, 793; AE 1980, 35; ILAlg. 1, 1362 (= AE 1903, 319 = AE 1904, 58 = AE 1904, 81 = *ILS* 7742ᶜ); IRT 647. *Iuris prudens: CIL* III, 141882 (bilingual, also νομικόν); *CIL* VI, 1853. *Iuris studiosus: CIL* III, 2936; *CIL* VI, 33868 (= *ILS* 7742); *CIL* VI, 38585; *CIL* VIII, 18348; *CIL* X, 569; *CIL* XII, 3339; *CIL* XII, 5900; AE 1908, 35; *Corpus de Inscripciones latinas de Andalucia*, IV: Granada, 131. Others: νομικόν *CIL* VIII, 15876 (= 1640), *iura peritus* AE 1926, 29, and *forenses* ILAlg. 1, 3064; *ILAlg. 1, 3071.
60 Magdelain 1950, 4–5.
61 Wieacker 1985, 80–83.
62 Cancelli 1987, 544, 546.
63 Vitr. 1,1,3 *responsa iurisconsultorum noverit*.

even without reasoning.[64] Quintilian noted how the interpretation of the *responsa* of *iuris consulti* relied on the interpretation of the words and the discrimination between good and bad.[65] Suetonius added the jurists to the long list of professions that were persecuted by Caligula, who threatened to put them out of business by proclaiming that they were not allowed to give advice contrary to his wishes.[66] Lactantius referred to the writings of the jurists as *disputationes iuris peritorum*.[67] Even Isidore, in his etymologies, observed that *responsa* were the opinions of the jurists.[68] Put simply, everything points to the likelihood that *responsa* were simply a mode of communication used by jurists, which did not make any distinction between different *responsa*.[69]

Furthermore, Cancelli noted that none of the Roman jurists refer to the possibility that the opinions of some jurists would have been more official than others, nor do any opinions seem to be in any way privileged. Neither do the jurists mention anything about the comparison between different *responsa*.[70]

This is confirmed by Fögen, who pointed out that not a single jurist speaks with the authority of the emperor in the Digest. The word *auctoritas* is mentioned 228 times, especially with regard to tutors, though also Plato, old jurists and some magistrates are also mentioned in connection with that word.[71]

A general survey of the Roman sources did not clarify the historicity of the institution, because the use of the words *ius respondendi* in the literature does not correspond to the theory of an imperial privilege. The oft-proposed link between the title *iuris consultus* and the *ius respondendi* was likewise not justified by either literary or epigraphic sources. Similarly the use of the word *responsum* in the Roman literature did not indicate a difference of rank between *responsa* given by different jurists, let alone that a jurist would have given opinions under imperial authorisation.

---

64 Sen. *epist.* 94,27 *Sic quomodo iuris consultorum valent responsa, etiamsi ratio non redditur.*
65 Quint. *Inst.* 12,3,7 *consultorum responsis explicantur aut in verborum interpretatione sunt posita aut in recti pravique discrimine.*
66 Suet. *Cal.* 34 *De iuris quoque consultis, quasi scientiae eorum omnem usum aboliturus, saepe iactavit se mehercule effecturum, ne quid respondere possint praeter eum.*
67 Lact. *inst.* 5,11,18.
68 Isid. *orig.* 5,14 *Responsa sunt quae iurisconsulti respondere dicuntur consulentibus.*
69 Cancelli 1987, 550.
70 Cancelli 1987, 551.
71 Fögen 2002, 205–206.

Sovereign power and the freedom of jurisprudence

The Roman sources on the *ius respondendi* are at best ambiguous. Pomponius' account has been subjected to intense text and source criticism because of the contradictions it contains and its general lack of consistency and elegance. Despite the vast amount of scholarly energy expended in this discussion over the years, the present *communis opinio* seems to be that we have ended up with approximately what Pomponius wrote, which is, in essence, that Augustus granted the right to give *responsa* on his own authority in order to raise the authority of the law. Sabinus was the first to give his opinions *publice* and Hadrian said that the *ius respondendi* should be earned, not applied for. Gaius maintained that unanimous *responsa* of jurists had the same status as law and that the *responsa* were the opinions of those with the right to compose law (*iura condere*). The Institutes of Justinian contain a similar passage formulated in an extended form: the *iuris consulti* were those whom the emperor had granted the right to give formal responses, which were binding on the judges.

This all adds up to a convincing mass of evidence for the existence of *ius respondendi*. The trouble is that the evidence is difficult to refute as long as one looks only at this material. When examining ancient sources in general, conclusive evidence on any aspect of the *ius respondendi* is noticeably lacking. There are a few references to *ius publice respondere*, but none of them make any allusions to an imperial intervention. Similarly, the theory based on the Institutes of Justinian that the title of *iuris consultus* is tantamount to *ius respondendi* is not corroborated by any evidence from literary or epigraphic sources. References to *responsa* in the literature in general indicate that opinions were simply the form of communication used by jurists, and that there were no special classes of *responsa* above the rest.

The situation regarding the sources has been so ambivalent that an interesting variety of scholarly opinions has developed. The research on the *ius respondendi* has basically wavered between two opposing stereotypes: that of the benevolent and the malevolent Augustus. While the former is said to have supported the jurists from altruistic motives and not to have used the *ius respondendi* as a means of interfering with the law, the latter usurped free Roman jurisprudence and used it as a tool to obtain total domination over Roman society.

In the earliest literature on the *ius respondendi*, the idea of the freedom of jurisprudence was dominant. The theme of *ius respondendi* emerged in Roman legal historiography with the commentaries on Pomponius' *Enchiridion*. One of the first to give it a lengthier treatment was the Humanist Ulrich Zasius, who wrote that the *ius respondendi* protected learned lawyers from the corruption of their ignorant colleagues. According to him, the *ius respondendi* resembled a college of learned doctors, which was created to prevent brash outsiders from speaking with the authority of the emperor. Zasius' legal ideal was the learned patrician jurist depicted so often by Cicero, the jurist who assiduously gave his opinions with knowledge and skill, not motivated by greed, incitement, pleasure or the drinking cup, as some scholars of his age did. In hindsight, Zasius' interpretations are individual, for example he hesitantly explained *pro beneficio* as a reference to jurists who worked more for glory than for gold. For the main part, his commentary is a polemic against both unlearned jurists who lack practical expertise and ignorant schoolmasters who have reached their positions by soliciting letters of recommendation and other dishonourable methods.[72] The privilege of the *ius respondendi* was a safeguard to protect the influence of the wise jurists that had dominated the field of law ever since the Republic. Independence of opinion was for Zasius one of the most valued virtues for a lawyer. This position was reflected also in his other writings.[73]

In order to grasp the significance of this view, it is necessary to look at the political and intellectual context in which it was written. J. Q. Whitman has described the importance of the *ius respondendi* for the professors of Roman law during the sixteenth century. The professors based their pride and dignity on the image of the ancient Roman jurists and their power, the clearest example of which was the *ius respondendi*, the right to give legal opinions that were binding on the judges. Even if the significance of the privilege in Rome was unclear, according to Whitman it provided the most important legal doctrine behind the power of the professors of law in Germany. The respect for scholarly legal authority it embodied was the basis of professorial lawmaking in the *Spruchkollegien*. The professors declared that Roman law as well as the professors who taught it were uniquely learned and impartial.[74] Such use of the *ius respondendi* as an argument in contemporary legal debates was not unique, as many scholars of the sixteenth century used Roman legal history and themes in it as points of inspiration and comparison for their contemporary domestic questions. The *ius respondendi* was used also in the ponderation of Etienne Pasquier on the authority of the jurists and their relationship with the emperors of Rome and kings of France.[75] However, due

---

72 Zasius 1541, 283–285 [ad Dig 1,2,2,47–50].
73 Erik Wolf, 'Ulrich Zasius (1461–1535): Monument historique ou exemple actuel?', in *Mélanges en l'honneur de Jean Dabin I*, Paris 1963, 388.
74 Whitman 1990, 29–38. Dieter Nörr, 'Romanistische Phantasien', *Rechtshistorisches Journal* 11 (1992), 163–165, criticised Whitman's reading as too bold.
75 Kathleen A. Parrow, 'Prudence or Jurisprudence? Etienne Pasquier and the *Responsa Prudentium* as a Source of Law', in A. T. Grafton and J. H. M. Salmon (eds.), *Historians and Ideologues*, Rochester 2001, 50–51, 55.

to the inferior position of Roman law in France, these discussions tended to be more academic and less practically oriented than in Germany.[76]

The interpretation established by Zasius was reversed by scholars of the following generations. Augustus was cast as an evil tyrant who was corrupting the jurists' profession to gain complete control over Rome. Jacques Cujas (1522–1590) reflected on Zasius' views in his commentary on the Digest and Institutes, but altered the consequences. He noted simply that, during the Republic, authority was vested in lawyers who frequented the forum, whereas, during the Empire, it came when the emperor granted permission to interpret the law. The purpose of the institution was to give imperially sanctioned lawyers an advantage over lawyers of higher learning.[77]

In his Franeker inaugural lecture in 1665, Dutch professor Ulrich Huber (1634–1694) described how Augustus degenerated the noble legal profession and obliterated the powers of the old Republican office of the praetor. Augustus wanted to eradicate the memory of the Republic, an era when the stern legal profession was still dignified, by encouraging endless litigation, sectarian disputes and general sweet indolence among the population.[78]

During the rise in power of German local princes in the seventeenth and eighteenth centuries, the orientation of the professors of Roman law was changed and the concepts of law and the place of lawyers were remodelled to suit the requirements of the new absolutism. Lawyers would henceforth be servants of the prince, not objective interpreters of impartial law. The reinterpretation of *ius respondendi* took the form of law emanating from the power of the emperor, and it was, therefore, the emperor whom the jurists should thank for their power. Samuel Stryk (1640–1710) even drew a parallel between the Roman *ius respondendi* and his contemporary jurists. At the

---

76   Kelley 1990, 203; Whitman 1990, 43–45.
77   Iacobus Cuiacius, *Opera quae de iure fecit I*, Frankfurt 1623, 4 [ad Inst. Iust. 1,2,8]: *quorum omnium: non quorumcumque sede eorum tantum qui à principe contendi & interpretandi iuris potestatem accepissent l. 1. c. de vet. iu. enucl. l. ult. c. de leg. id est, qui à principe Iurisconsulti iurisve interpretes pronunciati essent. In Rep. prudentium auctoritas ea tantum valuit, quae in foro usu frequenti recepta erat.* Iacobus Cuiacius, 'De origine iuris et iuris auctoribus ex Enchiridio Pomponii cum commentario', in *Opera II*, Frankfurt 1623, 102 [ad Dig. 1,2,2,48–49]: *superiores sine beneficio, ut subijcit, fiducia doctrine, iuxta illud, Qui sibi sidit dux, regit examen.* Similarly, Budaeus 1557 [1969], 11 [ad Dig. 1,1] affirmed that the right to give *responsa* publicly was given by the emperor. Gothofredus 1665, 32, 35 [ch. 1,4] denied this and claimed that the right to give binding *responsa* began only with Valentinian III.
78   Ulrich Huber, 'Oratio inauguralis habita Franekerae ... exhibens historiam juris Romani', in *Opera minora et rariora I*, Utrecht 1746, 109.

same time, authors like Thomasius were increasingly hostile to the corrupting influence of the emperors on lawyers.[79]

Christian Thomasius (1655–1728) blamed the jurists for falling into Augustus' trap because of their greed. The result of this entrapment was that their influence no longer emanated from their learning, but from the sovereign will of the emperor. Thomasius included the *ius respondendi* as birthmark number twenty of Roman jurisprudence: 'Jurisprudence suffered the gravest damage when Augustus conceded the right to respond as a privilege and made it impossible for the judges to deviate from the opinion of the jurist.'[80] Thomasius viewed the privilege as meaning the same as if Augustus himself had given the *responsa*, which consequently had the force of law. He echoed Zasius and others in his view that the *ius respondendi* corrupted the legal profession when avarice for money and power overtook certain lawyers.[81]

However, Gottfried Mascov (1698–1760) proclaimed that Augustus' actions had been a reaction to, not the cause of the decline. During the free Republic the right to give *responsa* remained pure and dependant on the dignity of the person. This splendor of science was destroyed with the collapse of liberty, honour and dignity at the end of the Republic. Augustus' legal programme did not only contain the dedication of a law library in the temple of Apollo, but also the restoration of the dignity of jurists by granting them the right to respond with his authority.[82]

In the writings of Enlightenment authors, such as Heineccius, Bach, and Gibbon, the interpretation was again reformulated. It was now the jurists who had the authority and influence that Augustus wanted to utilise to his advantage because of his political aims. Throughout the literature, there remained a marked distrust of Augustus' intentions, and with some exceptions, Pomponius' explanation about raising the authority of the law did not convince jurists. Heineccius and Bach wrote in sinister tones that Augustus wanted to use the dignity and respect enjoyed by the jurists to consolidate his

---

79   Whitman 1990, 56–65; Samuel Stryk, *Specimen usus moderni pandectarum I*, Halle 1713, 48–49. Grotius 1690, 102 [Sabinus] *Divus Augustus ex sua auctoritate de jure responderi voluit, itaque hoc posterioribus temporibus pro beneficio peti caepit; donec Hadrianus antiquum fere morem in usum revocavit.*

80   Christian Thomasius, *Naevorum jurisprudentiae romanae antejustinianae libri duo*, (2nd ed.), Magdeburg 1707, 67 [ch. 2.2.20]: *Naevus XX: Maximum damnum Jurisprudentia passa est, quod Augustus facultatem respondendi per modum beneficii concesserit, & judicibus necessitatem imposuerit, ut ne a responsis auctorum recederent*

81   Thomasius 1707, 68–70 [ch. 2.2.20].

82   Mascovius 1728, 31.

power. Heineccius favoured Huber's view that Augustus wanted to eliminate the power of the praetors, while Bach accepted that the authority of the law had been damaged during the turbulent years of the Republic.[83] The old theme familiar from Zasius and Thomasius of the greed of jurists propelling them into the service of the autocrat was again used. There was some disagreement regarding what Augustus wanted to control through the jurists: Bach suggested legislation,[84] Gibbon the *ius civile*,[85] and Christian Glück the judges.[86]

In his Roman legal history, Hugo wrote that the *ius respondendi* changed the nature of jurisprudence by making *responsa* one of the sources of law. His interpretation marked a profound change as he was clearly doubtful about the true nature and significance of the institution.[87] It was only some years later, in 1816, when the discovery of the text of the Institutes of Gaius brought new credibility to the *ius respondendi* that he was forced to reconsider his position.[88]

During the latter half of the nineteenth century, the discussion of the *ius respondendi* began to reflect a new distrust about emperors and codifications. There is again a marked rise in the status of the jurists, who are increasingly depicted as actors able to resist the emperor, not just helpless victims of imperial machinations. Puchta saw in the *ius respondendi* a parallel to all rulers who strived clandestinely to shackle jurists and to dominate the law.

---

83 Heineccius 1751, 239–241 [ch. 157–158], 267–268 [ch. 178]; Bach 1762, 217–218 [ch. 3.1.6.2–6].

84 Bach 1762, 218 [ch. 3.1.6.3].

85 Gibbon 1977 [1788], 392–393: 'Augustus and Tiberius were the first to adopt, as a useful engine, the science of the civilians; and their servile labours accommodated the old system to the spirit and views of despotism. Under the fair pretence of securing the dignity of the art, the privilege of subscribing legal and valid opinions was confined to the sages of senatorian or equestrian rank, who had been previously approved by the judgment of the prince; and this monopoly prevailed till Hadrian restored the freedom of the profession to every citizen conscious of his abilities and knowledge. The discretion of the praetor was now governed by the lessons of his teachers; the judges were enjoined to obey the comment as well as the text of the law; and the use of codicils was a memorable innovation, which Augustus ratified by the advice of the civilians.'

86 Christian F. Glück, *Ausführliche Erläuterung der Pandekten I*, (2nd ed.), Erlangen 1797, 433.

87 Hugo 1806, 336–339. Hugo took note of Pomponius' remark that as a matter of *ut obiter sciamus*, the founding of the institution could not have been very important.

88 Gustav Hugo, *Lehrbuch der Geschichte des Römischen Rechts,* (Lehrbuch eines civilistischen Cursus 3, 8th ed.), Berlin 1822, 596–603.

Theodor Mommsen's view was that Augustus destroyed independent jurisprudence by terminating the freedom to give *responsa*. On the other hand, the value of the *ius respondendi* to jurists' law was noted by authors like Johannes E. Kuntze, who advocated the modern revival of the institution.[89]

Puchta saw the *responsa* as the line that connected jurists to the judges, giving jurists a direct way to influence legal practice. In Puchta's opinion, Augustus' schemes were nothing more than a direct continuation of a plan to undermine the jurists' influence. It was a general quality of all reform-minded leaders to belittle the legal profession, and thus Cicero's antipathy towards lawyers mirrored the attitude of some mayors in Puchta's time, and Caesar's plans for codification had their counterparts in the codification plans of modern regents. Puchta gave Augustus credit for being wiser than his predecessors who had tried to impose a codification. Augustus' cunning plan was to make jurists dependent on him instead of trying to eliminate their influence, all the while claiming to be securing and supporting the jurists' authority. Thus, the expertise of jurists would seem to originate from the emperor, without the emperor having anything to do with the *responsa*.[90]

Mommsen, whose general dislike of Augustus is widely known, also contributed to the discussion. He wrote that in the Republic, legal science was applied to individual cases through the *responsa* of the jurists that were sought by the parties. Augustus moved against the freedom of jurists by banning *responsa* from jurists who did not have his special authorisation. Those who did not have the *ius respondendi* and continued to give *responsa* were acting in defiance. Mommsen compared Augustus unfavourably to emperors of better times, especially Trajan, who wisely refrained from giving their own *responsa*.[91]

One of the recurring features of the literature of the late nineteenth century was that Suetonius' story of Caligula's efforts to control the *responsa* of the jurists emerged as evidence of the emperor's incessant jealousy of the jurists' freedom in giving *responsa*. Karlowa, who otherwise followed Puchta and Mommsen, described the situation as a battle of equals between the emperor and the jurists. In this view, the freedom of giving *responsa* was seen by the emperor as a threat to his power.[92]

The dichotomy of the good and bad emperor obscures an even larger question, the function and significance of jurists' law. Paul Koschaker, one of

---

89   Kuntze 1858, 17–22.
90   Puchta 1875, 322–324.
91   Theodor Mommsen, *Römisches Staatsrecht*, Basel 1952 [1887], vol. II, 912.
92   Puchta 1875, 323; Mommsen 1952 [1887], vol. II, 912; Otto Karlowa, *Römische Rechtsgeschichte I*, Leipzig 1885, 659. Suet. *Cal.* 34 had naturally been evoked before, cf. Bach 1762, 218 [ch. 3.1.6.5].

the great authorities on the issue, has written that jurists' law and the centralised power of the state needed each other. The jurists needed some instance to give the factual power of law to their findings, and the emperor needed someone to formulate the law according to his wishes.[93] This view is in complete opposition to the idealism regarding the freedom of jurisprudence based on Puchta and the outlook that the jurists' law was based solely on the skill and authority of the jurists themselves.[94]

The nineteenth century debate between idealists in their conceptual heaven and materialists with their views of the inseparability of law and power may be observed here. As is well-established, the materialist turn, initiated by Jhering and Mommsen, stressed that behind the supposedly objective surface of the law lay a mass of contradictory interests and power struggles that were not taken into account by the traditional Roman law scholars.[95]

Rudolf von Jhering's criticism of the Pandectism of Puchta was mainly aimed at the tendency of seeing law merely as an abstract set of concepts that form a rigid system fully detached from extralegal matters. To Jhering, this conceptual jurisprudence was an antithesis of the real law, the organic, evolving law that was in constant interaction with society and the living human activity that formed it.[96] Jhering's criticism of Puchta and the jurisprudence of concepts was both humorous and scathing in its accusations

93 Koschaker 1966, 178–180. This perception was supported by von Lübtow 1953, 377, who claimed that the whole validity of the jurists' law depended on the imperial *ius respondendi,* and Horvat 1964, 715.

94 Arthur A. Schiller, 'Jurist's Law', in *An American Experience in Roman Law,* Göttingen 1971, reprinted from 58 *Columbia Law Review* (1958), 1236: 'Given *auctoritas prudentium,* the view of one jurist was as valid as that of another. It was the respect and confidence in the ability of a jurist, in the knowledge that his services were dedicated to the well-being of the Roman state, that gave his views legal force, not their adoption by a state official or even another jurist.'

95 Rudolf von Jhering, *Scherz und Ernst in der Jurisprudenz,* Leipzig 1892, 7–14; Rudolf von Jhering, *Der Kampf um's Recht,* (6th ed.), Wien 1880; Rudolf von Jhering, *Ist die Jurisprudenz eine Wissenschaft? Jhering's Wiener Antrittsvorlesung vom 16. Oktober 1868,* Göttingen 1998, 66–68; Mommsen 1952 [1887], vol. I, 6. Mommsen's legal ideology is insufficiently studied, but Kunkel has made some preliminary remarks on Mommsen's paradoxical beliefs in the permanence of legal concepts and institutions, see Wolfgang Kunkel, 'Theodor Mommsen als Jurist', *Chiron* 14 (1984), 369–380; Alfred Heuss, *Theodor Mommsen und das 19. Jahrhundert,* Kiel 1956, 33–57.

96 Rudolf von Jhering, *Der Besitzwille: Zugleich eine Kritik der herrschenden juristischen Methode,* Aalen 1968 [1889], ix–x; Dino Pasini, *Saggio sul Jhering,* Milano 1959, 3–4, 11–13; Jean Gaudemet, 'Organicisme et évolution dans la conception de l'histoire du droit chez Jhering', in F. Wieacker, C. Wollschläger (eds.), *Jherings Erbe,* Göttingen 1970, 29–39.

of *Weltsfremdheit* to the extent that it has subsequently modified our views of Puchta.[97]

While Puchta and Mommsen saw the jurists as the principled opposition to the emperors' ambitions, Jhering saw *ius respondendi* as the highest recognition a lawyer could achieve. Jhering's view of the Roman lawyers was traditional: it emphasised the honorary nature of the lawyers' activities and their strict detachment from extralegal matters in glorifying tones.[98] However, Jhering stressed that the path to 'A calling which brings only honour is closed to the man of no means.' The wealthy could afford to embark upon such a journey and reap their rewards later by plundering provinces as governors. Later, as the emperors took care of the exploitation of the provinces themselves, economic necessities forced jurists to become salaried labourers, some of which were trustworthy enough to be given the *ius respondendi* and to look after the emperor's wishes in particular cases.[99]

Jhering was clearly a supporter of the realistic school of thought, but the difference in the image of Roman lawyers was not drastic: Jhering's esteemed Roman jurist thought that the *ius respondendi* was an honour worth striving for, while Puchta's Roman jurist did not.

At the turn of the twentieth century Augustus was back in favour along with a general enthusiasm for all things imperial in Germany.[100] The advocates of the imperial rule saw in Augustus the ideal emperor, who increased the influence of the jurists without interfering with the content of the law. Helssig rejected the proposition that jurists were an influential and homogenous group that was in political opposition to the emperor. Although the early Republican lawyers used to be prominent patricians, who regularly rose to consulship, this link between law and politics was severed during the final years of the Republic. By granting the *ius respondendi*, Augustus actually increased the influence of the jurists without interfering with the content of

---

97 Haferkamp 2004, 46–68 refers especially to *Scherz und Ernst*. Coing 1969, 149–171 questions Jherings self-promotion and describes him as the culmination of conceptual jurisprudence, whose theory allowed for the internal development of the legal system. On the repercussions of Jhering's attacks, cf. Segrè 1892, 6–7, 10–11.
98 Rudolf von Jhering, *Law as Means to an End*, (translated by I. Husik), New York 1968, 85–86. Jhering writes of the Roman jurist: 'The highest goal of his ambition in the time of the emperors was the bestowal of the "jus respondendi", which stamped him as the official juristic oracle of the people.' (p. 86).
99 Jhering 1968, 84 (quote), 87, 324.
100 Ines Stahlmann, 'Vom Despoten zum Kaiser. Zum deutschen Augustusbild im 19. Jahrhundert', in K. Christ, A. Momigliano (eds.), *L'Antichità nell'Ottocento in Italia e Germania*, Bologna 1988, 318.

the law. Helssig denied the possibility that the emperor might have misused this power to advance his political agenda on the grounds that he had easier methods at his disposal. The emperor was largely benevolent towards the jurists, and juristic opposition was merely an unsuccessful campaign by a few individuals, such as Labeo and Cascellius.[101] Helssig's views were supported, among others, by Kipp who said that the significance of jurists greatly increased during the early Principate because of the *ius respondendi*.[102]

This view was quickly countered by realists who saw Augustus as a cunning despot who had managed to confuse both Pomponius and the contemporary advocates of imperial rule about his true intentions. The idea of the benevolent emperor did not gain universal acceptance, as traditional legal historians stressed the value of unhindered *responsa* in the evolution of the law. The *ius respondendi* was interpreted by Hahn as a part of the ongoing centralisation of the legal system towards the person of the emperor and his elevation above the law.[103] Berger wrote in his influential article in *Pauly's Real-Enzyklopädie* that Pomponius was gravely mistaken, as Augustus had no intention of increasing the authority of the law.[104] As several of Berger's contemporaries attested, the jurists were the highly esteemed elite of the Republic, and they did not need help from the emperor. In fact, according to Krüger and Berger, the high regard in which the jurists were regularly held was a threat to the emperor, which he sought to eliminate using his sovereign power.[105]

The detailed historical inquiry on the *ius respondendi* began relatively late with the discussion of the meaning of *auctoritas* and its use in the Augustan vocabulary. It was an offshoot of the extensive discussion around the Monumentum Ancyranum or the *Res Gestae Divi Augusti* 34.2 during the early twentieth century. Wenger and von Premerstein applied the redefined concept of *auctoritas* in the sense of a social and moral force to Pomponius' text. Wenger wrote that, because of their familiarity with *auctoritas* as the binding force behind their *responsa*, the jurists easily accepted the idea that a greater *auctoritas* would result from an imperial *beneficium*. Premerstein linked the *ius respondendi* to the general ideological programme and administrative structures of Augustus' principate. He was also the first to consider

101 Helssig 1891, 1318–20, 1322, 1332–1333.
102 Kipp 1909, 109.
103 Otto Hahn, 'Das Kaisertum', *Das Erbe der Alten VI*, Leipzig 1913, 74–77.
104 Adolf Berger, 'Iurisprudentia', in *Pauly-Wissowas Real-Encyclopädie* 10 (1919), 1159–1200.
105 Berger 1919, 1165; Hahn 1913, 73; Emilio Costa, *Storia delle fonti del diritto romano*, Milano 1909, 77; Krüger 1912, 120. Both Krüger and Berger evoked Suet. *Cal.* 34 to prove the emperor's animosity.

how exactly Augustus created this privilege, whether by edict or some other arrangement.[106]

From the 1930s onwards, attempts were made to reveal the historical context in which the institution developed. Many of Premerstein's questions regarding how the *ius respondendi* was really used and what effects it had were answered by F. de Visscher in the first ever article devoted entirely to *ius respondendi*. De Visscher claimed that what was said of the effects of the privilege in the previous literature were more assumed than scientifically proven. He probed the historical background of the institution, trying to discern between the actions of Augustus, Tiberius and Hadrian, during whose reigns the institution went through extensive changes.[107]

As more attention was paid to historical details and their accuracy, the old division of benevolent and malevolent emperor was supplemented by another, equally pervasive, division between a powerless and a powerful emperor. The powerless emperor theory was supported by Schulz, Wieacker, and Cancelli, who claimed that the *ius respondendi* never existed in practice despite the possible attempts of Augustus to install it. The powerful emperor theory revolved around Kunkel and Magdelain, who asserted that Augustus successfully controlled the jurists' profession with the *ius respondendi*. An extreme variant of this is Bauman's assertion that Augustus was in fact helping the jurists with the *ius respondendi*.

Fritz Schulz dismissed the whole existence of the institution as being contrary to the Augustan programme of reviving the Republic: 'A *ius respondendi* existed no more than a right to breathe.'[108] Schulz's denial prompted Kunkel to call for a critical evaluation of the sources instead of comparing constructed, doctrinal images of the Augustan system. In an interesting example of self-contradiction, Kunkel then proceeded to emulate Puchta and to describe how the jurists battled constantly against codifications which threatened jurists' law, the precondition for juristic creativity and the profession, from Caesar's reign up to the codification projects of the Enlightenment. Kunkel dismissed as false the image of the benevolent Augustan Principate and replaced it with the old view of juristic freedom.[109]

---

106 Leopold Wenger, 'Praetor und Formel', in *Sitzungsberichte der Bayerischen Akademie der Wissenschaften; Philosophisch-philologische und historische Klasse*, Jahrgang 1926, 3. Abhandlung, 108; Anton von Premerstein, 'Vom Werden und Wesen des Prinzipats', *Abhandlungen der Bayerischen Akademie der Wissenschaften; Philosophisch-historische Abteilung Neue Folge*, Heft 15 (1937), 158, 202.
107 Premerstein 1937, 204; de Visscher 1936, 615.
108 Schulz 1946, 113.
109 Kunkel 1948, 445–450.

According to Kunkel, juristic freedom did not mean that Augustus did not succeed in introducing the *ius respondendi*, but rather that a pact was made between him and the senatorial jurists. Kunkel claimed that the *ius respondendi* was a licence to practice law, without which no-one could act as a lawyer and give a *responsum*.[110]

The debate begun by de Visscher intensified as different solutions based on historical reconstructions of the Augustan principate appeared. Antonio Guarino interpreted the Augustan privilege as a social honour bestowed upon jurists he trusted; only later did this become a *beneficium*. He compared the privileged to 'purveyors of the Court' ('fornitori della Real Casa').[111] Like Kunkel, Magdelain proceeded from the assumption that Augustus wanted to control the jurists. Augustus, the master of indirect rule, did not want to attack the proud juristic profession, but used his silence to suppress other sources of law, the praetor and jurisprudence. In Magdelain's view, the history of *ius respondendi* was a chapter in the long campaign towards legal unity, a campaign that Augustus and his successors waged with stealth.[112]

In his later writings Kunkel restated his conviction that Augustus used the *ius respondendi* to return jurisprudence to the hands of the senatorial class and to exclude the avaricious and business-minded knights. Wieacker agreed that Kunkel was right about the *ius respondendi* being more a moral reorganisation than power politics, but the paucity of historical sources about the *ius respondendi* made him sceptical. His claim was that *ius respondendi* had been illogically self-evident to Romanists, who had never called it into question, despite the fact that we know next to nothing about the contents and scope of the privilege and those who gained it.[113]

---

110   Kunkel 1948, 455: 'Das von Augustus eingeführte *ius publice respondendi* war die vom Princeps verliehene Lizenz zu öffentlicher Erteilung von Rechtsgutachten. Wer es nicht besaß, durfte offenbar von Rechts wegen nicht respondieren.'

111   Guarino 1949, 411, 413–415 strongly criticised de Visscher's reconstruction: '... è tortuoso, contradittorio e, allo stato delle nostre conoscenze generali, inammissibile.' (p. 414)

112   Magdelain 1950, 1–3: 'Il n'hésita pas à agir par voie d'autorité, mais il le fit avec modération, en ménageant les principes. Parmi les *arcana imperii*, il faut compter avant tout le silence presque officiel qui enveloppait la limite des attributions de l'empereur et facilitait ainsi leur accroissement continu. Auguste exploita avec bonheur la marge d'indétermination qui entourait les siennes. Initiateur de la méthode, il l'utilisa avec tact. Il eût été absurde d'avoir décliné l'offre d'un pouvoir législatif personnel, manifestement contraire à la tradition républicaine, pour l'exercer en fait.' (p. 1–2).

113   Kunkel 2001 [1967], 272–282; Wieacker 1969b, 336, 338, 349; Wieacker 1985, 71–72.

Wieacker's refutation has more recently been followed by a marked suspicion about the *ius respondendi*. F. Cancelli's article was even entitled 'the presumed *ius respondendi*'. Cancelli noted how centuries of scholarly work have not produced reliable results, and that fictitious explanations have proliferated without regard for historical facts. In his opinion, the only clear conclusion should be that the *ius respondendi* had no effect whatsoever. Similarly, M. T. Fögen called the institution an ineffectual 'contact announcement'. The emperor perhaps had tried to lure jurists into a mutually beneficial association of authorities, but the jurists must have ignored the offer because the *ius respondendi* is not mentioned in the Digest at all or in any of the writings of the jurists.[114]

If the basic tenet in both Cancelli and Fögen was juristic freedom, Bauman took a completely different view in the third part of his jurisprudential trilogy. In his opinion, the *ius respondendi* was one of the most important changes in law during the Principate, along with the founding of the schools. With it, the emperor took complete control over jurists' law in the typical Augustan indirect mode, but with the permission of the jurists. Augustus had good reasons for his actions, which Bauman identified as the four problems that the *ius respondendi* was meant to solve. The chaotic state of the law would be clarified by creating indisputable law. Incompetent jurists would be banished from the profession by certification. The misuse and forgery of *responsa* would be halted by verification under a seal. Finally, judges would not dare to ignore a *responsum* given under the authority of the emperor. In Bauman's view, the context and significance of the *ius respondendi* was mostly political.[115]

How should the *ius respondendi* be interpreted? Should we believe authors like Cancelli, Fögen, and others, who maintain that the whole affair was merely a futile attempt by Augustus to encroach upon the liberty of jurisprudence, coupled with Late Antique misunderstandings about the nature of the sources of law? Cancelli has stressed that all the evidence points towards the complete lack of any authority outside the law, and that the jurists worked as a collective for the greater good of the law.[116] Fögen affirmed that the pursuit of *respondere* retained its freedom and remained uninvolved in politics. The influence of the emperors on the law came through legislation and later imperial constitutions that produced legal texts for the lawyers to

---

114 Cancelli 1987, 543–544; Fögen 2002, 203–206. Paricio 1996, 88–9, 105, among other recent authors, has taken a cautiously negative view of the institution.
115 Bauman 1989, xxvi, 8–10, 16–17.
116 Cancelli 1987, 552–553 sought his precedent from L. Valla and Leibniz.

comment on. There is no denying that the model for the future would be a combination of imperial constitutions and lawyers working in the imperial bureaucracy.[117] Cancelli dated the transformation of the image of the *ius respondendi* to the Dominate, when it was more difficult to understand how private individuals could create law. What remained was the juristic doctrine, which continued to evolve when the Law of Citations brought a new dimension to the *responsa*. The difference between jurists and lawgivers began to blur in the later literature, especially in Justinian.[118]

Or should we believe Kunkel, Magdelain, or Bauman, and their visions of a ruthless power struggle between the emperor and jurists? Kunkel saw the situation as a tradeoff; the senatorial jurists gained a monopoly over the interpretation of law in addition to the abandonment of Caesar's codification plans, and, in return, Augustus secured the support of jurists for his new regime.[119] Magdelain, Kunkel, and Bauman are self-described realists, who believed that the field of law was not immune to the power politics of the Roman Empire.

Similar to the difference between the two factions of Romanists in the late nineteenth century, the difference between the idealists and the realists in the present debate is also minor when we consider the areas in which they are in agreement.

The most poignant similarity is related to the concept of a patriotic narrative, or the construction of a heroic shared past. This term was originally used to describe historical writing with an agenda linked to nationalistic enterprises such as the glorification or construction of a national past. Lately it has been proposed that the concept can be applied to other situations as well, such as the histories of specific groups or entities, such as cities, associations, or companies.[120] The American historian William McNeill has

---

117 Fögen 2002, 206.
118 Cancelli 1987, 557–559 drew a parallel to early Greek lawgivers. A law found intact and unchangeable was seen as the work of a legislating sage. Cf. Amm. 27,9,5 *inventores iuris antiqui*.
119 Kunkel 1948, 448–456.
120 Thomas Hylland Eriksen, *Ethnicity and Nationalism*, London 1993, 82–120 discussed how ethnicity, nationality and the like are formed culturally through ideology and narratives in history. Benedict Anderson, *Imagined communities: reflections on the origin and spread of nationalism*, London 1991; Pierre Nora, 'Between Memory and History', in *Realms of Memory: Rethinking the French Past*, New York 1996, 10. Cf. also C. Steedman, 'Battlegrounds: History in primary schools', *History Workshop Journal* 17 (1984), 102–112; J. C. D. Clark, 'National identity, state formation and patriotism: the role of history in the public mind', *History Workshop Journal* 29 (1990), 95–102. For the nationalist debate in general, cf. John Breuilly, 'Historians and the Nation',

called this phenomenon shared truths. These are the beliefs, ideals, and traditions that unite certain groups of people. According to McNeill, shared truths are vital to the survival and preservation of a group, as they form the basis of its cohesion.[121] These shared truths are also a reflection of the self-image of that group. History in these circumstances tends to be mythical.

> All human groups like to be flattered. Historians are therefore under perpetual temptation to conform to expectation by portraying the people they write about as they wish to be. A mingling of truth and falsehood, blending history with ideology, results. Historians are likely to select facts to show that we – whoever 'we' may be – conform to our cherished principles ...[122]

To quote a classic example, this is what Nietzsche might have meant by monumental when he divided historiography into monumental, antiquarian, and critical kinds.[123] The patriotic narrative is simply the noble and uplifting version of history that reinforces the aspects that are seen as positive.

In applying the concept to the debate at hand, the first thing that one notices is that the fundamental issue is not whether to present a patriotic narrative, but what kind of patriotic narrative to present. There have been two major options used. The idealistic version of the patriotic narrative of the jurists' profession presents a powerless emperor attempting in vain to prevail over proud and powerful jurists. The realistic version is just as patriotic, even though the role of the emperor is different. In this case, the jurists or a group of them collaborate with the emperor, who allows them free reign over the law as long as his power is not questioned. Contrary to what one might think, this model of the disinterested emperor salvaged the idea of the freedom of jurisprudence by making the most out of available options.

To what extent is the proud profession of the jurists a Roman phenomenon and to what extent is it a later construct based on modern ideals? It is well documented that modern concepts and ideals influence our interpretations of ancient events.[124] The fact that the autonomy of the law and of the jurists' profession is one of the fundamental ideals of modern law raises questions of distortion or interference between the object and subject of history because of some form of loyalty. These loyalties may originate from a real or imagined

---

in P. Burke (ed.), *History and Historians in the Twentieth Century*, Oxford 2002, 55–87; Marc Ferro, *The use and abuse of history or how the past is taught*, London 1984, vii–xi.
121 William McNeill, 'Mythistory, or Truth, Myth, History, and Historians', *The American Historical Review* 91 (1986), 3.
122 McNeill 1986, 5
123 Friedrich Nietzsche, 'Vom Nutzen und Nachteil der Historie für das Leben', in *Unzeitgemässe Betrachtungen*, Leipzig 1930, 112–119.
124 Cf. Rhodes 2003.

similarity or an imaginary community of which both are members.[125] The historians of Roman law saw the Roman jurists as their predecessors, previous members of the same club, and proceeded to portray them unconsciously in their own image, thus projecting their own ideals and values on to Antiquity. This imagined community, as Benedict Anderson would call it, exists only on the level of ideas: 'It is imagined because the members of even the smallest nation will never know most of their fellow-members, meet them, or even hear of them, yet in the minds of each lives the image of their communion.'[126]

* * *

How does the concept of patriotic narrative apply to the central questions regarding the *ius respondendi*? These concern 1) the nature of the privilege, 2) its recipients, 3) the effects it had on law, 4) the purpose it served, 5) its evolution during the Principate. Can these problems be linked to the patriotic narrative of jurists and the contradictory images of the emperor as malevolent or benevolent, repressive or disinterested?

1) With regard to the individual questions surrounding the institution, the nature of the privilege is directly linked with the relations between Augustus and the jurists. Did the *ius respondendi* create a privileged class among jurists, whose *responsa* were held to be binding on the judges? Or was the *ius respondendi* a licence to practise law, without which no *responsa* could be given? In the earlier literature, the licence theory and the monopoly of the licensed jurists was dominant, as this theory agreed with the image of the sovereign power of the emperor.[127] From Puchta onwards, the interpretation began to shift in favour of the elite theory, which appealed to the idea of jurists' law. The jurists were accordingly divided into two classes, the small group of lawyers who had the privilege and the majority who did not.[128] Parallel to this

---

125 Cf. Hylland Eriksen 1993; Hingley 2000.
126 Anderson 1991, 6.
127 Thomasius 1707, 70 [ch. 2.2.20]; Gibbon 1977 [1788], 392.
128 Bach 1762, 217 [ch. 3.1.6.4]; Puchta 1875, 326; Karlowa 1885, 660; Kipp 1909, 111; Krüger 1912, 122; Krüger 1912, 123; Hahn 1913, 74; Berger 1919, 1166; Wenger 1926, 104; Bernhard Kübler, *Geschichte des Römischen Rechts*, Leipzig 1925, 257; Premerstein 1937, 203; Siber 1941, 401. Karlowa 1885, 660 suggested that only the *responsa* linked with a legal process were given under the *ius respondendi*, signed and sealed. Premerstein 1937, 204 claimed that the *responsum* had to be written and furnished with an imperial seal as a sign of imperial acceptance. He rejected Wenger's claims that *responsa* were stored in imperial archives (L. Wenger, 'Ueber Stempel und Siegel', ZRG 42 (1921), p. 633). De Visscher 1936, 625 pointed out that it was not unprecedented to give an imperial seal. Augustus gave Maecenas and Agrippa

the licence theory continued. This was popular among those who saw the Augustan regime as an authoritarian enterprise, such as Mommsen, Kunkel, and Magdelain. According to the licence theory, Augustus banned *responsa* from unprivileged lawyers.[129]

The debate over the competing theories subsided after Kunkel, the most ardent proponent of the mandatory licence theory, shifted to the elite theory.[130] After Wieacker denounced the mandatory licence theory as untenable given what we know about *auctoritas* and Augustus,[131] the theory is supported only by Bauman,[132] who has attacked the prevailing view fervently.[133]

The vital question here is whether these scholars believed that Augustus was benevolent towards the jurists, or whether he wished to gain complete control over them? The concept of the freedom of the jurists is not relevant in itself, since what is freedom to some is a chaotic legal confusion to others,

his seal so that they could act with his authority. Schulz 1946, 112–113: 'Unauthorized jurists were at liberty to continue to give *responsa* in the republican style, *propria et privata auctoritate*.' Guarino 1949, 415; Daube 1950, 517; Schönbauer 1953, 225–6; Provera 1962, 354; Schiller 1971, 1228–1229; Bretone 1982, 247; Wieacker 1985, 89, 92; Paricio 1996, 99.

129   Mommsen 1952 [1887], vol. II, 912 opted for the mandatory licence, but in a footnote acknowledged that unprivileged lawyers did give *responsa*. Helssig 1891, 1332; Kunkel 1948, 455; Magdelain 1950, 4–7, 13 was slightly more cautious. Kunkel was followed by Max Kaser in his *Römische Rechtsgeschichte*, Göttingen 1965, 158. However, Kaser was noncommittal in *Das Römische Privatrecht*, München 1955, 189 and later turned to the elite theory in *Römische Rechtsquellen und angewandte Juristenmethode*, Wien 1986, 19. Kunkel gained the wholehearted support of i. a. Vincenzo Arangio-Ruiz, *Storia del diritto romano*, (7th ed.), Napoli 1985, 271 and d'Ors 1965, 155.

130   Kunkel 2001 [1967], 282–283 still called the *ius respondendi* a 'Patent' but changed its definition.

131   Wieacker 1985, 83–87. Bauman 1989, 11–12, 15–16 conceded that the concept of *auctoritas* does not lend itself to exclusiveness, but explained that the word was used out of a sense of Republican nostalgia. He noted that there was perhaps no need to prevent unprivileged lawyers from giving *responsa*, because no client would trust his matters to an unauthorised jurist, nor would he know of his existence. Bauman was clearly attracted to the idea that a jurist would traditionally put up a sign saying LICET CONSULERE (p. 16). In the first part of his jurisprudential trilogy (Bauman 1983, 72), he imagined Tiberius Coruncanius simply putting up 'a sign reading LICET CONSULERE (Cic. *Mur.* 28).'

132   Bauman 1989, 10–13. Bauman 1989, 3 described the rather short list of supporters of the mandatory licence theory. He mentioned that the theory was popular during the nineteenth century but does not mention anyone besides Mommsen who had actually supported the theory.

133   Bauman's critique of the 'charismatic theory' is an attack on a straw man, because he simplified the arguments of his opponents, see attacks on de Visscher, Guarino and Schulz, in Bauman 1989, 2–3, 10–11.

and what is repressive control to one person is seen as a welcome order by another. The emergence of the patriotic narrative transformed the interpretations of the nature of the privilege. The elite theory, which was originally based on the idea that a malevolent emperor was promoting his henchmen above other jurists, gradually transformed into Schulz's and Guarino's theory of a mostly ceremonial honour given to jurists loyal to the emperor without any effect on other jurists. The mandatory licence theory underwent a similar transformation. The tones that dominated the discussion from the seventeenth century onwards, including the image of the evil emperor corrupting and repressing the jurists, gave way to the view that the *ius respondendi* was the result of a power-sharing agreement among the emperor and a group of lawyers. Kunkel, Magdelain, and Bauman shared the view that the legal elite gained a monopoly in law with the support of the emperor. Both approaches transformed the emperor from an evil oppressor into a partner of at least a group of lawyers.

2) To whom was the privilege granted? Why do we know of no other recipient than Sabinus? The identity of the recipients of the privilege was not a pressing issue for earlier scholars, but more recently the theories regarding this issue have been numerous, ranging from licensing jurists individually,[134] to the approval of single *responsa* by the emperor,[135] to the licencing of only upper-class jurists.[136] The answer to this question was also dependent on the nature of the privilege. The licence theory would solve the problem by requiring that all practising jurists would have to be recipients of the *ius respondendi*.[137] Magdelain, the most vocal advocate of this theory, claimed that all practising jurists mentioned in the Digest, some 30 in all, had had the *ius respondendi*.[138] At the other extreme was the theory that the *ius respondendi* never existed in practice, which would explain why we do not

---

134   Thomasius 1707, 70–71 [ch. 2.2.20].
135   de Visscher 1936, 622. The problem is that de Visscher's reconstruction called for Tiberius to have licensed individual jurists, whose absence from the sources he was unable to explain.
136   Gibbon 1977 [1788], 392.
137   Kunkel 1948, 436–441 admitted that it is a modern interpretation that Augustus granted the licence to some particular jurists; the text did not say so specifically. He thus tried a new approach: Augustus did not give the privilege to all jurists, but all jurists had to be licensed. As in Mommsen's theory, the *ius respondendi* was exclusive: those who did not have it simply were not jurists.
138   Magdelain 1950, 19–22. According to his calculations, about half of the known jurists from the reign of Augustus until the reign of Diocletian had the *ius respondendi*. Non-practising lawyers, such as Gaius, did not have it.

know of any recipients.[139] Thus it appears that the lack of known recipients leaves open only the possibilities of total freedom or total control.

One of the apparently incurable dilemmas of Pomponius' text is that on one hand Sabinus of the order of knights was the first to respond publicly and this privilege was given to him by Tiberius, but on the other hand, Augustus initiated the privilege.[140] Karlowa was the first to resolve this dilemma with a genial stroke of conjecture: Augustus had given the privilege only to senators and Tiberius was the first to give it to a non-senator, Sabinus.[141] In the core of Kunkel's reconstruction was the idea that Augustus wished to restore the authority of the law by returning it to the hands of the senatorial class.[142] Wieacker and Bauman have noted how most of the jurists in Augustus' inner circle (such as Trebatius, Ofilius and Alfenus) were actually knights, which makes it hard to understand why Augustus should have alienated his closest allies by establishing a privilege they were not eligible to apply for.[143]

Again the situation calls for either a total control or the total lack of it to enable the main theories to conform to the sources, which do not mention a single jurist holding the privilege except Sabinus. Either the privilege had to be strictly exclusive, which would mean that all jurists had to be licensed, as the Kunkel-Magdelain theory proposed, or completely inclusive, so as to include every lawyer, as de Visscher claimed, or none, as Cancelli and Fögen have maintained. This dilemma is the main obstacle to the credibility of the institution. The second main problem, the question of who was the first to grant the privilege, Augustus or Tiberius, provided the impulse for the senatorial

139 Cancelli 1987; Fögen 2002, 205–206.
140 de Visscher 1936, 626–628 tried to solve this dilemma by claiming that the passus in Pomponius that others have interpreted as Augustus giving the privilege as a *beneficium* actually refers to Tiberius. Pomponius' text from *ex illo tempore* onwards would refer to Tiberius: *Primus divus Augustus, ut maior iuris auctoritas haberetur, constituit, ut ex auctoritate eius responderent: et ex illo tempore peti hoc pro beneficio coepit.* Dig. 1,2,2,49.
141 Karlowa 1885, 661; Kipp 1909, 109; Krüger 1912, 124; Kübler 1925, 257.
142 The great senatorial jurists of the Republic were primarily responsible for the extensive authority of the law. As Cicero (*off.* 2,65) stated, this authority had been compromised by the social rise of ignorant, upstart equestrian lawyers. Returning the initiative in legal matters to the senatorial class was totally in line with Augustus' principate, which, according to Kunkel, restored the Republic by restoring the influence of the Senate. Kunkel 1948, 451–456; Kunkel 2001 [1967], 284.
143 Wieacker 1969b, 346–347. Bauman 1989, 17–21 even proved statistically that Kunkel's main thesis, the rise of the senatorial class to prominence in early Principate, was false. Cf. also Schönbauer 1953, 226; Paricio 1996, 93. In Wieacker 1985, 92–93 he surprisingly and without explanation reverted back to the senatorial theory.

theory. Its erosion by Kunkel with the admission that imperial control did not prevent all non-licensed jurists from practising law somewhere is symptomatic in the decrease of the credibility of the theory of total control. The beneficiary was the conception of juristic freedom, which was vital to the patriotic narrative of the jurists' profession.

3) The effect of the privilege was one of the earliest topics discussed regarding the *ius respondendi*. Did the *responsa* of the privileged jurists have a binding effect on the judges? Did the *responsa* have effects beyond the individual case they were addressing, by creating new law?

The presumed effect of the *ius respondendi* has changed according to the trends in jurisprudence. During the absolutist period the word of the emperor had the status of law and created law, and thus lawyers speaking with the authority of the emperor also created new law. This produced a practical problem if two or more lawyers spoke with the authority of the emperor and gave contradictory *responsa*, all binding on the judge.[144] However, the proposition that the *responsa* were binding on the judges was largely accepted and disseminated.[145] Puchta confused the situation even more by dividing the authority of the lawyer into an internal authority arising from his skill, and an external authority derived from imperial authorisation.[146] Unresolved practical problems led to the rejection of the universal binding effect in the early twentieth century,[147] and henceforth the idea of a binding effect in the single

144 For instance, Stryk 1713, 48–49 pondered at length how the binding nature of the *responsa* and their mutual relations were dealt with in ancient Rome and seventeenth century Germany.
145 Thomasius 1707, 67–72 [ch. 2.2.20]; Heineccius 1751, 239–241 [ch. 157–158], 267–268 [ch. 178]; Bach 1762, 217 [ch. 3.1.6.3]; Gibbon 1977 [1788], 393. Only Hugo 1806, 337 was puzzled by the fact that the classical jurists did not devote a single line to what a judge should do in the case of contradictory *responsa*.
146 The internal authority of the respected jurist added to the persuasiveness of his arguments, while the external authority of the licensed jurist gave his opinions the officially binding effect. This binding effect covered all legal opinions given by the *iuris auctores* in their other writings as well. Puchta 1875, 326–327. The *ius publice respondendi* served Puchta as an example of the inner and outer authority of jurists' law in modern law on several occasions. Haferkamp 2004, 174–176.
147 Mommsen 1952 [1887], vol. II, 912 agreed that the *responsa* were binding but did not see a difference between the *responsa* of the Republic and the Empire. Karlowa 1885, 659–662 questioned the practical implications of Puchta's universally binding effect, arguing that it would have been immensely unpractical if every single utterance of a jurist could create law. Furthermore, the existence of a universally binding effect would have precluded scientific discussion and critique among the jurists. Helssig 1891, 1332 limited the

case based on imperial authorisation prevailed.[148] Magdelain argued that the jurists did not exercise imperial power, which could have been interpreted as legislative, but gave binding *responsa* as authorised by the emperor.[149] This was opposed by the advocates of juristic freedom, who claimed that all *responsa* were mere recommendations in the manner of Republican jurisprudence and that the *ius respondendi* provided only additional authority.[150]

Although at first the sovereign authority of the emperor and the legal authority of the lawyer appear to have been incompatible, the patriotic narrative managed to combine these in an interesting way. Either the emperor was sovereign and granted the jurists the power to create law, thus increasing their influence, or the professional authority of the jurist was superior and the imperial privilege was merely an added bonus. The jurists' profession benefited regardless. The debate over universal or individual effect was a test of the limits and practical implications of jurists' law.[151] The patriotic

> response's binding effect to the case involved. Costa 1909, 77 still held that both the *responsa* and other writings had 'un valore obbligatorio'. Kipp 1909, 110–113; Krüger 1912, 120–122; Berger 1919, 1165–1166; Wenger 1926, 108; Leopold Wenger, *Institutionen des Römischen Zivilprozessrechts*, München 1925, 194; Kübler 1925, 256–257. Hahn 1913, 74 is an exception in claiming that unanimous *responsa* not only had the force of law but were also binding on the emperor.

148 de Visscher 1936, 623; Siber 1941, 402 believed that *responsa* became binding only with the rescript of Hadrian. According to Guarino 1949, 416 Tiberius gave Sabinus the first binding *ius respondendi*.

149 Magdelain 1950, 7–12 wrote that the words *ex auctoritate principis*, as proven by epigraphic evidence, were used to convey an imperial order. This order was used in the *ius respondendi* to authorise the jurists to give *responsa*. This theory was later adopted by Provera 1962, 347–350, 355, who claimed that the otherwise uncomfortable Inst. Iust. 1,2,8 was merely a fiction used by Justinian to justify the use of juristic writings as sources of law. In the most recent literature the binding effect in the single case has been almost universally accepted both on the account of the emperor's *auctoritas* and the testimony of Gaius Inst. 1,7. Kunkel 2001 [1967], 282–283; Bretone 1982, 245, 248; Wieacker 1985, 92; Bauman 1989, 12; Paricio 1996, 96–97.

150 Siber 1941, 401; Schulz 1946, 113: 'The jurisconsult remained simply a private citizen; he was not a magistrate, but he spoke *ex auctoritate principis,* and this would be an inducement for praetor and iudex to accept his opinion, although they were not legally bound to do so.' Because it has been widely accepted that at the time when Gaius wrote the privilege had a binding effect, the notion of its non-binding effect has continued only in the transformation theories. For instance, Guarino's idea that Augustus' *ius respondendi* was a non-binding social recognition that was gradually transformed to a binding force has been accepted by Paricio. Guarino 1949, 415; Paricio 1996, 93–94.

151 One of the more creative attempts to solve the problem was de Visscher's theory that during the reign of Augustus, jurists submitted their *responsa* to the emperor to have them validated. Tiberius then construed the *ius respondendi* as

narrative derived its force from the idea of jurists' law, but the assumption that every utterance of every single licensed jurist could create law was too impractical to gain popularity. The opposite view that the privilege only gave added *auctoritas*[152] to the opinions of the jurist on its own part reinforced the autonomous authority of the profession in contrast to the external authority of the emperor.

4) Although Pomponius quite clearly stated the motives of Augustus in founding the *ius respondendi* to be elevating the authority of the law, scholars have been rather sceptical whether that was really Augustus' main objective. Most of them have suspected Augustus of ulterior motives, such as wanting to use jurists as his servants or to seek the support of the profession for his political agenda.

Nearly all writers after Huber from the seventeenth century onwards have believed that Augustus intended to subjugate the jurists for his own purposes. With astonishing unanimity the core of jurist historians from Thomasius in the eighteenth to Fögen in the twenty-first century have affirmed that the authority of the jurists or the law did not need additional support. On the contrary, they have all held that Augustus was trying to steal the glory of the jurists.[153] Only Bauman objected by arguing that the jurists lured Augustus into the whole affair.[154]

> a privilege that was granted to jurists until further notice as he withdrew to Capri. de Visscher 1936, 623–626: 'L'autorité du Prince n'étant pas attachée à la personne du jurisconsulte, il faut bien qu'elle ait été imprimée au responsum lui-même.' (p. 623). This was proposed also by Premerstein 1937, 204 on account of the magnitude of the power given in the *ius respondendi*. Kunkel 1948, 427–429 condemned this theory as ludicrous, although his opinion was based more on his conviction of the jurists' status than on the actual evidence. In his opinion it was completely impossible even to speculate that proud men of the Republican opposition, such as Labeo and Cascellius, would humble themselves in front of the hated emperor with their *responsa*!

152 Wenger, whose opinion on the matter changed, stressed in Wenger 1926, 105–107: that *auctoritas* was just a social and political power and would not directly lead to any legal consequences. Von Premerstein 1937, 203–204 concurred, the binding effect was only produced by the jurists' own *auctoritas* and any imperial licence would merely serve as an added recommendation.

153 Thomasius 1707, 69–70 [ch. 2.2.20]; Heineccius 1751, 239–241 [ch. 157–158], 267–268 [ch. 178]; Gibbon 1977 [1788], 392; Bach 1762, 217–218 [ch. 3.1.6.3]; Puchta 1875, 324; Mommsen 1952 [1887], vol. II, 912; Karlowa 1885, 659–662.

154 Bauman 1989, 21–24 claimed that jurists close to Augustus actively sponsored and supported the institution and were the main beneficiaries. If Augustus had some agenda, it was perhaps to use patronage as a means of gaining control over the profession.

The second motive, the claim that Augustus was in fact seeking the support of the jurists, a continuation of the conspiracy theory popular from the early twentieth century onwards, further emphasised the power of the jurists.[155] This conviction was also invariably linked to the ardent defence of the independence of the profession.[156] Whether or not the *ius respondendi* was a great challenge to the independence of the profession seems to depend mostly on whether one believes Augustus succeeded in suppressing the jurists by introducing it. Recently, many seem to think that he at least tried to tempt the profession into the imperial fold.[157]

Pomponius' explanation that Augustus wanted to raise the authority of the law was accepted during the sixteenth century, discredited, and returned to favour sporadically, mostly with the help of Cicero's ridicule of the lawyers of his time.[158] The idea that Augustus wanted to enhance the authority of the jurists arose from Ferrini's edition of Pomponius and enjoyed brief acceptance.[159]

The main question about the motives of Augustus in creating the *ius respondendi* is not whether he tried and succeeded in subjugating the jurists' profession. The main issue is how the emperor was able to help the profession. While the earliest authors believed that Augustus succeeded in corrupting and subjugating the jurists, later this defeatist view was not compatible with the

---

155 Helssig 1891, 1331–2; Kipp 1909, 109: 'Die Macht, welche die Juristen durch die Erteilung von Rechtsgutachten über die Bevölkerung hatten, mußte es dem Kaisertum wünschenswert erscheinen lassen, die Jurisprudenz zur Freundin zu haben und sie zugleich in Abhängigkeit vom Kaiser zu bringen.' Krüger 1912, 120; Hahn 1913, 73–74; Kübler 1925, 257; Premerstein 1937, 203; Kunkel 2001 [1967], 286; Wieacker 1985, 92; Bauman 1989, 21–24.

156 Berger 1919, Kübler 1925, 257; Schulz 1946, 112; Magdelain 1950, 3; Fögen 2002, 205; Cancelli 1987, 543 claimed that the sacred independence and objectivity of jurisprudence, and its position as the voice of justice and law, could never have been compromised by political pressure.

157 Paricio 1996, 95; Fögen 2002, 205.

158 Cf. Thomasius 1707, 69 [ch. 2.2.20] with references to earlier authors and Cicero. According to Bach 1762, 217–218 [ch. 3.1.6.3] the authority of the law and the dignity and splendour of jurisprudence had been damaged during the civil wars of the Republic. Kunkel 1948, 451–456 stated that the incursion of equestrian lawyers had debased the authority of the jurists.

159 Helssig 1891, 1331–2; Siber 1941, 400. Bonfante, Fadda, Ferrini, Riccobono, and Scialoja (eds.), *Digesta*, Milano 1931, p. 36 added the word *consultorum* after *iuris*, so that the text read as *ut maior iuris consultorum auctoritas*. According to de Visscher 1936, 623, Augustus wanted to raise the authority of the jurists by helping them to find the most equitable solution and to avoid unfruitful disputes. Bretone 1982, 246–248 claimed that because Pomponius generally speaks of the authority of the jurists, *auctoritas* had to be connected with an *auctor* and there was no need to raise the authority of the law.

patriotic narrative. As if by common agreement, nearly all interpretations of Augustus' motives seem to glorify the jurists. Augustus either failed to repress the powerful jurists' profession, or he was actually asking for their support and in return granted them the privilege. According to some versions, Augustus acted as the jurists' loyal aid, either helping them to purge unsuitable elements from the profession or to increase their authority more generally.

5) Did the *ius respondendi* come to an end after the reign of Tiberius, as is alleged by the advocates of juristic freedom, or did it continue to evolve, as Gaius and the Institutes of Justinian seem to claim? The theory that the jurists were opposed to the emperors is supported by the various stories about the late Julio-Claudian emperors. Similarly Gibbon was the first to reshape Hadrian as the liberator of jurisprudence. Later on, it was argued that Hadrian abandoned the *ius respondendi* in favour of imperial constitutions.

The evolution of the institution is connected with several chronological questions. Augustus is generally credited with founding the *ius respondendi*. Because Tiberius was mentioned by Pomponius as granting the first privilege to Sabinus, the question has been what it was that Augustus actually did? Numerous explanations have sought to rationalise the primacy contradiction by arguing that one or the other either granted different things[160] or they granted the privilege to different people.[161] The problem with these explanations is that they have difficulties in explaining the change that was involved. For instance, Bauman envisioned a grand restructuring of the privilege, whereas Wieacker thought that the *ius respondendi* died out after Tiberius.[162]

The discussion of the fate of the *ius respondendi* after Tiberius has been dominated by Suetonius' observation that Caligula had suppressed several

160 According to Bach 1762, 218, 221 [ch. 3.1.6.5, 3.1.6.13] Sabinus was the first to grant *responsa signata*. De Visscher 1936, 621–622 and Siber 1941, 401 argued that Augustus authorised individual *responsa* and Tiberius gave a *beneficium*. Guarino 1949, 416 claimed that Augustus gave a social privilege and Tiberius started the real *beneficium*. Cf. also Schönbauer 1953, 227.
161 On the extension of the privilege to the knights, see Kipp 1909, 109; Krüger 1912, 124; Kunkel 1948, 455; and Provera 1962, 354–5.
162 Paricio 1996, 93–94, 101 wrote that the desire to invent some reform for Tiberius to implement is only natural; cf. also Bretone 1982, 247. Bauman 1989, 57, 63–67 argued that something had gone wrong with the *ius respondendi* during the reign of Tiberius, as a great number of contradictory laws are mentioned. Tiberius was unhappy with the concept of *auctoritas* or giving the right to respond in his authority, which is why he gave only a right to respond *publice* or *populo*, publicly or to the people. Therefore Bauman stated that it was possible that Augustus gave Trebatius the old *auctoritas* version and Sabinus was the first to receive the new *ius respondendi*. Bauman dated this change to between 23 and 31 AD. Wieacker 1985, 93.

different professions. According to the majority of accounts, this marks the beginning of the crisis of the institution, during which the *ius respondendi* was either banned[163] or not sought by the best jurists.[164] As none of the sources mention the *ius respondendi* during the later Julio-Claudian emperors, these theories have been criticised.[165]

Pomponius' narrative continued until the reign of Hadrian during which the institution is either revived in the original form or abolished. The mysterious *viri praetorii* asked for the right to respond and were given a rather curious answer. Gibbon wrote, reflecting Heineccius, that 'Hadrian restored the freedom of the profession to every citizen conscious of his abilities and knowledge.'[166] Heineccius' reinterpretation of the *ius respondendi* was transmitted through Gibbon to Haubold and Hugo, to fit the image of the age of the Antonines as the most auspicious of humankind. Whitman wrote that, during the late eighteenth and early nineteenth century imperial revival, Augustus was replaced by Hadrian as the ideal emperor. He liberated the lawyers by granting the *ius respondendi* according to merit, not blind loyalty. The jurists were again their own masters, commanding a high social status because of their learning and skill.[167]

Since then, scholars have desperately tried to decipher what Hadrian did.[168] From Hugo and Puchta onwards the theory of a privilege earned by

---

163   Bach 1762, 218 [ch. 3.1.6.5] wrote that Caligula wanted to get rid of the *responsa* of the jurists. De Visscher 1936, 630–632 argued that Caligula, Claudius, and Nero envied the influence of the jurists and possibly banned the *ius respondendi*. Sen. apocol. 12,2 *iuris consulti e tenebris procedebant pallidi graciles, vix animam habentes, tamquam qui tum maxime reviviscerent.* The jurists celebrate the funeral of Claudius. The above quoted Suet. *Cal.* 34 described how Caligula persecuted lawyers along with other professions. See also Tac. *Ann.* 16,9; Suet. *Nero* 37; Dig. 1,2,2,52. Cf. Magdelain 1950, 14–15.
164   Schulz 1946, 113: 'Like so many of Augustus' creations, this institution did not endure long. Under his successors some of the outstanding lawyers, being in opposition, probably preferred not to ask for imperial authorization, but to give their *responsa* in the proud old republican fashion, *propria auctoritate.*' Under the hostile reigns of Claudius and Caligula the privilege was probably forgotten. Similarly Wieacker 1985, 80–83 wondered why there is no trace of the *ius respondendi* between the reigns of Tiberius and Hadrian, as Suet. *Cal.* 34 is clearly not about the privilege.
165   Hugo 1806, 338 denied that there would be a way to deduce from Suetonius what Caligula really wanted to do to the jurists. Bauman 1989, 130–133 asserted that the hostility of the later Julio-Claudians is a myth.
166   Gibbon 1977 [1788], 392.
167   Whitman 1990, 84–89.
168   Puchta 1875, 324–325; Krüger 1912, 123; de Visscher 1936, 634–638. Karlowa 1885, 661 stated that Hadrian first confirmed the institution but later eliminated it.

merit has become the standard solution.[169] Parallel to this, the theory has persisted that Hadrian actually abolished the whole institution and completely ended state involvement in the *responsa* of the jurists.[170] Some have also suggested that Hadrian deceived the praetorians or denied their request on various grounds.[171] Bauman believed that Hadrian wanted to depoliticise and professionalise the institution as a part of his judicial reform, which he carried out with the co-operation of the jurists.[172]

[169] Puchta 1875, 324–325 held that Hadrian informed the men that the *ius respondendi* was not purely a *beneficium*, an honour, but an acknowledgement of skill that was placed in the service of others. That it can only be given, but not applied for, was already stated by Budaeus 1557 [1969], 61 [ad Dig. 1,2,2,49]. Modern supporters are numerous: Guarino 1949, 417, 419; Magdelain 1950, 16–18; Kunkel 2001 [1967], 295–296; Provera 1962, 355–356; Bretone 1982, 249–254; Bauman 1989, 287–304.

[170] Puchta 1875, 324–325 argued that Hadrian freed the right to respond from the emperor's power; Schulz 1946, 113–114; Schulz 1946, 118 on *consilium*: 'Its establishment by Hadrian is the counterpart of his codification of the Edict and his disuse of the *ius auctoritate principis respondendi*. The ancient right of the jurists to apply and develop the law was respected, but the bureaucratic tendencies of the times demanded centralization and officialization. The ancient aristocratic jurisprudence was gradually coming to an end.'

[171] Kipp 1909, 111; F. Pringsheim, 'Legal policy and reforms of Hadrian', *Journal of Roman Studies* 24 (1934), 148. Krüger 1912, 123 wrote that the emperor merely confirmed the free right to respond without the *ius respondendi* and nothing was granted. Kunkel 2001 [1967], 295–296 argued that the emperor's reply was a friendly denial, a suggestion that through serious study one might reach the level of proficiency needed to have the *ius respondendi*. Wieacker 1985, 92 suggested that the praetorians were in fact trying to resurrect an old and obsolete privilege, which the emperor deftly denied. According to Paricio 1996, 103–105, the whole passage is an amusing episode, meant to demonstrate that the *ius respondendi* was granted only to a select few, probably members of the *consilium*. Daube 1950, 511–517 considered that the men in fact asked for the renewal of *beneficia* that had ceased with the death of Trajan. Hadrian answered that he would renew the *beneficia* in due time. Bretone 1982, 249–254 dismissed Daube's explanation because the verb *praestare* was never used in the renewal of *beneficia*.

[172] Bauman 1989, 287–304. Bauman refuted most of the theories proposed by earlier scholars because they did not fit his master theory. Bauman 1989, 320 on his grand theory: 'The Principate was ready for a restructured legal system, and the lawyers were ready to supply it. Thus the main impetus now came from the profession itself – not entirely a new phenomenon, since the lawyers (or at any rate a segment of them) had promoted the *ius respondendi* and the schools from the start, but now their initiatives were more deliberate and more comprehensive. Behind every reform-minded emperor stood a group of legal luminaries. Imbued with a new professionalism, aware of the growing sophistication of their thinking and writing, conscious of the new juristic autonomy stemming from the *ius respondendi*, alive to the new opportunities for new

How long did the *ius respondendi* continue? Puchta wrote that the privilege continued uninterrupted and that the last person to have it was Innocentius, mentioned by Eunapius, who lived during the reign of Diocletian. This view has been accepted with reservations by those who believe that the privilege outlived Hadrian.[173] Whether the famed jurists Papinian, Ulpian, Paul, and Modestin had the privilege is uncertain, as is reported by Kunkel. Puchta noted that someone like Ulpian who was praetorian prefect hardly needed any added authority.[174] This theory has gone unchallenged since then.[175]

The whole discussion on the continuation of the institution highlights the problematic nature of the evidence. The traditional interpretation of Pomponius' text is that the *ius respondendi* continued from Augustus until Hadrian, who discontinued granting it as a privilege. How is this compatible with the view that Gaius Inst. 1,7 spoke of the *ius respondendi* as an existing institution?[176] As some explanations started with the assumption that the institution never existed in practice, or at least fell into disuse after Tiberius, they were at pains to explain Hadrian's involvement and the possible existence of the institution at the time of Gaius. Then again, if one argues that the institution continued in use, how can the complete silence of all other sources for one and a half centuries be explained?

The two main options, that the *ius respondendi* ended after the reign of Tiberius, either by itself or as a result of the actions of Caligula, and that Hadrian dispensed with it, either by abolishing it completely or by saying it would henceforth be given only on account of merit, are both useful to the patriotic narrative. The versatility of the patriotic narrative is in its ability to simultaneously present parallel alternatives. The details of the situation do

---

men in all spheres of post-Julio-Claudian Rome, jurists like Pegasus, Iavolenus, Neratius, Celsus filius and Julian began pressing for a new kind of *cursus honorum* adapted to their special skills. They persuaded the emperors to restructure the *ius respondendi* and the *consilium principis*, to give them systematic entry into the senate, and to open wide the doors of the imperial service. Hence such innovations as Pegasus' urban prefecture, the first to be held by a jurist and probably the first to be held without a prior consulship.'

173 Georg F. Puchta, 'Nachträgliches über das Ius respondendi', in *Kleine zivilistische Schriften* (reprint of the 1851 original), Aalen 1970b, 297–299; Puchta 1875, 324 held that Gaius' use of the present *est* and Justinian's use of the past *erat* must mean that the *ius respondendi* was brought to an end sometime between them. The continuous use was accepted by Wenger 1926, 108; de Visscher 1936, 634–638; Bauman 1989, 287–304.
174 Puchta 1970b, 297–299, 302; Kunkel 2001 [1967], 303.
175 Krüger 1912, 296; Schulz 1946, 114; Bauman 1989, 287–304.
176 Wenger 1925, 312; de Visscher 1936, 648.

provide the patriotic narrative of the jurists's profession with several uplifting examples. The juristic opposition to the dictatorship of the later Julio-Claudian emperors has been cited as proof of the independence of the profession, while Hadrian's reply to the praetorians has been seen as an indication that he accepted Puchta's division of legal authority into the external authority of the emperor and the internal authority of the skilled jurist and held the latter in greater esteem. In all of these cases, the patriotic narrative underlines the autonomy of the jurists and the independence of the profession.

The independent jurist and the creation of continuity

The fact that the patriotic narrative of the jurists has been, and still is, used to create a sense of union between ancient and contemporary lawyers is an example of the creation of continuity. The shared values and ideals of today are founded in the presentation of the past. The notions of a shared past and the continuity from the ancients to the present is one of the fundamental constants in the modern history of Roman law, which has had reflections in the writing of Roman legal history. The concept of legal continuity has its roots in the Historical School and its way of presenting itself as a direct descendant of a Roman legal tradition, and it may be divided into the original position of a direct legal continuity and its successor, the belief in the Roman foundations of modern law, or indirect continuity. Like all historical writing, the creation of continuity depends on narratives and their creative use.

The patriotic narrative is noticeable in the depiction of several themes of Roman legal history, where it has been used to portray themes of contemporary importance. A fine example of the idealising version of the patriotic narrative is the contrast between Labeo and Capito and the creation of the schools of jurisprudence[177] in the literature on Roman legal history. Labeo has played the role of the defender of republican freedom, while Capito has been allotted the role of the villain.

The controversy is based essentially on two sources, Pomponius and Tacitus. Pomponius recalls the creation of the schools:

---

[177] For a thorough analysis on the schools, see Gian Luigi Falchi, *Le controversie tra Sabiniani e Proculiani*, Milano 1981. Falchi noted how Sabinians were called conservative, Proculians innovators and vice versa, and given innumerable and contradictory epithets in legal history to explain the difference between the schools. Cf. also Dieter Nörr, 'I giuristi romani: Tradizionalismo o progresso?', BIDR 84 (1981), 9–33; Giaro 1992.

After him, the leading authorities were Ateius Capito, who was of Ofilius' school, and Antistius Labeo, who went to lectures of all the above, but who was a pupil of Trebatius. Of these two Ateius was consul. Labeo declined to accept office when Augustus made him an offer of the consulship whereby he would have become *consul suffectus* (interim consul). Instead, he applied himself with the greatest firmness to his studies, and he used to divide up whole years on the principle that he spent six months at Rome with his students, and for six months he retired from the city and concentrated on writing books. As a result, he left four hundred manuscript rolls (volumina) most of which are still regularly thumbed through. These two men set up for the first time rival sects, so to say. For Ateius Capito persevered with the line which had been handed down to him, whereas Labeo set out to make a great many innovations on account of the quality of his genius and the trust he had in his own learning which had drawn heavily on other branches of knowledge. (Dig. 1,2,2,47)[178]

Tacitus gives a more pointed version of the relationship, first describing the background of Ateius Capito:

> By his eminence as a jurist he had won the first position in the state; but his grandfather had been one of Sulla's centurions, nor had his father risen above a praetorship. His consulate had been accelerated by Augustus, so that the prestige of that office should give him an advantage over Antistius Labeo, a commanding figure in the same profession. For that age produced together two of the glories of peace; but, while Labeo's uncompromising independence assured him the higher reputation with the public, the pliancy of Capito was more to the taste of princes. The one, because he halted at the praetorship, won respect by his ill-treatment; the other, because he climbed to the consulate, reaped hatred from a begrudged success.[179]

---

178 *Post hunc maximae auctoritatis fuerunt Ateius Capito, qui Ofilium secutus est, et Antistius Labeo, qui omnes hos audivit, institutus est autem a Trebatio. Ex his Ateius consul fuit: Labeo noluit, cum offerretur ei ab Augusto consulatus, quo suffectus fieret, honorem suscipere, sed plurimum studiis operam dedit: et totum annum ita diviserat, ut Romae sex mensibus cum studiosis esset, sex mensibus secederet et conscribendis libris operam daret. itaque reliquit quadringenta volumina, ex quibus plurima inter manus versantur. hi duo primum veluti diversas sectas fecerunt: nam Ateius Capito in his, quae ei tradita fuerant, perseverabat, Labeo ingenii qualitate et fiducia doctrinae, qui et ceteris operis sapientiae operam dederat, plurima innovare instituit.* (Dig. 1,2,2,47, Mommsen-Krüger.) Translation by D. N. MacCormick in Mommsen-Krüger-Watson (eds.), *The Digest of Justinian*, Philadelphia 1985.

179 Tac. ann. 3,75 ... *principem in civitate locum studiis civilibus adsecutus, sed avo centurione sullano, patre praetorio. Consulatum ei adceleraverat Augustus ut Labeonem Antistium isdem artibus praecellentem dignatione eius magistratus anteiret. Namque illa aetas duo pacis decora simul tulit; sed Labeo incorrupta libertate ei ob id fama celebratior, Capitonis obsequium dominantibus magis probabatur. Illi quod praeturam intra stetit commendatio ex iniuria, huic quod consulatum adeptus est odium ex invidia oriebatur.* Translation by John Jackson, *Tacitus: the histories*, London 1962.

Historiographically, the story of Labeo and Capito is static, meaning that there is remarkably little change during the five centuries of legal historiography. The description of Johann Lorich from his 1545 rhymed biography of famed Roman jurists still illustrates the current attitudes. Of Labeo, Lorich wrote the following: 'Incorrupt he was, lover of freedom, constantly maintaining the old ways of knowledge.' Capito, in contrast, was treated more harshly: 'With servility he wished the powerful to oblige, a shameful toady he became.'[180]

In the more traditional literature, Bernard Rutilius' presentation of the jurists in 1537 is not unlike the ones presented in modern historiography. Rutilius shows Labeo and Capito in the spirit of Tacitus: Labeo is the stalwart defender of Republican freedom, whose opposition to the new order brought about the end of his rise in the magistracies, whereas Capito, an inferior legal talent, was advancing. Rutilius makes no secret of Capito's compliant adulation towards first Augustus and then Tiberius. The shame and ridicule that befell Capito because of this servility is mentioned frequently. He was particularly mocked when Rutilius mentioned Suetonius' and Dio's story of how Tiberius made a grammatical error in a speech (according to Dio in an edict). Capito rushed to explain that because Tiberius had used the expression it should now be correct classical usage. He was quickly discredited with the words 'You, Caesar, can confer Roman citizenship upon men, but not upon words'. The story has a parallel in the Holy Roman Emperor Sigismund I, who in 1414, in the council of Constance, tried to make his grammatical mistake a general rule.[181]

As early as during the sixteenth century, the stories of Labeo and Capito assume a near standardised form. In almost every book the profiles of Labeo and Capito are presented one after another, and reflect a kind of duality in which Labeo represents the proud and independent, and Capito the sub-

---

180   Johann Lorich, *Iureconsulti. Catalogus iureconsultorum veterum, quotquod aut vita, aut scriptis celebres sunt, succinto Carmine descripti*, Basel 1545, 21: *Incorruptus erat, tum libertatis amator, Constanti obtinuit scita vetusta modo*; p. 22: *Obsequiis voluit sibi devincire potentes, Assentatoris dedecus ergo tulit.*
181   Rutilius 1537, 140–146 [Capito]. Quote from Dio 57,17, translation by E. Cary, in *Dio's Roman history*, London 1924. The response Capito got was according to Suetonius *gramm.* 22 ... *tu enim, Caesar, civitatem dare potes hominibus, verbo non potes.* Sigismund's surely apocryphal words were *Ego sum rex Romanus, et supra grammaticam.* The phrase, refuted later famously by Molière (*Les Femmes savantes*, act 2, scene 6), were according to Renzo Tosi, *Dizionario delle sentenze latice e greche*, (4th ed.), Milano 1992, 457 first recorded by Johannes Cuspinianus (1473–1529), *De Caesaribus atque imperatoribus Romanis*, Strasbourg 1540, p. 601 and given their present form by Matteo Castiglione, *Elogi historici*, Madrid 1606, p. 234.

servient in a moral tale.[182] The interpretation of Pomponius, that the rivalry between the two jurists led to the establishment of the schools, was accepted and presented even here, but the composition was strengthened in the first general volume on the schools of jurisprudence by Gottfried Mascov. He underlines Labeo's great learning and the general tendency in his profile is positive. Of Capito he noted that there is little of his work in the Digest and that his reputation is poor because of the infamy he acquired as a result of his repulsive servility and compliance.[183]

Later, Thomasius and Heineccius connected the birth of the controversy to the *ius respondendi*.[184] The basic line of the argument, as perpetuated by Gibbon, remained largely the same. Thus, the story remained of the innovative oppositionist versus the lame and uncreative courtier.[185]

Hugo's juxtaposition went even further in the glorification of Labeo and the demonisation of Capito. His Labeo, unparalleled as a jurist, burns with an unrelenting hatred inherited from his father towards Augustus, the destroyer of the Republican order. In contrast, his Capito is of weak character and so inept as a jurist that his only chance to maintain a rivalry with Labeo is with heavy imperial support, which he paid for with adulation. According to

---

182   Aymar Du Rivail, *Civilis historiae iuris*, Lyon 1551, 253 [ad Labeo]; Hotomannus 1587, 166 [Capito, Labeo]; Iacobus Raevardus, 'Ad titulum de diversis Regulis Juris antiqui Commentarius anno 1568' in *Opera omnia I*, Napoli 1779, 146–150. Panziroli 1721, 34–37 [ch. 1.22–23]; Jean Bertrand, *Bioi nomikon, sive de jurisperitis libri duo*, Toulouse 1617, 40–49, 219–224 [Capito, Labeo]; Forster 1609, 478–483 [ch. 55–56], Grotius 1690, 95–101 [Capito, Labeo]. The quintessential story of the emperor and grammar is told in Panziroli p. 34 [ch. 1.22], Forster p. 482 [ch. 56]. Similarly Nicolaus Henel (c.1584–1656), *De veteribus jure consultis commentarius*, Leipzig 1654, 31–39 [Labeo]; Gravina 1704, 127–132 [ch. 73–74].
183   Mascovius 1728, 9–20.
184   Thomasius 1707, 73–81 [ch. 2.2.21]. Thomasius' chapter on the schools is mostly quoted from Huber. Heineccius 1751, 268–270 [ch. 179–180].
185   Gibbon 1977 [1788], 393: 'Capito distinguished by the favour of his sovereign; the latter more illustrious by his contempt of that favour, and his stern though harmless opposition to the tyrant of Rome. Their legal studies were influenced by the various colours of their temper and principles. Labeo was attached to the form of the old republic; his rival embraced the more profitable substance of the rising monarchy. But the disposition of a courtier is tame and submissive; and Capito seldom presumed to deviate from the sentiments, or at least from the words, of his predecessors; while the bold republican pursued his independent ideas without fear of paradox or innovations. The freedom of Labeo was enslaved, however, by the rigour of his own conclusions, and he decided, according to the letter of the law, the same questions which his indulgent competitor resolved with a latitude of equity more suitable to the common sense and feelings of mankind.'

Hugo, Capito was not appreciated by his contemporaries and even less by posterity.[186]

It was perhaps this tendency which provoked Puchta to dismiss the whole tradition as simply a convenient story on which to superimpose current controversial issues. Puchta said that this was the case with the question of the influence of Stoic philosophy and the question of strict interpretation versus equity, and even the controversies of the supporters and adversaries of the Historical School of jurisprudence. In every case, Labeo represents our man, the personification of virtue, whereas Capito is presented as mediocre, the bad opponent. Naturally this resulted in some inconsistencies with regard to what views the schools, and Labeo and Capito with them, were made to represent. Curiously enough, Puchta also repeated the same stereotypical portrayal of the jurists and made a similar adaptation to the one he criticised. Puchta lauded Labeo for opening jurisprudence to other sciences and giving it a new life with his versatile historical and philosophical education, so that it was saved from withering away in isolation. So, instead of an old-fashioned oppositionist, Puchta's Labeo is the creator of a new turn in jurisprudence, not unlike that advocated by the Historical School.[187]

Pernice's extensive portrait of Labeo's life and works used Capito as an anti-Labeo, a character that appears and disappears only to act as a contrast to the image of Labeo. The political position of Capito is not used as a moral weapon against him, and there is noticeable neutrality about any mention of the relationship between emperors and jurists. The republicanism of Labeo is noted as a personal trait, with nothing to do with his family or other affiliations. In contrast, in the discussion of their scientific impact, the scholarly mockery of Capito is pronounced. Pernice distills the few quotations of Capito that have made their way into the Digest into a single one that showed independent creative thinking from his part. Pernice doubts Capito's headmanship of a school, because there is no principal difference between the opinions of Labeo and Capito, and because Capito is not held to be a great authority.[188]

For a while after that, the moralistic tones in the literature all but disappeared and the characterisations became more neutral. At the same time, the role of Labeo and Capito in the founding of the schools was challenged as scholars tried to find the roots of the controversies in different juxtapositions.

---

186 Hugo 1806, 352–357.
187 Puchta 1875, 251–254.
188 Alfred Pernice, *Marcus Antistius Labeo*, Halle 1873, 4–5, 11, 16–17, 82–83, 90–91.

Nevertheless, as Kipp demonstrated, Labeo was subtly named the independent figure and Capito the compliant.[189]

Schulz mirrored the old theme and linked it with the founding of the schools by portraying Labeo as a good and active jurist, who founded his own school. Because of Labeo's republican beliefs, Schulz rejected the idea that Augustus had offered him the consulate. In contrast, Capito was an insignificant jurist, whose contribution to the development of private law is negligible. Therefore, the claim that he had a school is quite simply the product of later historians, who deduced that the antagonism between the schools was based on the antagonism between the two jurists.[190] Honoré developed this theory further and claimed that Cassius and Proculus were the real founders of the schools and Labeo and Capito were left with just their personal antagonism.[191]

Wieacker returned to this animosity and elaborated on the historical background, which brought him securely back to the old scheme. Labeo is again the hard-core republican, whose political views coupled with a tendency for sarcasm ended his political career. For Capito, all the sources for his servility are brought forth to prove that he was as spineless a toady as he is portrayed to be. According to Wieacker the depiction of the sources cannot be mere court gossip, even though one must take into account the biases of Tacitus and Suetonius, and thus the advancement of Capito must be the result of imperial patronage, especially if one takes into account his legal backwardness in relation to Labeo. Thus the portrayal we see in the sources is most likely to be the opinion of their contemporaries.[192]

Bauman took an epochal turn in the historical interpretation and rose to the defence of Capito, whom he depicts as an esteemed expert on constitutional and religious law. He points out that most sources like Pomponius, Gellius, Tacitus and Macrobius also praise Capito's abilities as a lawyer. Therefore the common assumption that because Capito is less cited than Labeo, he must be a worse lawyer is not sustained by the evidence. Bauman builds an elaborate scheme in which Capito is the house lawyer of the new administration, whereas Labeo is a good, but eccentric, lawyer with outdated political ideas, who constantly schemes against Augustus when he is not verbally insulting him. The animosity between the jurists would have been the result of the politico-legal battles they fought, which would have continued

---

189 Karlowa 1885, 663–664; Kipp 1909, 115 of Labeo: 'Kopf und Charakter', of Capito: 'ein gefügiger Mann'; Krüger 1912, 154–160; Cuq 1908, 53–55.
190 Schulz 1946, 102–103, 120.
191 Honoré 1962, 20, 37.
192 Wieacker 1969b, 342–345.

after they both founded their respective schools. Bauman's idealisation of Capito is clearly a reaction against the old image of him personified in Schulz.[193]

Nörr made an equally dramatic turn in the interpretation as he claimed that Labeo was actually the incorporation of the ideal type of man for the Augustan age, whose opposition to the new regime would have been wholly in accordance with the Augustan restoration of the Republic. Nörr's Labeo takes on the qualities of a good Pandectist lawyer, who turns to old Roman sources for legal innovations.[194]

The schools and their supposed founders have since been seen in different contexts. Peter Stein has written that Labeo and his school aimed for a more secure, logical, predictable, and rational law, in which rules are written out, whereas the Sabinians were more inclined towards practice.[195] The two schools could be divided according to their basic affiliations, which would for Labeo and the Proculians be *ratio* and for Capito and the Sabinians *usus*. Giaro has called this division a stereotypical portrayal of formal rationality and value rationality, which has then been projected upon both the Roman jurists and later Romanists.[196]

Following Stein, Lucio de Giovanni credited Labeo's fierce republicanism for the creation of a new model of legal science. This new model, which created the foundations of the great Roman jurisprudence, would have been based on such complicated techniques and logic that it would have been impossible for the emperor to interfere with it.[197]

The characters of Labeo and Capito are still the stereotypical models of the relationship between the emperor or political power and the jurist: Labeo as the supporter of the autonomy of law and the republican ideals and Capito as the active collaborator and imperial ally.[198]

193 Bauman 1989, 26–55.
194 Dieter Nörr, 'Innovare', *Index* 22 (1994), 75: 'Labeo war als Jurist und Innovator der perfekte Vollstrecker dieses augusteischen Programms.'
195 The writings elaborating this stretch from the 1960s to the present, one of the latest is Peter Stein, 'Le scuole', in D. Mantovani (ed.), *Per la storia del pensiero giuridico Romano da Augusto agli Antonini*, Torino 1996, 1–13. For a list of the earlier contributions, see Nörr 1994, 78.
196 Cf. Giaro 1992, 541–552; Nörr 1994, 77.
197 Lucio De Giovanni, 'Giuristi e principe. Aspetti e problemi', in D. Mantovani (ed.), *Per la storia del pensiero giuridico Romano da Augusto agli Antonini*, Torino 1996, 204. D. Nörr 1981, 9–33 had earlier criticised the use of this juxtaposition and the whole scheme of dividing the jurists as progressive or traditionalists as reflections of nineteenth century ideas.
198 Giuseppe Grosso, 'Labeone e Capitone: tradizionalismo e conformismo nei giuristi [1947]', in *Scritti storici giuridici*, Torino 2000, 144–150; Francesco Amarelli, 'Giuristi e principe. Conflitti compromessi collaborazioni', in

This model of juxtaposing the independent with the subservient is by no means unique, and like many good stories, has later replications or similar stories with similar morals. The most famous one in legal history is undoubtedly the story of the Holy Roman Emperor on a riding tour with two doctors. Savigny cited the version given by Otto Morena. The emperor Frederick I Barbarossa was riding with two doctors, Bulgarus and Martinus, during a break in the Reichstag of Roncaglia in 1158. The emperor asked them whether he is the ruler of the world. Bulgarus said that only with the exception of property, while Martinus said yes unconditionally. Upon hearing this, the emperor promptly donated his horse to Martinus. Bulgarus sourly remarked that *amisi equum, quia dixi aequum, quod non fuit aequum* (translates roughly as 'I lost the horse because I said it right; this is not right.'). The story is, like the one about emperor Sigismund, apocryphal, and different versions of it have been told with different emperors posing different questions to different lawyers in different places.[199]

The interesting phenomenon here is how the lawyers take on similar roles as Labeo and Capito. Bulgarus was the most famous and respected of the doctors, who gave counsel to the emperor with honesty and self-respect, whereas his rival Martinus' attitude towards the emperor is described with the same word that has been used repeatedly of Capito, *Schmeichelei*, (flattery, adulation, sycophancy).[200]

The stories of Labeo and Capito on one hand, and Bulgarus and Martinus on the other are basically moral tales about the relationship between jurists and power. The underlying morality of these stories is the notion that a good jurist holds true to his sense of self-worth, and does not need to flatter those in power in order to advance his career. The fact that an outstanding jurist is respected by his peers is the only advertisement he needs. Those who lack the abilities of the jurist compensate by becoming yes-men to those in power, constantly flattering their way to the top. The patriotic narrative works here as the narrative of the good and independent jurist against the narrative of unworthy yes-men, in which the ideal autonomy of the legal profession and jurisprudence is idealised and perpetuated.

The function of the patriotic narrative in the construction of continuity, which links the jurists from antiquity with those of the present, takes many different forms. Hugo, who was generally sceptical of established narratives

---

D. Mantovani (ed.), *Per la storia del pensiero giuridico Romano da Augusto agli Antonini*, Torino 1996, 183.

199 Friedrich C. von Savigny, *Geschichte des römischen Rechts im Mittelalter IV*, Darmstadt 1956 [1826], 180–182; Koschaker 1966, 54.
200 Savigny 1956, 82, 90–91, 178–179; Koschaker 1966, 54.

with convenient contemporary uses, exploited the possibilities offered by the story in furthering the glory of the independent jurist to the full. Puchta demonstrated a striking clarity of self-consciousness in denouncing the previous juxtaposition of the jurists, but nevertheless depicted Labeo as the independent innovator who founded a new style of jurisprudence. As in the example of the *ius respondendi*, the general trend in the patriotic narrative is towards idealisation. Even Bauman, the independent historical innovator, replaces the idealisation of Labeo with the idealisation of Capito. More generally, the realistic strand of the patriotic narrative, which relies on Jhering's vision, relativises the autonomy of jurisprudence to an inner autonomy of the legal system, where outside impulses can be channelled through the jurists to the law.

* * *

How is the writing of Roman legal history turned into a patriotic narrative? In historiography, narratives are generally assumed to be based on the historical sources. Hayden White has asserted that, in the writing of history, we necessarily make a leap into fiction, because the explanatory power of history is based on the narratives that historiography provides instead of a simple chronicle. Historians weave the isolated facts of a chronicle into a sequence, resulting in a plot, a narrative, which is a fiction by its nature. The claim that there is no fundamental difference between history and fiction was not welcomed by historians, who held true to the traditional view that fiction is a description of the imaginable while history is a description of what really took place, the argument of scientific objectivity. As White has pointed out, even according to its own self-image, history is a mixture of facts and their interpretation.[201]

---

201 Hayden White, *Tropics of discourse: Essays in cultural criticism*, Baltimore 1978, 83, 98–99; Hayden White, *Metahistory: The Historical Imagination in Nineteenth-Century Europe*, Baltimore 1990 [1973], 5–7. For a synthesis of the discussion on the so-called postmodernist school of history, see Matti Peltonen, 'After the Linguistic Turn? Hayden White's Tropology and History Theory in the 1990s', in Castrén et al. (eds.), *Between Sociology and History*, Helsinki 2004, 87–101. The basic proposition of White's is far more interesting to the present inquiry than the exegesis that has followed. Much of the criticism levelled against Hayden White has been irrelevant, especially since his views of narrativity have concerned history as a text. Cf. Frank Ankersmit, *History and Tropology*, Berkeley 1994, 9, 101; David Carr, 'Narrative and the Real World: An Argument for Continuity', in B. Fay et al. (eds.), *History and Theory: Contemporary Readings*, Oxford 1998, 137: 'Narrative is not merely a possibly successful way of describing events; its structure inheres in the events themselves.' Andrew Norman, 'Telling It Like It Was: Historical Narratives On

Without taking a stance in this old debate, it is still justified to claim that White's basic observation on the fundamental role of narratives in history enlightens an important aspect of this study. The transformation of the narratives in the examples presented earlier involved several factors, such as the different ideas about the continuity of the Roman law tradition, the development of legal history and the continuity of the narratives themselves.

The paradigm of continuity has a strong tradition in the history of Roman law.[202] For example, the continued use of the writings of classical Roman jurists by Justinian's compilers; the so called revival of Roman law in the eleventh and twelfth century; the continued use of Roman law as learned law, the reception of Roman law in Germany, and the *usus modernus Pandectarum*; the practical use of Roman law in Germany and the similarly named Roman-Dutch law.[203] The endurance of the idea of continuity and its narrative foundation were demonstrated by Jhering in his introduction to the *Geist des römischen Rechts*:

> Three times had Rome dictated laws to the world, three times bound nations to unity, the first time when the people of Rome were at the height of their power, to the unity of the state, the second time when already fallen to ruin, to the unity of the church, the third time through the reception of Roman law, in the Middle Ages, to the unity of law; the first time with external coercion through the force of arms, the both following times through the might of the spirit.[204]

Their Own Terms', in B. Fay et al. (eds.), *History and Theory: Contemporary Readings*, Oxford 1998, 153: 'Something is rotten in state-of-the-art narrative theory.', p. 169: 'The fact that a narrative is the product of a creative process, a construct that articulates the past anew, does not by itself compromise its truth.' Geoffrey Roberts, 'Introduction: the history and narrative debate, 1960–2000', in G. Roberts (ed.), *The History and Narrative Reader*, London 2001, 6: 'Historians, however, generally prefer to write narratives than to write about them.' Peltonen 2004, 99: 'Instead of issuing a radical challenge to the established order in historical methodology, the message of the collective work of White and Ankersmit is becoming a part of the most conservative ideas in historiography.'

202 Myron P. Gilmore, *Argument from Roman Law in Political Thought 1200–1600*, Cambridge 1941, 3: 'The appeal to an unchanging text creates the illusion of continuity.'
203 Cf. Wieacker 1995, 71–195; Philip J. Thomas, '*Usus modernus Pandectarum*; a spurious transplant', RIDA 47 (2000), 483.
204 Jhering 1993 [1907], vol. I, 1: 'Dreimal hat Rom der Welt Gesetze diktiert, dreimal die Völker zur Einheit verbunden, das erstemal, als das römische Volk noch in der Fülle seiner Kraft stand, zur Einheit des Staats, das zweitemal, nachdem dasselbe bereits untergegangen, zur Einheit der Kirche, das drittemal infolge der Rezeption des römischen Rechts, im Mittelalter zur Einheit des Rechts; das erstemal mit äusserm Zwange durch die Macht der Waffen, die beiden andern Male durch die Macht des Geistes.'

Jhering continued to describe how the significance of Roman law to the modern world was based on its rationality and universality, not its direct applicability. In the modern world, Roman law had become a cultural element that dominated the whole of legal civilisation, its thought, method, and conception of law. As he emphasises, this is a very different idea from the direct re-use of Roman law advocated by the Historical School.[205]

If we compare this with the criticism presented by Monateri in his recent article *Black Gaius*,[206] it is evident that the criticism, though effective against the Savignyan ideal, did not go to the core of the continuity argument. Inspired by Bernal's *Black Athena*, Monateri criticised the central role of Roman law in European legal history as ideologically based and called for a re-examination of Roman law in its Mediterranean context, especially with regard to its Afro-Semitic roots. According to Monateri, legal continuity is a specifically Western prejudice in which Roman law functions as a paragon for all modern law.[207]

> Of course the praise of Roman Law entails a highly positive (and positivistic) evaluation of the 'uniqueness' of the Western Law as the final outcome of a tradition, as an ongoing uninterrupted process, an inexorable teleology that lead us to where we are today.[208]

Monateri's claim that Roman law is the spurious root of the Western legal tradition is based on a criticism of a certain tradition of continuity, in which comparative lawyers see Roman law as a foundation of a unitary Western legal family.[209] Monateri has condensed their claims to four basic propositions:

> 1. Roman Law was the best developed and most sophisticated legal system in the ancient world;
> 2. Roman Law is at the root of the Western Legal Tradition, making it peculiarly 'Western';
> 3. Roman Law has a vigorous capacity to renew itself and still today can serve as a basis for actual governance;
> 4. Roman Law was the well-spring of a peculiar ethnic 'genius' for legal affairs and legal scholarship.[210]

---

205 Jhering 1993 [1907], vol. I, 10, 13–15.
206 Monateri 2000, published also as an Italian translation: Pier G. Monateri, 'Gaio nero', in P. G. Monateri, T. Giaro, A Somma, *Le radici comuni del diritto europeo: Un cambiamento di prospettiva*, Roma 2005, 19–76. Martin Bernal, *Black Athena: The Afroasiatic Roots of Classical Civilization I–II*, London 1987.
207 Monateri 2000, 483–485.
208 Monateri 2000, 487.
209 Monateri 2000, 488.
210 Monateri 2000, 489.

Monateri wants to challenge the originalist model of Roman law and the continuity model of Western legal tradition associated with it, which he has named 'the Aryan theory' (another loan from Bernal). He wants also to adopt a discontinuity model with an archaeological approach. This he terms 'the African-Semitic Theory', which is based on the writings of nineteenth century French Orientalists, but consists mostly of a criticism of the rationality of ancient Roman law.[211] Despite the concerns of Monateri, the inherent superiority of Western law has not been taken seriously for a long time.[212]

In the current work, I am not interested in whether the genealogy of the Western legal tradition should be traced to Rome. Even if the belief is false in a strictly historical sense, it is still a belief that helps to form an identity. I am more than willing to grant to Romanists that the tradition of Roman law can and should be traced to Rome. However, what is of more interest is the presence of nineteenth century Germans and their ideas among Romans. Monateri's weakness is that he repeats the doctrine of Roman legal history without inquiring into its foundations.

Peter Burke has argued that the emphasis on development or progress is the most obvious characteristic of Western historical thought.[213] Behind the idea of continuity lies a transhistorical identification of the past with the present. On a theoretical level, anachronistic interpretation is an extreme case of the preconceptions of scholars guiding the interpretative process. If Gadamer wrote that the small miracle of tradition is the fact that we may find in an ancient text something meaningful and appealing to us,[214] then the anticipatory structures in the anachronistic interpretation completely control the interpretation of the text. Meeting the other in the light of our preconceptions is turned into making the other meet those preconceptions. Whether we can draw the line between interpretation and invention is, however, another matter.

211 Monateri 2000, 489–502; Bernal 1987, 1: 'These volumes are concerned with two models of Greek history: one viewing Greece as essentially European or Aryan, and the other seeing it as Levantine, on the periphery of the Egyptian and Semitic cultural area. I call them the "Aryan" and the "Ancient" models. ... Most people are surprised to learn that the Aryan Model, which most of us have been brought up to believe, developed only during the first half of the 19th century.'
212 A case in point is the article by Ewould Hondius, 'The supremacy of Western law', in L. De Ligt et al. (eds.), *Viva vox iuris romani*, Amsterdam 2002, 337–342, which, despite its title, tries to prove that Western law is not intrinsically superior.
213 Peter Burke, 'Western Historical Thinking in a Global Perspective – 10 Theses', in J. Rüsen (ed.), *Western Historical Thinking: An intercultural debate*, New York 2002, 17–19.
214 Hans-Georg Gadamer, *Wahrheit und Methode*, (2nd ed.), Tübingen 1965, 274.

The idea of continuation in methodology and identity from Roman law to modern law raised the question of how direct that lineage should be. Savigny, the Historical School, and the Pandectists envisioned a direct continuation of Roman law from classical Rome to Byzantium, and from medieval Bologna to Germany, in which legal rules made in Rome were still applicable in Germany of the nineteenth century. In contrast, Jhering's theory was an inspirational scheme, in which the content of the law was new, but the deep structures of legal culture are derived from the Roman legal tradition. Even Jhering's interest in the history of Roman law was not purely historical, as he wished to follow its evolution and its purpose empirically like a natural scientist.[215]

How is it possible that so many historians employing the same sources can end up presenting different interpretations, which, in some ways, reflect their own ideals? It is essential to note how the significance of Roman law was not found but constructed, both legally and historically. To say that it was constructed implies that historians of Roman law consciously applied their own ideals to the history of Rome. It is unlikely that they were just bad historians, quite the contrary. They were writing the history of Roman law from the only viewpoint possible: their own. Despite this, some reasons for the permanence and evolution of the patriotic narrative can be found in the relationship between narrative, memory and tradition.

Legal history is a part of the tradition of history and follows the rules and conventions of history. One of the basic conventions of history is that it is a narrative formed on the basis of the material provided by the sources. In the formation of the narrative from the sources two important factors, memory and tradition are involved. The historian, as an interpreter of facts, proceeds with the formulation of the narrative equipped with numerous preconceptions such as previous scholarly interpretations, plot structures, other cultural material, personal opinions, and biases, and so on. Memory seeks to give meaning to facts and, with the help of the imagination, starts to construct a plot linking them together. Jan Vansina has described memory as a part of the general mindscape that creates our image of the self and which is therefore prone to change with that image. Tradition is involved with memory, giving past views an authoritative presence in the interpretative process through a process of identification,[216] which can be called an invented tradition, or a

215 Jhering 1993 [1907], vol. I, 48: 'Auch hier führt also erst die Kenntnis der Funktionen des Rechts zum Verständnis seiner Organe, die Physiologie zum wahren Verständnis der Anatomie.' Coing 1969, 158.
216 Vansina 1985, 8: 'Here we see the full power of memory at work. Events and situations are forgotten when irrelevant or inconvenient. Others are retained and reordered, reshaped or correctly remembered according to the part they play in the creation of this mental selfportrait.' Hoetink 1955, 7 writes how

patriotic narrative. Raphael Samuel has claimed that, despite their devotion to empirical research, historians are prone to unknowingly adopt the deep structures of mythical thought, the broad views of society manifested in ideas and media, in their desire to establish lines of continuity.[217]

Facts do not form history; the historian does. This limits the objectivity of scientific history and is one of the most important parts of narrative theory, a part which has, to some extent, also penetrated into the mainstream of history.[218] Like the human personal past, the historical past is in the process of constant modification (because the writing of history is a conscious process in which some parts are recollected and some not).[219]

For the theory of direct continuity, the autonomy of law was important, because the continued use of Roman law through the centuries demanded that it would remain relatively immutable and constant. Savigny used both the high standing of the classical civilisation during the nineteenth century and the writing of legal history for promoting of the continuing relevance of Roman law. For example, the image of the continuous use of Roman law as manifested, for instance, in the portrayal of the *usus modernus* in the seventeenth century is partly the product of Savigny's writing of legal history. The legal history of the Historical School was mostly cultural history that concentrated on legal scholarship. This approach overlooked the social, political or economic context and accentuated the effect of legal autonomy.[220] Still, to speak of an anachronism with regard to the Historical School

---

one's own past is constantly seen in a different light. Time modifies the past and different events compete for a place of honour. Similarly, Henry Gleitman et al., *Psychology*, (6th ed.), New York 2004, 256–268: 'Memory, it seems, is not a passive repository for our experience, recording the days of our lives and then permitting playback of these records later on. Instead, memory depends on a highly active set of processes, starting with the interpretation inherent in the initial encoding and continuing through the processes of reconstruction and interpretation used unwittingly to fill gaps in what we recall.' (p. 267)

217 Hingley 2000, 5; Raphael Samuel, *Theatres of Memory 1: Past and Present in Contemporary Culture*, London 1996, 3–11. Memory, myth, identity, and narrative have been explored in the current debate on France's recent past, cf. Henry Rousso, *The Vichy syndrome: History and Memory in France since 1944*, Cambridge 1991; Nora 1996, 3–7.

218 McNeill 1986, 2: 'Facts that could be established beyond all reasonable doubt remained trivial in the sense that they did not, in and of themselves, give meaning or intelligibility to the record of the past.'

219 Nora 1996, 10–14.

220 Savigny 1814, 12; Koschaker 1966, 265–269; Wieacker 1995, 308–316; Pugliese 1985, 424–425; Aldo Mazzacane, *Savigny e la storiografia giuridica tra storia e sistema*, Napoli 1974, 25–26. The traditional view has been criticised by Maximiliane Kriechbaum, 'Römisches Recht und neuere Privatrechts-

of the first half of the nineteenth century is in itself misleading or anachronistic, because history and legal science were inseparable in the works of Savigny.

The emphasis on direct continuity made the Historical School one of what Whitman called the 'backward-looking reformist movements'.[221] Their vision of continuity and their mode of historical writing have been continued by the contemporary comparative Romanistic scholarship. It denies the importance of legal mutation and sees the development of law as an organic process, in which Western law develops primarily as an interpretation of the past. According to Giaro, the Neopandectistic School sees Roman law as a ready package, which contains the seeds of all later dogmatic developments.[222]

The same idea of continuity explains the ease with which respected nineteenth century authors like J. E. Kuntze could juxtapose and compare the ancient and modern cultural landscapes. Without going into detail about Kuntze's fascinating book 'The Jus respondendi in our times', it is noteworthy how Kuntze recreated the idea of both ancient Rome and modern Germany being essentially part of the same Romano-Germanic cultural world. Kuntze suggested that it was time to emulate Roman jurists again and to revive the *ius respondendi* in the development of law. Kuntze's vision of history was both historical and ahistorical in the sense that it used the historical precedent of the Reception of Roman law in Germany and the foundation myth of the Historical School to justify the totally ahistorical re-use of a supposed Roman legal institution. Kuntze's short treatise illustrates how much classical civilisation and Roman law were part of the intellectual world of contemporary jurists.[223]

While Romanist scholars of the nineteenth century mostly strove to adapt Roman laws and Roman jurisprudence to the modern world, it has been claimed that they have modernised the Roman jurists in the process. Even when Bremer, a scholar explicitly conscious about the difference between Roman jurists and modern lawyers, wrote about legal education in Rome, he classified teachers as 'Professors' and 'Asessors' according to modern types.[224]

geschichte in Savignys Auffassung von Rechtsgeschichte und Rechtswissenschaft', in R. Zimmermann (ed.), *Rechtsgeschichte und Privatrechtsdogmatik*, Heidelberg 1999, 41–63.
221 Whitman 1990, 98.
222 Tomasz Giaro, 'Diritto romano attuale. Mappe mentali e strumenti concettuali', in *Le radici comuni del diritto europeo: Un cambiamento di prospettiva*, Roma 2005, 111–112.
223 Kuntze 1858, 5–10, 32.
224 F. P. Bremer, *Die Rechtslehrer und Rechtsschulen im Römischen Kaiserreich*, Berlin 1868, 33–34.

A more profound use of modern models of the profession was found in the historical interpretations of the *Causa Curiana* by J. W. Tellegen and O. E. Tellegen-Couperus. They argued that the explanation of the case as an example of the strict division between law and rhetoric and lawyers and rhetoricians is based on the application of the German concept of *Fachjurist* (a university trained professional lawyer) to the Roman jurists in the nineteenth century. This division was not supported by the Roman sources, but has continued into the present day because of the paradigm created by the Historical School of jurisprudence.[225]

The idea of continuity was also given more practical uses such as the conservation of established order. The supposed value neutrality of the Pandectists has generally been interpreted as social conservatism. The fact that they promoted legal norms derived from an ancient society that did not reflect current values and the fact that they promoted a legal system that would give jurists a large role in deciding the content of the law were a symptom of the distrust Pandectists held for popular legislation. The opposition to legislation, and especially codification, reflected a fear of popular power and the threat it posed to the existing order. This fear was heightened by the recurrent revolutions in several European countries during the nineteenth century.[226] The law the Pandectists promoted was an antidote to reforms and social justice, which they excluded from law as belonging to politics. The jurists' law was seen as an instrument of scientific justice, which dealt with purely normative questions, free of values.[227] The autonomy of law, which has since been interpreted as the protection of legal interpretation from the repressive intrusions of political power, served to protect conservative legal policies from liberal calls for change.

Why these narratives continued was, to a large extent, also dependant on the inner dynamics of the narrative and their use and re-use. Elements like the patriotic narrative of jurists, for example, have maintained their influence over the history of Roman law because of the significance of narratives in ancient history itself.[228] In modern history, the task of the historian would be to evaluate the narratives of the sources and to form a scientifically enlightened recreation of the events. As is clear from the cases presented earlier, one

---

225 Tellegen and Tellegen-Couperus 2000, 180–202.
226 Pugliese 1985, 453.
227 Giaro 1991, 210.
228 M. I. Finley, *The use and abuse of history*, London 1986, 28–30; M. I. Finley, *Ancient History: Evidence and Models*, London 1985, 9: 'The ability of the ancients to invent and their capacity to believe are persistently underestimated.'; Egon Flaig, *Den Kaiser herausfordern*, Frankfurt am Main 1992, 14–25.

of the problems for Roman legal history is the lack of sources. Those that do exist are often obscure in their meaning.

The recourse taken by most historians is to rely on the context, the general scheme of things and what we already know of the actors and circumstances, to help bridge the gaps between the sources. What is often called the context, is another narrative. For example, the *generatim* of Quintus Mucius is a confusing piece of information, which became intelligible to most scholars only after it was linked with the general scheme of Greek philosophical influences. The Greek scientific roots provided something that in screenplay-speak is referred to as a 'back story', an explanatory framework that links together the various pieces of information in the sources. Likewise the explanations of the *ius respondendi* rely on the different back stories of what the Augustan Principate was like and thus what were the aims of Augustus for the institution. Similarly the *edictum perpetuum* is seen as a part of the narrative tradition surrounding Hadrian, and enlivened with what is known of the Antonine Empire.

The concept of a back story is admittedly rather unscientific. A back story may be described as a kind of metanarrative, or, as in the case of history, overarching syntheses of the preceding scholarship, current trends in science, literature, politics and other matters that we use to determine what is reasonable. The metanarratives are fixtures of the imagination, which is in constant contact with a plethora of cultural products. Even popular culture is reflected in the metanarratives through their influence on the subconscious level of the imagination.

General presentations of Roman history were one of the ways in which these metanarratives were formed and perpetuated. Gibbon's Chapter 44 and Hugo's translation of it with a commentary brought to a wide readership the history of Roman law in a short, understandable, and highly readable form. Hugo's contemporaries had noted that law was one of the fields in which Gibbon's autodidactism was apparent and as such the book did not present any real progress in relation to Gibbon's sources like Heineccius.[229] Hugo was more interested in how Gibbon had managed in so few pages to bring the Romans and their law back to life, whatever the small mistakes might have been. Gibbon was a master story-teller and that was what counted if interest in Roman legal history was to be awakened.[230] Hugo's interest in Gibbon was based on Gibbon's abilities as a narrator. Gibbon could, according to

229 Gustav Hugo, 'Vorrede', in E. Gibbon, *Historische Übersicht des Römischen Rechts, übersetzt, eingeleitet und kommentiert von Gustav Hugo*, Göttingen 1996 [1789], 14: 'wozu brauchen wir einen Auszug aus Heineccius, da wir diesen und mehr als diesen selbst haben?'; Craddock 1989, 201.
230 Hugo 1996 [1789], 14–15; Craddock 1989, 201.

later historical interpretations, forget contemporary morals, rules, and religion and meet the Romans as themselves, not as antitheses or ideas, but as living men living their history and developing their law.[231]

Gibbon's narrative perpetuated the narratives of Heineccius and others, but this was not exceptional. As cultural products scholarly narratives have elements of surprising permanence, which enable them to live on through the centuries. To say that the stories lived on is admittedly a reification of non-corporeal entities. Nevertheless, their corporeal form as text contributed to the permanence by liberating them from the need of retelling and the limits of human memory. Still, the fact that the narratives remained in use and written down is the main cause for their long life. As anthropologists have demonstrated, material things have an ability to cross great spans of time in a way myths and other manifestations of oral tradition cannot. As in the case of the replication of myths, even here reproduction causes slight changes each time.[232]

The narratives of Roman legal history were constantly used for new purposes. For instance, the defence of the independence of the jurists by Zasius still lives, albeit in a modified form, in the interpretation presented by Schulz. The narrative of legal science has continued uninterrupted from its sixteenth century beginnings to the present, just as the narrative of Greek philosophical roots for Roman legal science will continue its obscure existence for many years to come. Likewise, the narratives of bad emperors are as much a staple of Roman legal history from Huber in the seventeenth century to Bauman in the present day.

The spread and permanence of the narratives of Roman legal history was enhanced also by the use of Latin, as scholars could easily build on the basis of an extended previous literature and knowledge would spread far beyond national and linguistic boundaries. The use of the vernacular spread to Roman legal science only gradually during the eighteenth century, but made considerable progress during the nineteenth.[233]

The use and re-use of historical narrative, both consciously and unconsciously to legitimate and propagate a certain viewpoint was not confined to

---

231   Hugo 1996 [1789], 15.
232   Greg Urban, *Metaculture: How Culture Moves through the World*, Minneapolis 2001, 19, 45–46, 48.
233   Anderson 1991, 18–19 discussed how 'the fall of Latin exemplified a larger process in which the sacred communities integrated by old sacred languages were gradually fragmented, pluralized, and territorialized.' He compared the wide continental renown of Hobbes, who wrote in Latin, to the virtual obscurity of Shakespeare outside the English-speaking world during the seventeenth and eighteenth centuries.

Roman legal history. For much of the post-war period, intellectual history has discovered and analysed anachronistic interpretations and their use as legitimating ideologies for certain styles of political thought.[234] Still, examples of the lure of anachronistic interpretations reappear constantly. A good case is the recent American 'Republican synthesis' debate, in which liberal lawyers argued that the intellectual history of American Revolutionary period can be used as a source for implications on current legal policy or the legitimation thereof. In the ensuing debate historians accused lawyers of an opportunistic use of history as a legitimation of a political agenda by imagining present contradictions and themselves with it as the latter-day incarnations of an old battle. In that case, lawyers were accused of using altruistic ideologies of the past as a legitimating source for contemporary arguments against liberal policies in the present.[235]

Historical accuracy proved to be the undoing of Pandectism. It is perhaps not so surprising why the Pandectist project began to fail. More difficult to understand, though, is why it was possible in the first place. The Pandectistic construction of modern legal rules from ancient Roman legal texts was a product of a great process of adaptation, in which the system based on Roman law was revamped to fit the emerging industrial society. This unlikely process was only possible as the continuation of a tradition dating back to the Middle Ages. That attempt failed, as the need for change proved to be beyond the possibilities available with regard to the tension and distance between the obsolete source material and the end product of the normative construction. Such a situation was not easily tolerated in an environment that valued historical accuracy and the rule of law.[236] By the end of the nineteenth century the dominant role of classics was beginning to come under criticism even in other fields, such as art and architecture.

The failure of the concept of direct continuity left the notion of Roman law as the foundation and inspiration of modern law as the main argument for its use. The narratives that had been used to support the claim of direct continuity did not lapse into history with it, but continued in the history.

---

234 See, for instance, Kari Palonen, *Quentin Skinner: History, Politics, Rhetoric*, Cambridge 2003, 22, 65, 118–120.

235 The debate continued from the 1980s to the 1990s. It is admirably documented with ample references to the literature in Laura Kalman, *The Strange Career of Legal Liberalism*, New Haven 1996. Cf. for insights also Nomi Maya Stolzenberg, 'A book of laughter and forgetting: Kalman's "Strange career" and the marketing of civic Republicanism', *Harvard Law Review* 111 (1998), 1025–1028, 1035–1037.

236 Giaro 1991, 230; Whitman 1990, 150–199 used the example of the *Agrarfrage*.

Conclusions

The discussion on the autonomy of the jurists was of such importance that it also came to be projected on to the writing of Roman legal history. In this chapter it was examined through the institution of *ius respondendi*, the possible imperial grant of a legal privilege to give opinions binding on the judges. The Roman sources on the matter are indecisive and unclear despite the textual exegesis that they have been subjected to. The tradition of the *ius respondendi* of Augustus was based on Pomponius' *Enchiridion*: Augustus, to enhance the authority of the law, established that opinions might be given under his authority. Gaius wrote that the unanimous *responsa* of jurists had the force of law. This formulation was later changed by Justinian so that the *iuris consulti* were those whom the emperor had granted the right to give formal answers. Beyond the traditional sources, Pomponius, Gaius, and the Institutes of Justinian there is a void.

I attempted to find out if some clarity could be achieved through a more extensive search through the Roman sources. However, a survey of the sources did not yield any texts that would have supported the exclusive interpretation of *publice respondendi* as an official privilege, because all sources seemed to be using the words in their general meaning. The connection presented in the Institutes of Justinian between the the title *iuris consultus* and the privilege *ius respondendi* was not supported by either the literary or the epigraphical sources. In both groups of sources the title *iuris consultus* was used only as a general professional title, synonymous with other professional titles of the legal profession. Finally, in the use of the concept of *responsa* there were no references to different responsa, for instance between a *responsum* given by the imperially certified lawyer and the opinion of the humble uncertified jurist.

This contradiction is clearly reflected in the literature from the sixteenth century to the present. The earliest authors have followed the traditional sources quite literally, while recent scholars have been increasingly sceptical. The ambivalence of the sources has been reflected in the rather free interpretations, which have vacillated between two stereotypical representations of the relationship between the emperors and jurists: the benevolent and malevolent emperor.

What is more noteworthy is that the interpretations of *ius respondendi* followed the general trends of law in an intriguing fashion. Most of the interpretations proceed from a certain view of the Augustan Principate and then explain the passage accordingly. The elegant jurisprudence of the sixteenth century stressed the significance of the jurists' abilities, while seventeenth century absolutist authors followed the dictum that the word of the emperor was law. From the late eighteenth century onwards, the power of the jurists returned and law flowed again as jurists' law.

Zasius stressed the intellectual freedom of the good lawyer and how the purpose of the *ius respondendi* was to protect that freedom by preventing misuses. As early as the late sixteenth century, however, it was recognised that the power of the jurist was derived from the emperor's power. This led to the malevolent emperor theory, as scholars began to question the motives of Augustus. Some of the eighteenth century Enlightenment authors believed that Augustus was after the influence exerted by the lawyers, whom he wanted to control. The belief in the authority of the jurist and jurists' law continued through the nineteenth century when lawyers and jurists were considered to be equal powers. Puchta saw a parallel between Augustus and the modern reforming leaders, because both tried to attack and subjugate the legal profession.

There was a notable break in the development of research on the *ius respondendi* during the early twentieth century. At that time, scholars began to search for corroborative evidence from outside the traditional sources. Because the results of these efforts were disappointing, scepticism persisted. Scholarly debate developed along two main lines of thought. The first, led by Schulz, denied the existence of the *ius respondendi*, while the second line, developed by Kunkel and others, claimed that Augustus took control over the legal profession through the *ius respondendi*. The basic question in this debate concerned the freedom of jurisprudence from imperial control.

Upon close examination, the two main theories expressed in the literature, the one emphasising the freedom of jurisprudence and the one stressing the power of the emperor, emerge as two sides of the same coin. Both reflected a self-aggrandising form of historiography, a patriotic narrative of the jurists. The narrative topic of the good emperor stressed how the emperor never wanted to interfere with the activities of jurists, whereas the theme of a malevolent emperor pointed out how, in spite of his will, he was unable to do so because of the great authority of the jurists.

These two versions of the patriotic narrative could be compared to the nineteenth century debate between idealists and materialists over the impact of power and politics on the law. Despite the difference the most influential factor is their similarity, because both forms of the patriotic narrative are a demonstration of the construction of a shared past. The difference is that they promote either an idealistic or a realistic version of the narrative.

Despite having traced the Roman sources and the history of interpretations on the *ius respondendi*, we are still unable to say anything conclusive about the historical events themselves. The *ius respondendi* remains an unsolved puzzle by its very nature. The value of the *ius respondendi* and its power as a catalyst seem to be based on the ambiguous nature of the historical event as seen in the light of the evidence, which has elicited such a wide variety of interpretations.

The ambiguous nature of the *ius respondendi* clearly highlights the patriotic narrative of the jurists' profession and the modern ideal of the autonomy of law projected on the past. The imaginable historical events behind the tradition have been completely separated from the interpretative tradition that has been based on its sources.

The patriotic narrative of the jurists' profession is strikingly visible also in other themes, such as the different portrayals of the Augustan lawyers Labeo and Capito. The stories are used and re-used in the historiography as moralistic tales to underline the glory of the independent jurist. The Roman sources Pomponius and Tacitus describe the two jurists on nearly equal grounds, both as esteemed jurists. However, Capito is described as seeking the favour of the emperor, while Labeo declined the consulship offered to him. Based on these stories, legal historians from the sixteenth century onwards have labelled Labeo as the good and independent and Capito as the worthless and subservient. The Romans do not claim that Labeo would have been a better lawyer: that is something that later scholars have imagined. The stories of the jurists and the emperor have been duplicated in the history of the Holy Roman Empire as stereotypical portrayals of the relationship between the emperor and lawyers.

The duality was extended also to the schools of Sabinians and Proculians. Puchta was the first to doubt the historical nature of the story and to suspect that it had been used as a convenient narrative on which to project contemporary issues. However, the old narrative was perpetuated by leading scholars and is still alive in the current discussion. Basically, it is a moral story of the relationship between jurists and power, which asserts how the good lawyer is an independent one. The permanent feature of the patriotic narrative is that the idealisation of lawyers is constant: the idealisation of Labeo can only be replaced by the idealisation of Capito.

The continuation of different narrative tendencies such as the patriotic narrative draws its strength from the opinion of scholarly continuity from the Roman lawyers to modern jurists. There are two models of continuity, direct and inspirational. The direct continuity was the scheme advanced by Savigny, but it was based on the conviction of cumulative progress, a constant feature in the Western historical thought. The inspirational theory was formulated by Jhering and assumes that the rationality of Roman law forms the foundation of legal method and culture and is an inspiration to future lawyers.

Virtually all the main theories were advanced without any reference to the rich variety of assumptions needed to make them even remotely plausible.

The narratives form frameworks of interpretation that guide scholars to their foregone conclusions. The explanations are based on various types of assumptions concerning the roles of the emperor and the jurists that can be traced back to earlier traditions. The theme of the bad emperor, for example, can be traced back to the sixteenth century, as can the topic of the importance of the jurists' law. The narratives are perpetuated by both the memory of the historian and the respect for scholarly authority.

Chapter 4

The Disputed Codification of Law

The codification of law, or the coherent collection of legal norms, is one of the basic components of modern western legal culture. The significance of codifications has produced an interest in the earliest variations and forms in the history of codifications.[1]

The lack of a true codification in the history of Roman law has puzzled Romanistic scholars considerably. Francesco Paolo Casavola wondered why the Romans did not produce a codification of law, despite the interest they apparently had in collecting legal norms. From the last years of the Republic we have notions that Pompey and Caesar made tentative attempts to organise the material of law. If the turbulence of the final years of the Republic explained why these plans led to nothing, why did the emperors and jurists of the classical age not manage to produce a codification?[2]

The two famous collections of law the Romans arguably produced, the Twelve Tables and the Justinianic compilation, are too primitive and too unsystematic, respectively, to serve as example of a systematic and conscious codification. The modern terminology draws a distinction between a compilation of law, which is a collection of legal norms without any apparent internal order, and a codification of law, which is defined by a systematic order with which legal institutions and norms are related to one another.

In order to examine the influence of the idea of codification in Roman legal history, there is a third option available, the *edictum perpetuum* or the Perpetual Edict, supposedly compiled by the jurist Salvius Julianus during the reign of Hadrian. In the literature, the compilation or codification of the praetor's edict has been seen as highly influential, both on the sources of law and indirectly on the schools of jurisprudence and the creation of an imperial bureaucracy.[3]

1 Cf. Jean Gaudemet, 'La Codification. Ses formes et ses fins', in J. Roset Esteve (ed.), *Estudios en homenaje al Profesor Juan Iglesias I*, Madrid 1988, 309–327. On the historical codification studies, cf. Pio Caroni, 'La storia della codificazione e quella del codice', *Index* 29 (2001), 55–81.
2 Francesco Paolo Casavola, 'Verso la codificazione traverso la compilazione', in L. De Giovanni, A. Mazzacane (eds.), *La codificazione del diritto dall'antico al moderno*, Napoli 1998, 304.
3 Gaudemet 1988, 316 cited the *edictum perpetuum* as an example of a technical codification in contrast to a social or political codification.

The Roman sources for the collection of law form only the material basis of the present inquiry. What interests us here is the emergence of different theories of codification, various explanatory traditions, and the narratives they contain.

Edictum perpetuum, Salvius Iulianus and the supposed codification

In the textbooks on Roman law the praetor's edict occupies a central position in the history of legal sources. In classical Rome, the praetor was the magistrate charged with the administration of justice. At the beginning of his year each praetor published his edict, which set out the legal remedies which he would grant together with the formulae for those remedies.[4] The conventional wisdom is that, during the Principate, the praetor's edict slowly assumed a standardised form, which was then set into a final mould by the jurist Julian under orders from Hadrian. This final composition was called the *edictum perpetuum*, or the Perpetual Edict.[5]

As is often the case, the clarity of the textbooks does not reflect the state of the scientific debate. Despite the massive amount of literature that has appeared on Salvius Julianus and the *edictum perpetuum*,[6] the discussion is

---

4   David Johnston, *Roman Law in Context*, Cambridge 1999, 3.
5   Johnston 1999, 4; Robinson 1997, 16; Mayer-Maly 1999, 22.
6   Heinrich Buhl, *Salvius Julianus,* Heidelberg 1886; Theodor Mommsen, 'Salvius Julianus', ZRG 23 (1902), 54–60; Louis Boulard, *L. Salvius Julianus: Son œuvre, ses doctrines sur la personalité juridique*, Paris 1903; P.-F. Girard, 'L'Edit perpetuel', RHDFE 29 (1904), 117–164; Ernst Kornemann, 'Der Jurist Salvius Julianus und Kaiser Didius Julianus', *Klio* 6 (1906), 178–184; Kipp 1909, 57–59; P.-F. Girard, 'La date de l'édit de Salvius Julianus', RHDFE 34 (1910), 5–40; Krüger 1912, 93–101; Otto Lenel, *Das Edictum Perpetuum: Ein Versuch zu seiner Wiederherstellung*, (3rd ed.), Aalen 1956 [1927]; Pringsheim 1934, 144–149; Fritz Pringsheim, 'Zur Bezeichnung des Hadrianischen Edictes als edictum perpetuum', in *Symbolae Friburgensis in Honorem Ottonis Lenel*, Leipzig 1934b, 1–39; Franz Wieacker, 'Studien zur Hadrianischen Justizpolitik', in A. Ehrhardt et al. (eds.), *Romanistische Studien: Freiburger Rechtsgeschichtliche Abhandlungen* 5 (1935), 43–81; Alfred Merlin, 'Le jurisconsulte Salvius Julianus proconsul d'Afrique', *Mémoires de l'Académie des inscriptions et belles-lettres* 43.2 (1941), 93–122; Schulz 1946, 127; Bernard d'Orgeval, 'La carrière de Salvius Julianus e la codification de l'édit', RHDFE 26 (1948) 301–311; Wolfgang Kunkel, 'Über Lebenszeit und Laufbahn des Juristen Julians', IVRA 1 (1950), 192–203; Bernard d'Orgeval, *L'Empereur Hadrien: Œuvre législative et administrative*, Paris 1950; Heinrich Vogt, 'Hadrians Justizpolitik im Spiegel der römischen Reichsmünzen', in *Festschrift Fritz Schulz II*, Weimar 1951, 193–200; Adolf Berger, 'Due note su Salvio Giuliano',

no nearer to a conclusion. In the current debate, there are three distinct main theories on the nature of the Perpetual Edict: that it was a rational and systematic codification of the praetor's edict;[7] that it was a simple compilation not much different from previous edicts;[8] and finally, that it never existed in practice.[9]

The main theme of this chapter is the difference between the historical interpretations on the Hadrianic Perpetual Edict and what those differences reveal of the ideological, cultural, and political presuppositions of the historians. Roman sources and their past interpretations are compared to highlight the roots of different historical reconstructions. Of particular interest is the development of the idea of a legal codification and how this has affected the evolution of historical interpretations on the Perpetual Edict. Again, the

> in V. Arangio-Ruiz (ed.), *Studi in memoria di Emilio Albertario I*, Milano 1953, 605–621; Pietro de Francisi, 'Per la storia dell'editto perpetuo nel periodo postclassico', RIDA 4 (1950), Mel. F. de Visscher III, 319–360; Antonio Guarino, 'La pretesa codificazione dell'editto', in V. Arangio-Ruiz (ed.), *Studi in memoria di Emilio Albertario I*, Milano 1953, reprinted in *Le ragioni del giurista*, Napoli 1983, 265–288; Feliciano Serrao, 'Il giurista Salvio Giuliano nell'iscrizione di "Thuburbo Maius"', in *Atti del III Congresso Internazionale di Epigrafia Greca e Latina*, Roma 1959, 395–413; Antonio Guarino, 'Alla ricerca di Salvio Giuliano', *Labeo* 5 (1959), 67–78; Honoré 1962, 46–55; Antonio Guarino, 'Salvius Iulianus: Profilo biobibliografico', *Labeo* 10 (1964), 364–426; Antonio Guarino, 'Spunti sul metodo di Giuliano', *Labeo* 12 (1966), 393–395; Timothy D. Barnes, 'A senator from Hadrumentum, and three others', in A. Alföldi (ed.), *Bonner Historia-Augusta Colloquium 1968/1969*, Antiquitas 4.7, Bonn 1970, 45–51; Antonio Guarino, 'La pista dell'"avunculus"', *Index* 3 (1972), 421–426; Dieter Nörr, 'Drei Miszellen zur Lebensgeschichte des Juristen Salvius Julianus', in Alan Watson (ed.), *Daube Noster: Essays in Legal History for David Daube*, Edinburgh and London 1974, 243–245; Elmar Bund, 'Salvius Iulianus, Leben und Werk', ANRW II. 15, (1976), 408–454 Antonio Guarino, 'La formazione dell'editto perpetuo', ANRW II. 13, (1980), 62–102; Armando Torrent, *Salvius Iulianus liber singularis de ambiguitatibus*, Salamanca 1971; Armando Torrent, 'La ordinatio edicti en la politica juridica de Adriano', *Anuario de Historia del Derecho Español* 53 (1983), 17–44; Willem J. Zwalve, 'Einige Bemerkungen zur Constitutio Tanta/Dedoken § 18', TR 51 (1983), 135–149; Bauman 1989, 250–260; Sandro Serangeli, 'Abstenti', 'beneficium competentiae' e 'codificazione' dell'editto, Ancona 1989; Antonio Guarino, 'L'editto in casa Cupiello', *Labeo* 36 (1990), 50–57; Antonio Guarino, 'Inter amicos', *Labeo* 40 (1994), 349–352; Sandro Serangeli, 'Ancora su Dio 36,40,1 e la codificazione dell'editto', in S. Romano (ed.), *Nozione formazione del diritto II (Mel. F. Gallo)*, Napoli 1997, 267–278; Mantovani 1998; Dario Mantovani, 'L'édit comme code', in E. Lévy (ed.), *La codification des lois dans l'antiquité*, Paris 2000, 257–272.

7 Torrent 1983.
8 Bund 1976.
9 Guarino 1980.

objective is not to propose a solution to the original historical problem, but rather to understand how the different interpretations reflect the competing theories of law upon which they are based.

* * *

The main sources for the *edictum perpetuum* date from several centuries after the event, from the post-classical period. They can be divided into three distinct groups. First, there are Roman historians; secondly there are references in the Codex Theodosianus; and, thirdly, Justinian's *Corpus Iuris*.[10]

The first group consists of Eutropius, Aurelius Victor, and those later Roman historians who commented on their texts. Eutropius, an imperial court historian writing in the late fourth century, mentioned how, after the reign of Pertinax, a Salvius Julianus rose to the imperial throne:

> After him Salvius Julianus seized possession of the state, a man of noble birth and highly skilled in the law, the grandson of Salvius Julianus who composed the 'Permanent Edict' under the deified Hadrian.[11]

The text of Eutropius gained considerable standing during Late Antiquity. Bird maintained that its easy readability and compactness made Eutropius' *Breviarium* the common history textbook during the Middle Ages.[12] Earlier, Eutropius was commented upon and paraphrased by Paulus Diaconus, Jerome, Paeanius, and Landolfo Sagax. Paeanius' translation of Eutropius states that Julian's work was later called *edictum perpetuum*, while in the early fifth century St. Jerome dated the event at 2147 after Abraham, which has been traditionally interpreted as 131 AD. The other versions of the *Breviarium* by Paulus Diaconus and Landolfo Sagax are more or less loyal reproductions.[13]

10   Antonio Guarino, 'La leggenda sulla codificazione dell'editto e la sua genesi', in *Atti del congresso internazionale di diritto romano e di storia del diritto, Verona 27.–29.9.1948, II*, Milano 1951, 174–181.

11   Eutr. 8,17 *post eum Salvius Iulianus rem publicam invasit, vir nobilis et iure peritissimus, nepos Salvi Iuliani, qui sub divo Hadriano perpetuum conposuit edictum.* Translation by H. W. Bird, *The breviarium ab urbe condita of Eutropius*, Liverpool 1993.

12   H. W. Bird, 'Introduction', in Bird 1993, lv–lvii.

13   Paeanius in H. Droysen (ed.), *Monumenta Germaniae historica, Auctores antiquissimi 2*, Berlin 1879, 147; Hier. *Chron. a. Abr.* 131 *p. Chr.* (R. Helm [ed.], 'Die Chronik des Hieronymus', *Eusebius Werke 7.1*, Leipzig 1913, 200): *Salvius Iulianus perpetuum composuit edictum.* (On the dating, see Bund 1976, 426). Paulus Diaconus, *Historia romana*, (Droysen 1879, 316); Landolfo Sagax, *Historia miscella*, 146 (Droysen 1879, 316): ... *sub divo Antonino perpetuum composuit edictum.* Cf. also Girard 1910, 6; Guarino 1980, 84–85.

Also writing in the late fourth century, the Roman historian Aurelius Victor mentioned the same unfortunate emperor, but like later historical accounts called him Didius. However, Aurelius Victor gave him the credit for the compilation of the edict:

> Of noble origins, he distinguished himself with his knowledge of the civil law; he was the first, in effect, to organise the edict of the praetors.[14]

It is important to note that while the emperor Didius Julianus and the jurist Salvius Julianus were different persons, perhaps relatives, their identities were constantly confused by historians. Another version of the relationship is given by Spartianus, who in his biography names Salvius Julianus, twice consul, city prefect and jurist, as the great-grandfather of emperor Didius Julianus.[15] The confusion over the name of the maker of the *edictum perpetuum* was a continuing subject of debate from at least the sixteenth century onwards, and even in modern literature the possible relationship between Salvius and Didius Julianus has been under intense scrutiny.[16]

Eutropius and Aurelius Victor are believed to have one or more models or sources in common for their historical narratives, but the exact nature of the transmission is disputed. The close resemblance and shared errors between the two texts and parts of *Historia Augusta* have led to the *Kaisergeschichte* debate about their provenance. As a result, it is now recognised that it is possible that both Eutropius and Aurelius Victor drew from a common source now lost, but it is not known which one of them is more loyal to the original.[17]

The second group of sources are two references in the Codex Theodosianus to an edict *per divum Hadrianum conditum*[18] and to an *edictum Hadriani*.[19] Neither of them makes any mention of Julian or the nature of the edict.

14 Aur. Vict. *Caes.* 19,1–2 *At Didius (an Salvius?) Iulianus, fretus praetorianis, quos in societatem promissis magnificentioribus perpulerat, ex praefectura vigilum ad insignia dominatus processit. Genus ei nobile, iurisque urbani praestans scientia; quippe qui primus edictum, quod varie inconditeque a praetoribus promebatur, in ordinem composuerit.*
15 Hist. Aug. *Did.* 1,1 *Didio Iuliano, qui post Pertinacem imperium adeptus est, proavus fuit Salvius Iulianus, bis consul, praefectus urbi et iuris consultus, quod magis eum nobilem fecit…*
16 Diplovatatius 1919 [1550], 254–257, 268–269. On modern literature, see Mommsen 1902; Kornemann 1906; Barnes 1970, 49–51.
17 Guarino 1951, 176–177, n. 36; Bird 1993, xlvii–xlix.
18 Cod. Theod.11,36,26 (Imppp. Grat., Valent. et Theodos. ad Hypatium 379 AD.) *Quisquis, ne voluntas diem functi testamento scripta reseretur, vel ne hi, quos scriptos patuerit, heredes edicti per divum Hadrianum conditi beneficium consequantur…*
19 Cod. Theod. 4,4,7pr (Imp. Theodos. Asclepiodoto 424 AD.) … *ita ut, sive bonorum possessionem secundum tabulas vel secundum nuncupationem cete-*

The third group of sources consists of Justinian's praise of Julian both in the Codex and in the confirmation of the Digest. In the Codex emperor Justinian called Julian a man of supreme authority and the organiser of the praetor's edict.[20] Justinian's words have also been reproduced in later texts, of which the *Epitome legum* mentions a Servius Cornelius as Julian's aid in the compilation.[21] In the confirmation of the Digest, Justinian lauds Julian as 'the most acute author of legal writings and of the Perpetual Edict.' *Dedoken*, the Greek version of the text, is not identical to the Latin and describes the *edictum perpetuum* as a small book.[22] Justinian clearly made a comparison between his Digest and the Perpetual Edict and their respective compilers.

Furthermore, the name Salvius Julianus is mentioned in a number of epigraphical sources. The most important is the Pupput inscription found in present-day Tunisia in 1899, which lists details of the career of a Salvius Julianus. Hadrian doubled his salary as a questor because of his outstanding learning, and he later proceeded on the *cursus honorum* up to the consulate.[23] This is almost unanimously accepted to be an honorary inscription for the jurist Julian, even though his first name is said to be Lucius instead of Publius as in the literature.[24]

> rasque similes postularit, aut certe ex edicto divi Hadriani se mitti ad possessionem ex more petierit, statim inter ipsa huius iuris auspicia propositum suae intentionis explanet.

20 Cod. Iust. 4,5,10,1 ... *huiusmodi sententiae sublimissimum testem adducit Salvium Iulianum summae auctoritatis hominem et praetorii edicti ordinatorem.*

21 C.E. Zachariä, *Ius Graeco-Romanum* vol. 2, Leipzig 1856, 280.

22 Const. Tanta/*Dedoken* 18§ ... *ipse Iulianus legum et edicti perpetui suptilissimus conditor.* Friedrich Ebrard, 'Das zeitliche Rangverhältnis der Konstitutionen De confirmatione Digestorum 'Tanta' und *'Dedoken'*, ZRG 40 (1919), 113-135; Wieacker 1935, 72-76; Zwalve 1983, 139-145; Tammo Wallinga, *Tanta / ΔΕΔΩΚΕΝ: Two introductory constitutions to Justinian's Digest*, Groningen 1989.

23 *CIL* VIII, 24094, abbreviations completed, the text reads: *L. Octavio Cornelio P.f. Salvio Iuliano Aemiliano xviro quaestori imp[eratoris] Hadriani cui divos Hadrianus soli salarium quaesturae duplicavit propter insignem doctrinam trib[uni] pl[ebis] pr[aetori] praef[ecto] aerar[ii] Saturni item mil[itaris] co[n]s[uli] pontif[ici] sodali Hadrianali sodali Antoniniano curatori aedium sacrarum legato imp[eratoris] Antonini Aug[usti] Pii Germaniae inferioris legato imp[eratoris] Antonini Aug[usti] et Veri Aug[usti] Hispaniae citerioris proco[n]s[uli] provinciae Africae patrono d[ecreta] d[ecurionum] p[ecunia] p[ublica].* Because the jurist Julian's first name is Publius, the name Lucius has usually been interpreted as a scribe's mistake, see Berger 1953, 608–609.

24 Honoré 1962, 47: 'It would be a strange coincidence if there were two such prominent men in the reign of Hadrian called Salvius Iulianus.' Cf. also Kunkel 1950, 192; Serrao 1959, 397-398; Honoré 1962, 46; Bund 1976, 413. The only voice to the contrary is Guarino 1964, 370-372, who claims that the

Salvius Julianus' consulship in 148 is documented in three inscriptions and the Fasti Ostienses.[25] Of the more varied kind, there is a dedication of a temple in Thuburbo Maius by Salvius Julianus,[26] an honorary inscription naming a Salvius Julianus as the *curator aedium sacrarum* in 150 AD.[27] To make matters more difficult, three inscriptions mark the consulship of another Salvius Julianus in 175 AD.[28] Of the more curious sort is the funerary inscription of a philosopher, who was a friend of Salvius Julianus.[29] There is also a probable fake, which mentions that Salvius Julianus organised the *edictum perpetuum* and was born in Milan.[30]

Julian is frequently mentioned in Roman literature, though no reference is made to the *edictum perpetuum*. The Historia Augusta refers to him three times, one of which has already been mentioned. In the biography of Hadrian, Julian is a member of Hadrian's *consilium* among other jurists.[31] A Salvius Valens is named as one of the jurists consulted by Antoninus Pius in his *vita*.[32] One of the orations of Aristides has a god appear to his foster father in the form of Salvius, one of the consulars.[33] Finally, Marcus Aurelius names Iulianus as one of those who lived a particularly long life, and Fronto refers to him in two letters to the same emperor.[34]

The compilation and the significance of the *edictum perpetuum* is seldom explicitly mentioned by the Roman authors. The length to which scholars have been willing to go in finding references is illustrated in how a chapter in Dio's Roman history has been interpreted as a reference to the *edictum perpetuum*:

> politician of the inscription and the jurist are two different people. Students of Latin onomastics have pointed out that such variation in *praenomina* in inscriptions is common and should not be used to draw far-reaching conclusions. Of the declining significance of the *praenomen*, see Olli Salomies, Die römischen Vornamen, Helsinki 1987, 390–413.

25 CIL VI, 375; CIL XVI, 95; Fasti Ostienses 28,148 (*Inscriptiones Italiae* XIII. 1, ed. Degrassi, 207).
26 ILA 244.
27 CIL VI, 855.
28 CIL VI, 30865; CIL X, 7457; CIL XV, 7240; Mommsen 1902, 60.
29 ILS 7776.
30 CIL V, 714*.
31 Hist. Aug. Hadr. 18,1 *Cum iudicaret, in consilio habuit non amicos suos aut comites solum sed iuris consultos et pracipue Iuventium Celsum, Salvium Iulianum, Neratium Priscum aliosque, quos tamen senatus omnis probasset.*
32 Hist. Aug. Pius. 12,1 *Multa de iure sanxit ususque est iuris peritis Vindio Vero, Salvio Valente, Volusio Maeciano, Ulpio Marcello et Diavoleno.* Diavoleno is probably a corrupted form of Iavolenus Priscus, which makes it probable that Salvius is in fact Salvius Julianus. On this discussion, see Bund 1976, 428.
33 The orations of Aristides, 48,9.
34 Marc. Aur. *Ta eis heauton* 4,50; Fronto p. 54–55 v. d. H. (Ad. M. Caes. 4.1–2.)

The praetors themselves had always compiled and published the principles of law according to which they intended to try cases; for the decrees regarding contracts had not all yet been laid down.[35]

According to Serangeli, this juxtaposes two situations, the earlier one before the *edictum perpetuum* and the one after the compilation, in which the praetors would not need to publish any more edicts.[36]

The concept of *edictum perpetuum* was already in use during the Republic,[37] but began to appear in the legal literature only by the third century, decades after the supposed Julianic compilation. It appeared simultaneously in both jurisprudence through Papinian[38] and imperial constitutions through Septimius Severus.[39] Later it all but disappears from the texts of the jurists.[40] In the imperial constitutions its use is limited mainly to two periods, the first during Gordian,[41] and the second during Diocletian and Maximianus.[42] Even if this does not support the theory that the *edictum perpetuum* was merely a post-classical invention, neither do the sources support the claim that it was used consistently or simultaneously with the supposed compilation. Pringsheim examined the use of the words *edictum perpetuum* in connection with other terms used of the edict in his article on the labelling of Hadrian's edict as *edictum perpetuum*. He also noted the same periodicality and claimed that the term is alien to classical jurisprudence and only came into use for the first time

---

35   Dio 36,40,1 Οἱ στρατηγοὶ πάντες τὰ δίκαια καθ' ἃ δικάσειν ἔμελλον αὐτοὶ συγγράφοντες ἐξετίθεσαν· οὐ γάρ πω πάντα τὰ δικαιώματα τὰ περὶ τὰ συμβόλαια διετέτακτο. Translation by E. Cary, *Dio's Roman History III*, London 1914, 67.

36   Serangeli 1997, 275; Serangeli 1989. Guarino's rebuttal, cf. Guarino 1990, Guarino 1994, questions the plausibility of such a reading.

37   Ascon. *Corn.* Stangl p. 48, Clark p. 59 *Aliam deinde legem Cornelius, etsi nemo repugnare ausus est, multis tamen invitis tulit, ut praetores ex edictis suis perpetuis ius dicerent: quae res studium aut gratiam ambitiosis praetoribus qui varie ius dicere assueverant sustulit.*

38   Dig. 31,77,29 (Papinian); Dig. 47,11,5 (Ulpian); Dig. 49,5,7,1 (Paul); Dig. 44,7,52,6 (Modestin); Dig. 49,14,1,1 (Callistratus); Dig. 50,13,5,2 (Callistratus).

39   Cod. Iust. 2,1,3 (Severus, Antoninus, 202 AD); Cod. Iust. 2,12,5 (Antoninus 212 AD).

40   The only one is Dig. 1,5,2 (Hermogenian).

41   Cod. Iust. 2,2,2; Cod. Iust. 2,11,15; Cod. Iust. 2,12,13; Cod. Iust. 2,19,3; Cod. Iust. 2,19,4; Cod. Iust. 6,10,1; Cod. Iust. 2,11,18.

42   Cod. Iust. 2,4,13pr; Cod. Iust. 2,25,1; Cod. Iust. 2,32,1; Cod. Iust. 2,54,1; Cod. Iust. 5,71,11,1; Cod. Iust. 7,50,2; Cod. Iust. 4,26,12; Cod. Iust. 8,30,3; Cod. Iust. 5,21,2; Cod. Iust. 6,2,18; Cod. Iust. 6,9,6; Cod. Iust. 6,20,9; Cod. Iust. 6,20,11; Cod. Iust. 4,29,19; Cod. Iust. 7,16,21; Cod. Iust. 7,75,6; Cod. Iust. 8,46,9; Cod. Iust. 9,35,8; Cod. Iust. 8,6,1.

during Diocletian. The earlier instances he accounts for as interpolations.[43] The text of the edict was used by jurists as a source well into the reign of Justinian. According to de Francisi, however, from the Severan period onwards the edict was identified with imperial legislation.[44]

At the heart of the evaluation of these sources has been a debate over two questions: 1) did Julian compile the *edictum perpetuum* and 2) what was the *edictum perpetuum*? The currently prevailing view clearly supports the credibility of the sources on the first question. The second question is much harder to answer as it involves making a leap beyond the sources. The edict was stabilised and was the work of Julian, but what did it mean?

The discussion on the sources has, to a large extent, been dominated by a debate between Antonio Guarino and nearly all others, in which the indomitable neapolitan has stood his ground despite overwhelming odds. Guarino believes that the whole theme of the codification of the edict is based on a misunderstanding by Eutropius, which then spread to the works of later historians relying on him, and finally to Justinian. Guarino's theory is based on the assertion that the now lost common model of Eutropius and Aurelius Victor did not mention a codification. Aurelius Victor, who Guarino argues had a superior legal understanding and a loyalty to the original text, would have referred to Julian's commentary of the edict. As he did not mention any codification, it is fair to assume that there was none mentioned in the original text.[45]

These arguments have not persuaded the majority of scholars to abandon the idea of the *edictum perpetuum*, although the debate has added to our understanding of the textual tradition. Guarino's analysis has been criticised because his argument does not rest on the extant sources. Bund has sourly noted that the final editing of the edict is better proven than many things in the history of legal sources. Honoré conceded that if the historical accounts stood by themselves, they would not be convincing, but the quantity of evidence makes it improbable that the whole affair would have been a mere misunderstanding.[46] These positions may be said to reflect the majority opinion, despite the obstinacy with which Guarino has for half a century defended his argument.[47]

43 Pringsheim 1934b.
44 de Francisi 1950, 319–360.
45 Guarino 1951, 176–177; Guarino 1980, 86–89 of the Const. Tanta: 'insomma rappresentassero solo una fiorita variante bizantina della leggenda che si era andata formando e diffondendo nel mondo postclassico' (p. 89).
46 Bund 1976, 422–423; Honoré 1962, 47; Berger 1953; Serrao 1959, 404; Torrent 1983, 35–38; Serangeli 1997.
47 Serangeli 1997, 270–274.

The relationship between the sources is not clear, but the fact that Justinian often mentions the *edictum perpetuum* is a good indication that the matter was of great importance to him. Whether or not this can be said to prove that he had extensive knowledge of the actions of Hadrian and Julian is wholly another matter. Nevertheless, as Mantovani has demonstrated, Justinian clearly wanted to establish a line of descent between himself and Hadrian as codifiers, as well as between Julian and Tribonian as drafters, and between the two codes.[48]

Does the mass of evidence then contain irrefutable proof that the event did occur as we are led to believe? Can the lack of contemporary evidence convince us that all this is a Late Antique misunderstanding? The multiplicity and challenges of historical interpretation are a direct result of the state of the sources. There is a strong narrative tradition supporting the claim that Julian compiled the *edictum perpetuum*. However, the contemporary sources make no mention of it and we do not know what exactly it was or what it meant.

The ideals of legal positivism and the transformation of the Praetor's edict

The Roman sources on the *edictum perpetuum* are slightly patchy with regard to finding consistent proof for the claim that Julian, under orders from Hadrian, compiled the final form of the praetor's edict, which was then called the *edictum perpetuum*. In fact, to deduce this from the sources requires some interpretation. Individually, there are sources that maintain that there was an *edictum perpetuum* by Julian (Eutropius and Justinian), that the edict of the praetor was organised by Julian (Aurelius Victor and Justinian), and that there was an edict of Hadrian of some importance (Codex Theodosianus). However, the connection between these facts is a product of historical interpretation.

From the epigraphical material we learn that there was a Salvius Julianus, who received from Hadrian double pay for his service as a questor and later attained the consulship. In the literature in general it is mentioned that the jurist Julian was also a consul and sat at Hadrian's council. The use of the term *edictum perpetuum* does not support the theory that it would have been promulgated during Hadrian's reign.

---

48 Mantovani 1998, 136–139. The claim by Justinian that his compilation is a direct descendant of the *edictum perpetuum* was already discredited by Cornelius van Bynkershoek, in *Observationes Juris Romani I*, Leiden 1735, 207–211 [ch. 2.25].

What is then the final word on the Roman sources? The existing sources are generally in agreement that there was an edition of the praetor's edict and that this was made by Julian. The criticism presented about the existing sources being post-classical and the absence of contemporary sources[49] does not mean that the sources are exceptionally bad for that period. Honoré has explained that the lack of contemporary sources simply means that the event was not significant to contemporaries as it did not alter the contents of the edict, but, in contrast, to Justinian's compilers it was an interesting forerunner of their work.[50]

The journey of the *edictum perpetuum* through historical literature mirrors the general trends in jurisprudence. Through the sixteenth century the belief in the authority of Roman sources resulted in the neutral reporting of the sources without many attempts at source criticism or analysis,[51] and earlier historiography accepted the composition of the *edictum perpetuum* as a given fact. Authors like Diplovatatius, Du Rivail, Panziroli, Forster, and Hotman took their cue from Eutropius and St. Jerome; Julian composed the *edictum perpetuum* under orders from Hadrian.[52] The antiquarian nature of scholarship was reflected in the first attempts to reassemble the *edictum perpetuum* from the fragments in the Digest by Equinarius Baron (1495–1550) and Guillaume Ranchinius (1560–).[53]

How the collection and composition of the *edictum perpetuum* was done was generally not a matter of debate, only Rutilius described how Julian diligently compiled the edict and inserted his own additions to the text.[54] It may only be guessed whether the increasing interest in the *edictum perpetuum* can be attributed to the fact that new collections aimed at the centralisation of law were published all around Europe during the sixteenth century.[55]

---

49 Guarino 1980, 91–97 also pointed out that Hadrian's speech in the Senate has not survived, nor has any separate mention of the event, and that the edict does not seem especially well ordered.
50 Honoré 1962, 54.
51 Franz Wieacker, *Privatrechtsgeschichte der Neuzeit*, Göttingen 1952, 135.
52 Diplovatatius 1919 [1550], 254–257, 268–269, 306–307; Du Rivail 1551, 257 [ad Adriano Imp.]; Forster 1609, 501 [ch. 73]; Panziroli 1721, 46 [ch. 1.38]; Hotomannus 1587, 169 [Salvius].
53 Equinarius Baron, '*Ad omnes partes Digestorum seu Pandectarum iuris enucleati Manualium*', in *Opera*, Paris 1562; Guilelmius Ranchinius, *Edictum perpetuum Adrianeum*, Parma 1721, reprint of the 1597 first edition.
54 Rutilius 1537, 163–164 [Salvius].
55 Vincenzo Piano Mortari, 'L'idea di codificazione nel rinascimento', in L. De Giovanni, A. Mazzacane (eds.), La codificazione del diritto dall'antico al moderno, Napoli 1998, 325–336. The most important examples are the Spanish Nueva Recopilatión (1567) and the Habsburg *Constitutio criminalis*

The first to analyse the significance of the *edictum perpetuum* was Jean Bertrand (1527–1594), who hailed it as the prototype of the Digest. Bertrand envisioned the *edictum perpetuum* as a perfect legal text that combined the eternal wisdom of true philosophy with the combined learning of the jurists, made with such painstaking care that later emperors used it as a source for true and unbiased law. 'It drew upon not only unparalleled learning, but also philosophy true and pure as the light.' There is a marked emphasis on the contemporary legal theory which stated that in order to be valid, law had to be also right and just. He aspired to give the Edict more legitimacy by proposing that when in doubt, Julian would not have hesitated to consult other jurists.[56] The terms true philosophy and reason were catch-phrases of sixteenth century French jurisprudence, which strove to systematise law and make it a science.[57] There was also a noticeable shift within the sources during this period. The medieval favourites, like Eutropius and St. Jerome, are marginalised and Justinian was promoted as the main source.

During the seventeenth century literature began to reflect the ideals of rationalist natural law. The *edictum perpetuum* was idealised as the crowning of human wisdom and the common will of the jurists' profession. There was a marked emphasis on the contemporary theory which stated that in order to be valid, law also had to be right and just. The way to reach this correct law was though juristic reasoning.[58] Gerhard Feltmann described how the *edicti perpetui conditor* burned with an extraordinary passion for learning, and as Godefroy wrote in his manual, the *edictum perpetuum* represented the most impartial law.[59]

> *Carolina* (1532). Gaudemet 1988, 318–319 claimed that these too were examples of technical codification, meant to clarify and simplify the law.
> 56 Bertrand 1617, 2 [Salvius]: *Verum hoc ideo factum puto, quod Salvius Julianus perpetuum composuerit Edictum. Imperator autem Justinuanus ad Edicti perpetui imitationem totum Pandectarum opus confecit.* p. 5: *Ceterum in hac Edicti perpetui compilatione, si quid Julianus dubitatione, vel animaversione dignum inveniret, alios Jurisconsultor consulere non dubitavit.* p. 6: *Tanta autem ingenii sedulitate hoc Edicti perpetui opus confectum est, ut in posterum Impp. Romani uti eo, tanquam vero & aequissimo iure voluerint. ... A quo non solum ociofa illa doctrina, & in scholarum umbris delitescente institutus, & imbutus est; sed veram & puram, quae in solem, & lucem perducitur, Philosophiam hausit.*
> 57 Kelley 1990, 197–198.
> 58 Wieacker 1952, 148.
> 59 Henel 1654, 54 [Salvius]; Feltmannus 1678, 87 [ad Dig. 1,2,2,47]: *mira discendi cupiditate flagravit ... jussu Hadriani Imperatoris perfecit, & publica auctoritate anteriorum praetorum edicta in unum corpus conlegit ordinavitque congrua titulorum serie.* Gothofredus 1766, 25–26 [ch. 3]. Cf. also Egidius Menagius, *Juris civilis amoenitate*, (3rd ed.), Frankfurt & Leipzig 1680, 123–136 [ch. 24]; Grotius 1690, 142–144 [Salvius]. The Salvius-Didius confusion

Underlying the whole theory was the idea of progress, the conviction that the *edictum perpetuum* was the final, perfected version of earlier edicts, which in turn served as the prototype for the Digest. This corresponded with the view presented by Justinian, though the implications were different. Julian was elevated to one of the great organisers of law and attempts to reconstruct the organisation of the edict were made. Nothing, said van Giffen, was as beautiful and useful as order.[60]

Towards the early eighteenth century the idea of the *edictum perpetuum* as a reasoned restatement of the law was raised. The uncertainty and confusion caused by the ever changing yearly edicts was seen as the main reason for its compilation. Thomasius claimed that Hadrian attempted also to smooth the discord among jurists resulting from the division between the schools with the *edictum perpetuum*, but failed. Mascov wrote that the *edictum perpetuum* eradicated the authority of the jurists' opinions and completely changed the nature of the *ius civile*. Thomasius began to investigate the various dilemmas surrounding the *edictum perpetuum*, such as the influence of the previous revision of the edict by Ofilius and the various cases of mistaken identity, but accepted Julian's authorship without question.[61]

In the eighteenth century scholars led by Heineccius transformed the *edictum perpetuum* into a codification of law, which was made by a rational scholar with the help of a sovereign imperial power. While other authors had overlooked it as a minor detail in the life of Julian, Heineccius turned the compilation of the edict into a scholarly undertaking. He wrote how Julian, during his praetorship, perused the edicts of his predecessors collected in the Bibliotheca Ulpia and composed his edict based on their work, meticulously gathering the finest pieces. There was an order, but it was mostly pedagogical, not systematic, and this was illustrated in his preliminary sketch of its outline. Likewise, Antoine Terrasson portrayed Julian as an editor, organiser and mender, who solved questions others had not dealt with, finally producing a work that earned the title 'perpetual' because of his great authority. The result

---

still reigned, cf. Bertrand 1617, 7–8 [Salvius]; Feltmannus 1678, 87 [ad Dig. 1,2,2,47]; Grotius 1690, 142 [Salvius].

60 Jacobus Gothofredus, *Fontes quatuor iuris civilis in unum collecti*, Geneve 1653, 351; Giphanius 1612, 1–2, 118–165 suggested that the *edictum perpetuum* would have contained 100 books, since 100 is a round and perfect number (p. 118).

61 Mascovius 1728, 32, 109–110, 117–120; Bach 1762, 229, 249–251 [ch. 3.2.1.1; 3.2.4.1–6]; Gerard Noodt, 'Commentarius ad Digesta seu Pandectas', in *Opera omnia III*, Napoli 1786, 15 [ad Dig. 1,1]; Thomasius 1707, 81–85 [ch. 2.3.22]. In contrast, his contemporary Gravina 1704, 79–85, 141–143 [ch. 38, 86] was remarkably neutral about the whole institution.

was a code, which, under the auspices of the great Hadrian, perfected law and relegated factional strife to history. The finished work was enacted with an oratio in the Senate during Hadrian's quindecennalia and could be altered only with the order of the emperor. According to Heineccius, Hadrian emulated ancient Roman lawgivers like Numa Pompilius, while for Terrasson, Julian was the esteemed servant of the *prince legislateur* Hadrian, a patron of arts and sciences.[62]

Edward Gibbon, who followed closely Heineccius' opinion, understood the *edictum perpetuum* as the culmination of the codification process:

> It was reserved for the curiosity and learning of Hadrian to accomplish the design which had been conceived by the genius of Caesar; and the praetorship of Salvius Julian, an eminent lawyer, was immortalised by the composition of the PERPETUAL EDICT. This well-digested code was ratified by the emperor and the senate; the long divorce of law and equity was at length reconciled; and, instead of the Twelve Tables, the Perpetual Edict was fixed as the invariable standard of civil jurisprudence.[63]

Another contemporary theme reflected above by Heineccius, Terrasson, and Gibbon was the replacement of contested and contradictory sources of law by the harmonious and sovereign law of the ruler. All other sources of law are subordinated to the one emanating from the top of the pyramid of power.[64]

---

62   Johann Gottlieb Heineccius, 'Salvio Iuliano iurisconsultorum sua artate coryphaeo, seu exercitatio XXIV', in *Opera II*, Geneve 1746, 799; Heineccius 1751, 360–367 [ch. 267–273]. Johann Gottlieb Heineccius, 'Historia edictorum edictique perpetui', in *Opera XI*, Napoli 1777, 120–127 [ch. 2.1.1–7]. He evaluated and rejected the theory of an earlier *edictum perpetuum* by Ofilius due to the lack of sources, Heineccius 1777, 118–120 [ch. 2.1.8]. Heineccius' reconstruction: 'Edicti perpetui, ordini et integritati suae restituti', in *Opera XI*, Napoli 1777b, 195–340 was later copied and translated by Bouchaud. Even Terrasson 1750, 256–259 delves into the question of mistaken identity with Didius, this time against Grotius (p. 259). According to Mantovani 1998, 133–140, the interpretation of Heineccius is simply another reflection of the Justinianic representation. Since Gibbon wrote before any of the codifications of the Enlightenment, Mantovani asserts that the meaning of Gibbon's 'well-digested code' cannot be deduced from the modern concept, but rather reflects a synthetic use of the word. The two explanations are by no means exclusive, it could be said that they reflect two different stages of the interpretation: the reading of the sources and the formulation of a contemporary outlook.

63   Gibbon 1977 [1788], 384.

64   A similar mental change is observed by de Martino in the discussions in Naples in early nineteenth century when the Code Napoléon was to be implemented. Armando de Martino, 'Illuminismo e codificazione', in L. De Giovanni, A. Mazzacane (eds.), *La codificazione del diritto dall'antico al moderno*, Napoli 1998, 340–342.

The similarity of this historical image with the ideas behind Enlightenment natural law codes is striking. In both cases, rational and benevolent reasoning guides the sovereign power.[65] Just law was to be found by scientific inquiry motivated by reason.

This uncritical idealism and the echoes of rationalistic natural law were attacked by Gustav Hugo, who, in the spirit of historical inquiry, claimed that there was nothing perpetual in the edict and certainly nothing resembling a modern codification. He claimed that the existing tradition was a long-lasting distortion in the history of law intended to glorify the age of Hadrian. According to him, the facts all point to a misconception. There was no contemporary evidence for the *edictum perpetuum,* because the different edicts continued to exist in legal literature before, during, and after the purported codification, and the evidence for the *edictum perpetuum* is shaky. Even the words *edictum composuit* are according to Hugo merely a reference to a commentary written on the edict such as that by Ofilius. He admitted that the book of Julian might have gained a special position during the time of Hadrian, but denied vehemently that it was a codification or perpetual in the way that modern authors wished to portray it.[66]

Hugo managed to discredit the tradition of identifying the *edictum perpetuum* and the Digest, but his excessive anti-codificationalism made his contemporaries interpret his text as a commentary on the codification debate of the time.[67] The doubts Hugo expressed about the comprehensive nature of the *edictum perpetuum* as a codification were quite simply a manifestation of the fundamental doctrine of the Historical School. Thus, for Hugo, the jurists were the ones that were at the heart of legal development; not the organs of state. As the classical period was supposed to be the purest example of this model, a codification in the middle of it would have been disastrous for this theory.[68]

Hugo's attack did have some immediate effect,[69] but most scholars continued on the traditional paths. For example, M. Berriat-Saint-Prix praised

---

65 Wieacker 1952, 197–216; Gaudemet 1988, 322–323 called these political codes. The prototypes were the *Grandes ordonnances* of Colbert (1667–1681), among the natural law codes are usually named the Bavarian, Prussian, Austrian and Lombardian codes, and also the French *Code Civil.*
66 Hugo 1806, 328–336. In the seventh edition of the same work (1820) Hugo doubts that Julian should be compared with the men who drafted the Napoleonic, Prussian or Austrian codes (p. 571).
67 Of Hugo's influence, see Mantovani 1998, 142–144.
68 Of the development from Gibbon though Hugo and Savigny, see Stein 1999, 116–117.
69 See Mantovani 1998, 143.

indiscriminately both Julian for the codification, and Hadrian, the man of amazing virtues, talent, and shameful vices, for the wisdom of choosing Julian for the task.[70]

Puchta maintained that the *edictum perpetuum* was simply a regular edict with an irregular purpose, the transfer of power to the emperor. He gave Hugo credit for exposing the tendency of earlier literature to read too much in the way of extensive codification into the reform of Hadrian. However, he did not accept that all the sources could be the result of a misunderstanding, because few things are as well proven as the *edictum perpetuum*, the only thing that is contested is its interpretation. Puchta proposed that Julian had composed his edict as any praetor before him, as a collection of actions, interdicts and exceptions. What separated it from other edicts was its purpose, to transfer power from the praetor to the emperor and his council, which was manifested by the fact that all changes and supplements had to be made by the emperor.[71]

Puchta held on to jurists' law but only as one of the sources of law together with legislation. The emphasis of his theory had shifted to the system of law instead of its organic development, which meant that nothing crucially important turned on whether the already petrified edict was officially confirmed as perpetual.[72] It is also worth noting that Puchta was more rigorous in his examination of the Roman sources than the authors of previous centuries and would therefore have had more qualms about discrediting sources without sufficient consideration.

The edict was again labelled a codification by A. E. Rudorff, a pupil and a friend of Savigny. Rudorff made a systematic presentation of the order followed in the edict. According to him, the edict itself was not a scientific system but a practical codification of law. The edict was 'eine Reichsprozessordnung',[73] a true codification that permanently altered the way sources of law were seen. Regarding the systematic presentation of the order followed in the edict, Rudorff stressed that the inner order of the edict was not conceptual, but rather the different parts were arranged according to unscientific categorisations such as economic importance and chronology. However, his edition of the edict invoked a strict system. More importantly, he saw it as a turning point in the history of Roman law in that it changed the edict of the praetor into law, ending the division between *ius honorarium* and

---

70 M. Berriat-Saint-Prix, *Histoire de droit romain*, Paris 1821, 102–106.
71 Puchta 1875, 319–320.
72 Koschaker 1966, 260–261 claims that Puchta was not interested in developing the Savignian concept of Volksgeist.
73 A. F. Rudorff, 'Ueber die Julianische Edictsredaktion', ZRG 3 (1864), 88.

ius civile. Julian's code was ratified through Hadrian's speech in the Senate and became law, *lex*, making it valid everywhere in the Empire. The future of legal development was in the hands of the emperor.[74] Old edicts vanished into history, and Julian was the last person to change the edict: '... his revision of the edict was the final and last.' Despite the fact that there was now only one edict, the singular *edictum perpetuum*, the disputes among the schools continued.[75] Rudorff's theory of the *edictum perpetuum* as a codification and his explanations for the imperial quest for total legislative control gained acceptance immediately afterwards.[76]

Codification was one of the main trends in European law during the 19th century, beginning from the French Code Civil and its uses and influences outside France, the numerous other codification ventures in continental Europe (for example Italy 1865, Belgium, Luxembourg, The Netherlands 1838, Romania 1865), and finally the many German codification projects that began in earnest after 1848 and culminated in the common civil code (*Bürgerliches Gesetzbuch*, BGB 1900). The codification movement spread also outside Europe, to Japan (Meiji Civil Code of 1898) and South America, where the Chilean Código Civil (enacted in 1855) became the model. The colonies were not unaffected either, of which examples are the Civil Code in 1849 of the Dutch East Indies and the Anglo-Indian Codes beginning from the 1860s.

Only 14 years after Rudorff, Otto Lenel, who belonged to the next generation of the heirs of the Historical School, published his magisterial edition of the edict, which again made a sweeping change in its interpretation. Lenel heavily criticised the conception of the edict as a systematic codification. If it was a codification, Lenel asked, why did it omit so much and leave so many matters to a mere reference? He also rejected other labels and definitions that had been given to the edict, claiming that it would be foolish to try to force the edict under some or other modern definition. The content of the edict was what the praetor would need in his office, collected by Julian from the works

---

74   Rudorff 1864, 13: 'Die Fortbildung des Rechts blieb der kaiserlichen Staatsgewalt vorbehalten.'
75   Rudorff 1864, 11, 13, 24–26, 30, 88. The quote is from page 30: '... sein Edictabschluß ist der endgültige und letzte.' This idea of the edict is evident in his edition of the *edictum perpetuum*: A. F. Rudorff, *Edicti perpetui quae reliqua sunt*, Leipzig 1869. That the *edictum perpetuum* became statute law was accepted also by Bryan Walker, *The fragments of the Perpetual Edict of Salvius Julianus*, Cambridge 1877, 21.
76   D. Huschke, 'Ueber den Gregorianus und Hermogenianus Codex', ZRG 6 (1867), 324; Karlowa 1885, 628–629; Louis Jousserandot, *L'édit perpétuel*, Paris 1883, xxv–xxvi, xxx.

of previous praetors and as such more the result of historical coincidence than any systematic or scientific effort.[77]

Lenel's view of the unsystematic edict, as the regulation of the praetor's office, which did not entail the combination of *ius civile* and *ius honorarium*, penetrated the textbooks of the early twentieth century.[78] The research on the *edictum perpetuum* began to concentrate on the historical position of the institution in the Roman Empire building on Lenel's views. Despite this the claim that the edict was a systematic codification reflecting an orderly legal system lived on in the writings of Kipp and others.[79]

The development of the debate during the twentieth century was transformed by the discovery of the Pupput inscription in 1899. This invigorated historical research on Julian and boosted the importance of the *edictum perpetuum* in the history of Roman law. The mention of a double pay during his questorship was soon declared by Mommsen to be connected with the *edictum perpetuum*.[80] If we compare Buhl's 1886 biography of Julian to Boulard's biography dating from 1903, after the discovery, the prominence of the *edictum perpetuum* is remarkable. Where Buhl held the *Digesta* to be the culmination of Julian's life, Boulard saw it as *edictum perpetuum*. Boulard followed Lenel's view on the nature of the edict; it was a work of organisation, harmonisation and compilation, not a codification.[81]

Fritz Pringsheim and his students claimed that the codification of the edict could only be understood as a part of Hadrian's programme for the organisation of the imperial civil administration. The edict signalled the beginnings of bureaucracy, because its composition was the most important manifestation of the rationalising tendency brought about by the bureaucratisation of the Roman Empire. Through the reform, a homogenising imperial law thrust aside the unpredictable and uncertain *ius honorarium*. This was because the new bureaucratic model of administration was not compatible with the development of law through elastic formulations and the

---

77 Lenel 1956 [1927], 14–16.
78 Kipp 1909, 57–59; Krüger 1912, 93–101.
79 Kipp 1909, 57–58; d'Orgeval 1950, 41–42; Torrent 1983.
80 Mommsen 1902, 56.
81 Buhl 1886, 25–28; Boulard 1903, 10–11, 27, 38–68. Before the inscription was found the majority of scholars thought that Julian had done the compilation during his praetorship, but after the find, during the questorship. Boulard 1903, 44–47. Girard 1910, 9 collected the different opinions presented in the earlier literature about the date of the compilation. In the later discussions both options are presented, see Merlin 1941, 110–112; Serrao 1959, 409; Bund 1976, 426. Both of the later authors support the praetorship and the years 135–138.

repeated changing of the edict, and thus the praetor had to make way for the imperial council. The purpose of the reform and the *edictum perpetuum* was to provide law that was certain, rigid and predictable. In fact, Wieacker made the connection between this development and Weber's model of bureaucracy. It is curious, however, that both Pringsheim and Wieacker also see the bureaucratisation as the beginning of systematisation.[82] This would mean that the idea of systematisation lived on despite the positivism of Lenel, which had removed the significance that system had had in law.

Similarly, Fritz Schulz called the *edictum perpetuum* a codification in the style of the Principate, in which the Republican form remained, but the content was stereotyped and the praetor bound to the will of the emperor. Schulz maintained that this amounted to the closing of a chapter in the history of Roman jurisprudence.[83]

The consensus was broken by Antonio Guarino, who returned to the argument concerning the lack of sources, a theme first promoted by Hugo. He claimed that the identification of the Puput inscription with the jurist Julian is false and that the whole tradition that the double pay and remarkable learning were signs of Julian having compiled the edict as questor was wrong. Guarino's conclusion was that the whole tradition of *edictum perpetuum* was spurious, because no contemporary author mentions it, not a single contemporary or later jurist refers to it (not even Gaius or Pomponius), and the only source to support it is the untrustworthy Eutropius.[84]

Guarino later declared that the whole tradition surrounding the *edictum perpetuum* is merely a post-classical legend and there is no convincing evidence that the codification ever took place. He conceded that there are facts behind the legend, namely that the edict became petrified and formalised after Hadrian, and that Julian was a famous jurist, whose writings on the edict would have given him a place in history as the organiser of the edict. The references to a compilation he explained as belonging to a provincial edict.[85]

Guarino's claims provoked criticism from every quarter, which elicited some further discussion. Bernard d'Orgeval said that Guarino had completely misunderstood the political nature of the codification: it was in fact a *coup d'etat* by the emperor, not a simple legal procedure.[86] D'Orgeval's own

---

82 Pringsheim 1934, 144–149, 151; Wieacker 1935, 43–81; Honoré 1962, 46–55; Mantovani 1998, 150–153.
83 Schulz 1946, 127.
84 Guarino 1964, 370–379.
85 Guarino 1951, 169–174; Guarino 1953; Guarino 1980, 62–102.
86 d'Orgeval 1948, 301, 307–311. He also satirised some of Guarino's stranger claims, such as that *doctrina* never could have signified legal learning in as a young man as a questor, when he could have had philosophical and historical

biography of Hadrian combined Pringsheim's glorification of Hadrian with Lenel's view of the edict.[87]

The criticism Guarino has received is fairly uniform, it defends attributing the inscription with the jurist and the real existence of the *edictum perpetuum* in contrast to the view of it as a post-classical legend. Berger accused Guarino specifically of using arguments *ex silentio* and of unfounded mockery of post-classical sources. Bauman, who most recently has made a thorough analysis of the sources, maintained that while fourth century authors are notorious for their ability to get details wrong, they were not in the habit of inventing things.[88]

Pietro de Francisi's argument of the later use of the *edictum perpetuum* had a more profound impact. He demonstrated that, while the text of the edict remained in use as a reference, modifications of its contents ceased. Therefore, it may be safely assumed that at some point the edict was stabilised.[89]

Heinrich Vogt's oft-cited article on the dating of the edict with the help of Hadrianic coins is one of the more creative approaches to the *edictum perpetuum*. Vogt interpreted the emergence of coins with figures of Justitia as advertisements for the *edictum perpetuum*, but the insecure dating and small number of coins make this a very tentative conclusion.[90] Nörr gave some, although probably unintentional, support to Guarino's theory, by stating that the Puppet inscription's mention of double pay for outstanding learning could refer to some other feat by Julian. Nörr compared it to a reference in a papyrus to Hadrian having given double pay to an outstanding magician.[91]

Apart from Guarino, the two modern models of codification are still strongly present in the recent literature. The Lenelian view of a compilation with slight changes is presented by Bund and Zwalve, whereas Torrent supported the idea of a full-blown codification with major changes and reorganisations.

---

learning. Guarino 1964, 375; d'Orgeval 1948, 307. Kunkel 1950, 192–203 condemned Guarino's use of inscriptions.

87 d'Orgeval 1950, 40–48.
88 Even a select list of Guarino's critics is rather long: Serrao 1959, 397–398, 404–405; Berger 1953, 612–620; Honoré 1962, 46, 54–55; Barnes 1970, 45–51; Torrent 1971, 42–43; Bund 1976, 413, 419, 422; Torrent 1983, 19, 35; Bauman 1989, 252. Guarino has replied to his critics with numerous articles. Guarino 1959, 67–78 (to Serrao); Guarino 1966, 393–395 (to Bund); Guarino 1972, 421–426 (to Barnes).
89 de Francisi 1950, 320–322.
90 Vogt 1951, 193–200.
91 Nörr 1974, 243–245.

The compilation theory has remained virtually unchanged after Puchta, and it has secured a dominant position in the historical literature. Bund portrayed the event as a revision and stabilisation of the edict, when unused material was removed, some alterations were made, and some minor clauses were added. He claimed that the nature of the event might have been distorted and its significance increased by the lengthy period of time between the event and the first written accounts of it. Zwalve added that the compilation did not alter the nature of the edict as *ius honorarium* and the praetors continued to interpret the edict and change it through new clauses, which were accepted by the emperor. This is why lawyers make no mention of the edict, whereas they do comment on Julian's new clauses.[92] It should be noted that the use of terminology is no indication of the position an author has chosen. For instance Honoré, a supporter of this theory, spoke of codification as editing in a definite form.[93]

The systematic codification theory has had less success. In the specialised literature it has been supported only by Torrent, who combined Pringsheim's theory of Hadrian's grand plan of legal restructuring with the idea of a logical and systematic codification. The purpose of the *edictum perpetuum* was to sideline the praetors and to place complete control of the law in the hands of the emperor.[94]

The most recent references to the problem have mostly been arguments for or against these established positions. Sandro Serangeli advanced a new source, Dio 36,40,1, to prove that the compilation of the edict had happened. If the interpretation is accepted that Dio described historical change through situations before and after the *edictum perpetuum*, Dio would provide much needed near contemporary support for the compilation. Dio wrote his Roman history in 196–218 AD, which explains Serangeli's claim that Dio would have needed to enlighten his readers about the time when the edict was not fixed. In the Italian discussion Serangeli's interpretation has been viewed favourably, despite Guarino's disapproval.[95]

Dario Mantovani examined the use of the concept of codification in the discussions concerning the *edictum perpetuum* and found it less than consistent. Although often disproved, the concepts of 'codification' and 'to codify' have been regularly used to describe the *edictum perpetuum*. In more recent articles the word codification has been placed inside quotation marks to emphasise that the edict did not in any way resemble a modern codifica-

---

92   Bund 1976, 423–424; Zwalve 1983, 146–149.
93   Honoré 1994, 15.
94   Torrent 1983, 38–40, 43–44.
95   Serangeli 1997, 270–278; Serangeli 1989; Guarino 1990, Guarino 1994.

tion. Mantovani reflected how the process of making the *edictum perpetuum* is still called codification, although the end product is not, making it a codification without a code. The use of modern legal terminology is not in any way neutral, as it brings with it connotations of modern law.[96] Mantovani claimed that the interpretations have oscillated between two different models of codification, Justinian's model of the Digest and the modern idea of the codification of law.[97]

Though I basically agree with Mantovani on the reconstruction of the history of interpretations, except for the position of Heineccius, the division between a modern codification and a Justinianic compilation does not fully take into account the modern context of these themes. The different theories may also be analysed through the concept of legal positivism.

The theory of a systematic and scientific codification was first developed by Heineccius, then popularised by Gibbon, supported by Rudorff and some of his contemporaries, and later presented by Torrent. This theory also reflected a certain approach to legal positivism. The idea that law is expressed through the explicit statement of rules, as the codification of law, was first brought to the fore by Heineccius and his contemporaries in the form of Enlightenment codification. This was later resurrected by Rudorff as the modern codification. According to the theory of codification, the edict is changed into a unifying and centralising state law, which irons out local particularisms and enhances the idea of exclusive state control over law. As Mantovani writes, the model used by Rudorff was a projection of modern European state sovereignty and the codification of law into antiquity.[98] However, the way Rudorff examined the *edictum perpetuum* was through the conception of a codification in the spirit of the jurisprudence of concepts, an off-shoot of the Historical School, which emphasised the importance of a rational system of law. It was

> ... an equalising and centralising codification of the utmost significance. In the field of contentious civil law it should be undoubtedly seen as the peak and turning point of Roman legal culture.[99]

Rudorff was clearly obsessed with the systematisation or rather the lack of it and how it related to the writings of Roman jurists. Borrowing the traditional

---

96 Mantovani 1998, 129–131, 156.
97 Mantovani 1998; Mantovani 2000, 257–272.
98 Mantovani 1998, 146–148.
99 Rudorff 1864, 11: '... eine ausgleichende and centralisierende Codification von der nachhaltigsten Bedeutung. Man darf sie im Gebiet des streitigen bürgerlichen Rechts unbedenklich als den Gipfel und Wendepunkt römischer Rechtsbildung betrachten.'

division of legal positivism presented by Wieacker, Rudorff's framework was that of scientific legal positivism. Scientific or scholarly legal positivism was a view that 'a legal system is necessarily a closed system of institutions and rules',[100] a conceptual system coherent and free from gaps.[101] However, Rudorff did not claim that the *edictum perpetuum* itself was a modern systematic codification, but he did present it against the model of scientific legal positivism.

By juxtaposing the *edictum perpetuum* and the model of a systematic and comprehensive codification it was possible to see it in modern terms. The prerequisites of the modern codification, as described by Wieacker are sovereignty of power and the existence of a legal system. The sovereignty may be absolutist imperial power or the modern constitutional sovereignty of the state produced by a legal monopoly. The existence of a legal system requires the idea of an autonomous and universal justice and the actuality of a systematic legal science.[102] By emphasising the Roman precedent to a modern codification, Rudorff's interpretation essentially transformed the Romans into modern legal theorists.

The second theory, which described the edict as an unsystematic, uncomprehensive compilation not much removed from the previous edicts was formulated by Puchta and Lenel, and represents more or less the prevailing view as expressed by Bund. It was changed radically by Lenel, who gave it a legislative aspect. Should we again use Wieacker's definition, there is a shift apparent in Lenel's view of the edict, that from scientific legal positivism to the textual legal positivism of statutory law (*Gesetzespositivismus*).[103] Textual legal positivism understood law as solely the legal norms produced by the organs of state. This had important consequences for understanding Roman legal history, since it removed jurists' law from the sources of law. The task of the jurists was to interpret, not to create law. He criticised Rudorff's codification as a continuation of the systematising tendency, but despite the claims of Lenel, the main impetus of Rudorff's theory was not systematisation or a system, but the comprehensive codification of law.[104]

Lenel's legal positivism constituted the first break from the traditions of the Historical School. He saw elements like the law, state, and nation as historically given, rather than entities that needed to be metaphysically constituted. He made a clear distinction between his contemporary constitu-

100 Wieacker 1995, 343.
101 Wieacker 1952, 271–273; Wieacker 1995, 342–345.
102 Franz Wieacker, 'Aufstieg, Blüte und Krisis der Kodifikationsidee', in *Festschrift für Gustav Boehmer*, Bonn 1954, 35–36.
103 Wieacker 1995, 342.
104 Rudorff 1864, 88–89; Lenel 1956 [1927], 19–20.

tional state and ancient Rome, and his criticism of Rudorff was aimed at Rudorff's blurring of the boundary between ancient and modern phenomena and ideals. Lenel's handling of the edict, both in *Das edictum perpetuum* and the plethora of articles he published, was dogmatic in the true sense of the word. Thus, he proceeded from a thorough textual exegesis of the sources to the strict interpretation of the rules. For Lenel, the edict was a historical legal text made and validated by a Roman state authority and he set out quite simply to interpret the rules in that text. He consistently maintained that the Romans never held systematisation in the high regard his contemporaries did.[105] Lenel's description of the *edictum perpetuum* as a modest unsystematic compilation that was simply to serve the praetor in his office ended speculation that the edict was an early example of a modern codification.[106] After Lenel's critique, the *edictum perpetuum* was cited only rarely as the predecessor of the BGB.

The final theory, the complete refutation of the codification and the gradual petrification of the edict was the work of Hugo and is currently supported by Guarino.[107] It may also be analysed in the framework of legal positivism. The edict was transformed by Lenel into a simple authoritarian statement of law and further developed by Pringsheim and Wieacker into bureaucratic regulation. The antithesis of this kind of legal positivism is jurists' law, which was taken from its seventeenth century roots by the scholars of the Historical School and developed into a theory expounding the leading role of the jurists in developing the law. Hugo and Puchta thought that the jurists' law, not statutory law, was the main element in the development of Roman law. This viewpoint is continuously supported by scholars, whose way of thinking I have referred to as the patriotic narrative of the jurists.[108] Hugo and Guarino

---

105 Lenel 1956 [1927], 17: 'Bei dem Versuch, das System des Edikts zu ergründen, darf man niemals vergessen, daß die Römer und zumal der Ediktredaktor auf ein durchgeführtes System bei weitem nicht den Wert legten wie wir Modernen.' Okko Behrends, 'Otto Lenel', in O. Behrends, F. d'Ippolito (eds.), *Otto Lenel, Gesammelte Schriften I*, Napoli 1990, xix–xxxiii; Behrends 1991, 173.
106 Mantovani 1998, 150.
107 Guarino has himself upheld the image of himself as the sole opponent of the conservative codification theory, whereas both Bund and Torrent note that his view is not so much removed from the mainstream, both in his refusal to accept the concept of modern codification and the belief that some changes were made to the edict. Guarino 1980, 82; Bund 1976, 423; Torrent 1983, 40.
108 Letizia Vacca, 'La "svolta adrianea" e l'interpretazione analogica', in S. Romano (ed.), *Nozione formazione del diritto II (Mel. F. Gallo)*, Napoli 1997, 447 explained that the whole idea that the autonomy of the interpretation of jurists was reduced to a mere explanation of norms is totally contrary to the casuistic nature of the jurists' activities.

both supported the continuing influence of the jurists and argued that the development of law should remain in their hands.

Good indications regarding the positivistic tendency are the theories on how the *edictum perpetuum* influenced the schools of jurisprudence. Until Heineccius scholars were fairly unanimous that the compilation of the edict resolved the dispute between the schools and represented a victory for the Sabinians.[109] Raevardus wrote how the *edictum perpetuum* led to the decline of the schools, as later jurists from Papinian onwards did not mention their affiliation and cited the writings and opinions of both schools.[110]

By virtue of his role in the compilation, Julian was the last of the Sabinians,[111] the 'friends of monarchy' as described by Gibbon. It is worth noting that, though many of the disputes were solved, the schools remained, because Heineccius did not believe that all the disagreements were resolved by Julian's small book. The confrontation was less severe, but the existence of the sects continued.[112] Nevertheless, the basic idea is the same: the *edictum perpetuum* brought about certainty in the law, it laid down the law, and hence disputes over the content of the law ceased.

The authors linked to the Historical School form a stark contrast to this view. Hugo is sceptical about the existence of the schools, calling them mere instructional tools for understanding the history of legal literature. He rejected altogether the claim that Hadrian's edition of the edict caused some profound change, as there were still so many controversies after Hadrian.[113] Puchta's account of the demise of the schools cited internal development and general aimlessness as the reasons for their gradual decline. There is not a single remark of any sudden turn, let alone any reference to the influence of the *edictum perpetuum*. The previous authors that have so implied were quite simply wrong.[114]

However, the legal positivistic argument concerning the demise of the schools returned, but in a different shape. The new form is outlined by Karlowa, who explained that the internationalisation or 'unnationalisation' (Entnationalisierung) of law during the Principate, especially by Hadrian, made the controversies redundant. The importance of the matter was declining. For instance, authors like Krüger make no mention of it.[115] The con-

---

109 Giphanius 1612, 121; Gothofredus 1766, 28 [ch. 4].
110 Raevardus 1779, 148–149.
111 Thomasius 1707, 81–85 [ch. 2.3.22]; Mascovius 1728, 109–110, 117–120.
112 Gibbon 1977 [1788], 394; Heineccius 1777, 127–128 [ch. 2.2.8.], 132–135 [ch. 2.2.11–14].
113 Hugo 1806, 347–348, 361.
114 Puchta 1875, 265–266.
115 Karlowa 1885, 666; Krüger 1912, 163.

nection between the increasing imperial authority and the decline of the schools was conceded even by the staunchest defender of juristic authority, Schulz, who maintained that Julian's authority laid to rest most of the controversies. For Schulz, 'the leadership of legal thought' in the future rested on the great lawyers of the imperial *consilium*.[116] Despite this, he was still reluctant to say that the imperial authority of the state became dominant.

The analysis of different theories of codification from the viewpoint of legal positivism reveals the fundamental change in the modern context of the interpretations of the *edictum perpetuum*. It also illuminates how Hadrianic Rome was made a setting for modern debates.

Hadrian and the phantom modernity of Rome

The narrative themes that appear in the discussions on Julian, Hadrian, and the *edictum perpetuum* figure prominently in the conceptual framework of modernity. The sovereign statement of law as a codification or a compilation is a theme appealing to the adherents of legal positivism; the centralisation of power through the building of a permanent imperial machinery of government is familiar to those acquainted with the workings of bureaucracy. The picture would not be complete without the third narrative element, the narrative of the Golden Age of Hadrian.

The idealisation of the reign of Hadrian has been a theme much used by ancient historians and legal historians alike. There has been a constant stream of glorifying biographies of Hadrian, which speak of the virtues of his administrative reforms. Hadrian himself is placed on the pedestal, not only as an ideal character, but also as a modern ideal.[117]

> He was a man of great versatility and achievement: soldier, statesman and humanist, a political innovator whose views more than any other Roman emperor find a response in our own contemporary ideals.[118]

In the narrative sense, Emperor Hadrian has been generally portrayed as a positive character. The theme of the enlightened sovereign gained unprece-

---

116 Schulz 1946, 122. In a similar vein, Bauman 1989, 315 wrote that the demise of the schools was both cause and effect of the imperial *consilium*.
117 The archetype of Hadrian biographies is Gregorovius, *Geschichte des römischen Kaisers Hadrian und seiner Zeit*, Königsberg 1851. B. W. Henderson, *The Life and Principate of the Emperor Hadrian*, London 1923, 3–4, 201 compares Julian to Lord Mansfield and the Viceroy of India; Anthony R. Birley, *Hadrian: The restless emperor*, London and New York 1997.
118 S. Perowne, *Hadrian*, London 1960, 15.

dented popularity during the imperial revival of the early nineteenth century. This elevated Hadrian as an example of an ideal monarch who was civilised and well versed in Greek culture. The new theme of the Golden Age had entered into the literary conscience when Gibbon had described the age of the Antonines as the happiest and most prosperous in the history of mankind.[119] For the portrayal of the Golden Age ancient precedents and literary texts were skilfully used. There was an ample supply of precedents, since the theme of the Golden Age emerged in ancient literature as early as Hesiod and has been a recurrent theme ever since. The idea of the Rome of the Antonines as the Golden Age was presented in 143/144 AD by the Greek rhetorician Aelius Aristides in a speech to Rome. According to Schiavone, Aristides praised Rome as being 'in a state of grace: an era in which the high-minded rule of order and reason, instituted by the demiurgic action of the Romans, was able to develop to its highest potential, bestowing civilization and opulence'.[120]

The considerable influence of Hadrian on the law has regularly been connected to Julian, who was thought to have carried out Hadrian's plans. Julian has been linked to two inter-dependent processes. First, to the diminishing significance of the praetor, and, second, to the rising influence of the emperor on the law. With regard to the first process, Julian and the *edictum perpetuum* symbolise the final professionalisation of law. Before that the praetor, advised by the jurists, gave edicts, which were interpreted by jurists. After that the emperor, advised by the jurists, gave constitutions, which were interpreted by the jurists. The one to fulfil this change and to end the praetorian power, Julian, was naturally a jurist.[121]

With regard to the second process, Julian is generally believed to have been instrumental in the process of transferring legal power to the emperor because of his position in the imperial administration and his role in the making of the *edictum perpetuum*. The fact that Hadrian's reforms were largely responsible for the destruction of the Republican way of jurisprudence has been seen as a negative development by the supporters of juristic freedom. The legal ideology of Julian would be fitting for this new system, as Scarano Ussani maintained that Julian identified the state with the emperor. Julian wrote that the matters jurisprudence cannot resolve should be dealt with by imperial legislation. Legal certainty could be achieved by the co-operation of jurisprudence and imperial actions; Julian is demonstratably norm-oriented, but, as Seidl has

---

119   Edward Gibbon, *The Decline and Fall of the Roman Empire I*, London 1980 [1788], 78.
120   Aristeid. *oratio* 26,90–109; Aldo Schiavone, *The End of the Past: Ancient Rome and the Modern West*, Harvard 2002, 7.
121   Cf. J. M. Kelly, *Roman Litigation*, Oxford 1966, 88–95; Johnston 1999, 4.

noted, there has been a tendency to modernise Julian in the earlier literature.[122]

The appearance of themes familiar from a modern context such as codification, legal positivism, centralisation, and bureaucratisation tempted scholars into making their historical reconstructions unconsciously similar to their contemporary circumstances. They followed a well-established practice. Earlier scholarship on Roman legal history had long tended to project their contemporary themes onto the Antonine age. The early romantic writers of the late eighteenth century saw Hadrian as the reformer who restored the dignity of jurisprudence through his union of imperial power with scholarly lawmaking. When the powers of the republican institutions were left largely unused, the legal authority of the jurists in the imperial council grew. Similarly, for the Historical School the common conviction of the lawyers as presented in the *edictum perpetuum* was a true reflection of Roman *Volksgeist*.[123]

As Aldo Schiavone described it, modernisation of Hadrian's Rome can be called 'the phantom of modernity'. Schiavone called the phantom of modernity the image of a possibility lost. Scholars who had observed the industrial revolution and the advent of the modern world, from Gibbon to Rostovtzeff, were intrigued by the dilemma of why a highly developed ancient civilisation was destroyed, and the world plunged into the dark ages, instead of continuing to develop into a modern civilisation?[124]

> But now we can see that the "modernity" attributed to the ancients was also the expression of something different from error. The image contained the remnants, eroded but still perceptible, of what the opportunity for a precocious but suddenly botched evolution had imprinted on the environment in which it had taken shape. ... The phantom of modernity was discernible, not its substance – but it still counted for something, because every new possibility that history presents, no matter how fragile or fleeting, transforms history as a whole in some way. It was the glow of a disembodied one-dimensional form suspended in the void – an incandescent meteor speeding through cold space.[125]

---

122 For instance the Dig. 1,3,11 mentioned before. Erwin Seidl, 'Wege zu Julian', in W. Becker (ed.), *Sein und Werden im Recht: Festgabe für Ulrich von Lübtow zum 70. Geburtstag*, Berlin 1970, 215–222; Vincenzo Scarano Ussani, *L'utilità e la certezza. Compiti e modelli del sapere giuridico in Salvio Giuliano*, Milano 1987, 82–87.
123 According to Whitman 1990, 84–90, 128 the idealisation of Hadrian can be traced back to a remark of Heineccius utilised and diffused by Gibbon; Giaro, 'Römisches Recht, Romanistik und Rechtsraum Europa', *Ius commune* 22 (1995), 13.
124 Schiavone 2002, 24–29, 202–203.
125 Schiavone 2002, 202–203.

Scholars of the late nineteenth and early twentieth centuries repeatedly translated their passion for the classical world into modernising it in their works. For example, M.I. Finley wrote that Eduard Meyer wanted to rid the study of antiquity of romantic idealisation and antiquarianism by reconstructing the 'real picture', which turned out to be a virtual mirror-image of the modern world.[126] The theme of a phantom modernity was supported greatly by the practice of projecting contemporary themes into history. One of the most obvious projections was the identification of a modern codification with the *edictum perpetuum*.

The bureaucratic model has echoed throughout the discussion on Hadrian's centralisation of law. In the current literature there is a marked consensus regarding the fact that Hadrian wanted to take control over the whole field of law. The legal reforms were simply a culmination of the centralisation policy initiated by Augustus. This aimed at placing the emperor at the heart of the legal system. There is also agreement that the stripping of the praetors of their powers and the subordination of lawyers as the emperor's servants was achieved without resistance.[127]

The bureaucratic model continued the themes of the idealising narrative employed in the literature on the *edictum perpetuum*. This model was rejected by scholars emphasising the importance and vitality of jurists' law, but most attempted to combine the two. It was recognised that the reign of Hadrian marked a profound change in the history of Roman law. Under Hadrian's rule the emperor began to create law in earnest for the first time.[128] Mascov's reconstruction is a good example of how the two models were combined to the benefit of both the emperor and the jurists. Mascov saw in Hadrian an enlightened sovereign, who was both wise and learned, and whose abilities were matched by his insatiable curiosity in new learning. Hadrian's reforms completely transformed the old *ius civile* by abolishing the *ius respondendi* and removing the praetorian element in legal change. This put an end to the schools of jurisprudence and returned the jurists to the ways of the Republic, where every lawyer would act according to his learning. In the future, jurists would have a major influence on the law as members of the imperial *consilium*. However, the authority of the emperor would be so strong that the lawyers would occasionally submit their differences to the emperor to

---

126 Moses I. Finley, *Ancient Slavery and Modern Ideology*, New York 1980, 44–45.
127 Pringsheim 1934, 148–150; Honoré 1962, 54; Guarino 1980, 96; Torrent 1983, 34–35, 38–39, 43–44.
128 Gothofredus 1766, 28 [ch. 4].

solve. It was clear that the emperor was the lawmaker to whom the jurists were subordinate.[129]

Heineccius was more appreciative of the jurists' authority. He wrote that the roles of the emperor and jurists supplemented each other. As Julian could not have made his edition without Hadrian, neither could Hadrian have sat in judgement without the jurists counselling him. The *edictum perpetuum* was, therefore, a crowning moment of this fusion of imperial power and juristic authority.[130]

Unlimited power made many uneasy about how beneficial sovereign rule really was. Whether Hadrian is seen as an ideal autocrat, an enlightened despot, or simply a despot, depends on the reader. Nörr created an intriguing and humorous vision of Hadrian in the role of an oriental sultan, who on a theatrical whim grants Julian twice the pay because of his great learning.[131] Even Torrent suspected that the real purpose of the learned, Hellenistic, and centralising Hadrian was to diminish the freedom of jurisprudence.[132]

These objections have done little to curb the enthusiasm with which the reforms of Hadrian have been interpreted as the advent of the bureaucratic model of government. The weberian concept of bureaucracy, which was imported into Roman legal history by Pringsheim and Wieacker, took root quickly and became the dominant model of describing Late Antiquity.[133]

Pringsheim described how Hadrian wanted to create a new epoch of peace, prosperity, and culture. It was for that purpose that he wished to stabilise the Empire with a new administration based on a regular civil bureaucracy. The most important of his reforms was the *edictum perpetuum*, which, in addition to the imperial council and the *ius respondendi*, laid the basis for a professional administration for a new Golden Age.[134] D'Ors stated that, through his reforms, Hadrian united, developed, and harmonised law, strengthened the position of provincials and the bond between the provinces and Rome proper. He remodelled administrative structures according to Hellenistic principles, which was as much a revolution as the reforms of Augustus had been. The reorganisation of the imperial government, the granting of jurisdiction to the prefect of the city, the formation of the imperial *consilium*, the legislation of the Senate and the codification of the praetor's edict all com-

129 Mascovius 1728, 113, 117–120.
130 Heineccius 1777, 128–130 [ch. 2.2.9].
131 Nörr 1974, 245.
132 Torrent 1983, 43.
133 Mantovani 1998, 154–155 questioned whether this bureaucratic tendency is something that can be observed in the sources, or merely another distortion.
134 Pringsheim 1934, 141–148: 'His aim was to maintain eternal peace in his eternal and world-wide Empire, and to secure the happiness of his people by the wisdom of their omnipresent ruler.' (p. 141).

bined to create a new law and new legal authority, which was instrumental in the transformation of jurisprudence. To maintain the illusion of free jurisprudence, Hadrian abolished the *ius respondendi*, but that had little practical meaning, since all jurists of authority were now members of the *consilium*.[135] In short, d'Ors saw the reforms of Hadrian as similar to the creation of an integrated state.

Honoré's interpretation of the beginnings of the system of imperial rescripts has a similar tone. According to him, Hadrian apparently wanted to improve the Roman judicial administration by reinforcing both imperial control and the standing of lawyers. The administration was generally professionalised and extended. Hadrian offered lawyers new career prospects, which culminated in the inclusion of lawyers in the *consilium*. To Honorè, the *ius respondendi* was aimed at restricting the freedom of lay judges from deviating from the opinions of the jurists. However, the greatest of Hadrian's reforms was the activation of the system of rescripts. He began to systematically answer petitions from private persons, which explains why, during Hadrian's reign, five times as many written replies have survived as from all the previous emperors. Hadrian's aim was clearly to make the statements to have wide-ranging implications. This was achieved through the combination of imperial authority and the ability of the jurists who handled the petitions. Hadrian widened the scope of imperial jurisdiction to encompass the creation of new law. Consequently, the *responsa* of the jurists were gradually superseded by the imperial rescripts. The rescript system began to function as a kind of imperial legal aid, which gave lower classes and provincials a new way of access to justice.[136] The image one easily gets from the portrayal of these reforms is that of modernity. The possibility of an appeal and the existence of legal remedies against the state bring to mind connotations of the modern ideal of the rule of law.

The image of a growing state machinery that would dominate Late Antiquity and its Hadrianic roots was adopted by Jill Harries, who depicted Hadrian as the first Late Antique law-giver. Hadrian was the initiator of the imperialisation of law, which manifested itself in the *edictum perpetuum* and the imperial constitutions.[137] Palazzolo has similarly described the reforms of Hadrian as a true revolution, in which the structure of the Roman state was reorganised to ensure the imperial hegemony. It is no coincidence that the first imperial constitutions in the codes are from Hadrian.[138] The gradual advent

---

135   d'Ors 1965, 147–158.
136   Honoré 1994, 12–16, 28, 33.
137   Jill Harries, *Law and Empire in Late Antiquity*, Cambridge 1999, 14–17.
138   Palazzolo 1996, 290–291, 304, 321.

of imperial sovereignty in law-making is currently accepted to be the prevailing opinion.[139]

This idealisation of the imperial power and the possibilities it offered lawyers was however deplored by many who saw the authority of the jurists and their freedom as the true vehicle of legal development. Schulz saw in the rise of imperial power the demise of juristic freedom. He named the time between Diocletian and Justinian as the bureaucratic period, explaining how the bureaucratic elements entered into Roman jurisprudence gradually beginning from the Augustan era. For Schulz, it was a sign of intellectual fatigue, because while the jurisprudence of the Republic and the Principate had rejected petrifying the law with immutable statutes, the codification of the edict was the first sign of stabilisation. Statute law, or positive law, would substitute jurists' law.[140] Guarino described the whole of the Principate as an era of continuing incapacitation of Republican legal organs. Parallel to this was the growth in new methods of social discipline used by the imperial bureaucracy. Even Guarino accepted that the edict was not immune to the growing uniformity of law.[141]

However, these events have been given also opposite interpretations. For instance, Vacca claimed that it would have been manifestly impossible that statutes would have become the primary source of law. At best, the emperors could give the jurists new authority and make them the official interpreters of the law. This is not to say that the jurists would have ignored imperial norms, but rather to underline that the interpretation of the jurist was primary.[142]

In the debate over the bureaucracy there is a marked emphasis on the importance of the jurists, of which Vacca's opinion is only the most blatant example. Only Nörr seems to suggest that, even though Hadrian is often portrayed as the prototype of the legal emperor, no direct conclusions can be drawn from that. Things may have been more human and erratic than our presentations of legal history suggest. Maybe even the status of the jurists' profession was not as high as we like to believe.[143]

Still, the dominant model seems to be of the bureaucratic lawyer. It may be interpreted as a manifestation of the patriotic narrative of jurisprudence adapted to a situation dominated by imperial power. Within this schema,

---

139 Cf. Casavola 1998, 309–310.
140 Schulz 1946, 263–264, 286.
141 Guarino 1980, 62, 81.
142 Vacca 1997, 447–448, 450, 456–457 claimed that the order in Julian's Dig. 1,3,11 proves that juristic interpretation is more important than imperial constitutions.
143 Nörr 1974, 245: 'Vielleicht war auch die "Würde" des Juristenstandes dieser Epoche gar nicht so hoch, wie wir es uns glauben machen wollen.'

the role of the emperor and the imperial government is to provide legal certainty and continuity, while the jurists are eager assistants helping the state to formulate and interpret legal rules.

* * *

The transformation of the Hadrianic Empire as a phantom modernity represents a new phase in how the ancients were seen. When combined with modern legal positivism, the role of Roman law and Roman jurists was transformed into something that could be described as a classical model. The direct applicability of their opinions and rules was for the most part abolished by legislation. Whitman described the situation at the beginning of the latter half of the nineteenth century with the words: 'In the end, of course, there *was* no future of Roman law.'[144] That was not to be exactly true, because the future of Roman law was in its classicism. This was evident already in Mommsen's 1852 speech on the meaning of Roman law in legal education, where he stressed how rich, well-reasoned, and universal it was. These were the main reasons why Roman legal history was necessary for a legal education, not its practical utility: 'Alle Wissenschaft ist Luxus wie alle Kunst.' (All science is luxury like all art.)[145]

The change in the role of Roman law is visible in the writings of Max Weber, whose image of modern law was strongly influenced by the Romanistic tradition. Weber's ideal type of rational modern law was fashioned in part after the Pandectistic idea of rational and pure Roman law. Roman law and Roman jurists were no longer practical examples but historical ideal types.[146] Gerhard Dilcher wrote that Weber marked both the endpoint of the Historical School and the beginning of its new influence.[147] As for Jhering, for Weber, the value of Roman law was its rationality.[148]

Classicism was one of the most permanent of the ideals of Roman law. Yan Thomas has noted that, from Savigny to Kaser, Romanists have defined Roman jurisprudence as classical. The criteria have changed during two centuries, but the judgement of dogmatic value and aesthetic appeal has remained

---

144 Whitman 1990, 228.
145 Theodor Mommsen, 'Die Bedeutung des römischen Rechts', in *Gesammelte Schriften III: Juristische Schriften III*, Berlin 1907, 591–600, quote from p. 598.
146 Max Weber, *Economy and Society, an outline of interpretative sociology II*, Berkeley 1978, 792–798; Kaius Tuori, 'Weber and the Ideal of Roman law', *Current Legal Issues* 6 (2003), 201–214.
147 Gerhard Dilcher, 'Von der Geschichtlichen Rechtswissenschaft zur Geschichte des Rechts', in P. Caroni, G. Dilcher (eds.), *Norm und Tradition*, Köln 1998, 125–128.
148 Weber 1978, 657–658, 798; Whitman 1990, 232.

the same.¹⁴⁹ The decline of the practical example of Roman law is evident when we consider that the Pandectists of the late nineteenth century did not use the term 'classic' to refer to Roman jurists, but to their near contemporaries. For later Romanists like Kaser, however, the Romans were again classics signifying a normative ideal with an overhistorical (*überhistorische*) value.¹⁵⁰ The classics were the free Roman jurists and their unparalleled practical genius of rational legal thinking:

> The Roman private law achieved its timeless greatness first under the 'classical' jurists of the first two and a half centuries of our chronology.¹⁵¹

In Kaser's paradigm, the value of classical Roman law was its inherent goodness and the wisdom of the jurists' reasoning. This inherent worth was independent of the later reception of Roman law, let alone its compatibility with some scientific system, modern or Greek.¹⁵²

The aesthetic ideal of classical Roman law was formed in earnest at the same time as its practical use was disappearing. Mario Bretone described how in just a few years during the late 1880s and early 1890s the significance of classical Roman law was altered. During that short period of time a plethora of important works on Roman legal history were published, among others Lenel's *Palingenesia*, Krüger's *Geschichte der Quellen*, Jörs's *Römische Rechtswissenschaft*, Gradenwitz's *Interpolationen*, Mommsen's final parts of *Staatsrecht*, and Mitteis's *Reichsrecht und Volksrecht*. In, and through, these works the whole concept of Roman law was changed as historical accuracy became the new ideal. Philology was the favourite tool of historically oriented Romanists. The knowledge of ancient Roman law multiplied and Roman legal history became a part of ancient culture. This process of the expansion of the past produced results of immense richness.¹⁵³

During these scholarly advances, the aesthetic ideal of Roman law was manifest in the belief that our sources of Roman law, which are mostly Late Antique, were corrupted by the ignorant Byzantine jurists, who simplified the

---

149 Yan Thomas, 'La romanistique allemande et l'état depuis les pandectistes', in H. Bruhns et al. (eds.), *Die späte römische Republik*, Paris 1997, 121; Wolf 1951, 472: [of Savigny] '… auch sein Kunstideal war ein klassisch-formales …'
150 Tomasz Giaro, 'Max Kaser', *Rechtshistorisches Journal* 16 (1997), 282–293. On classicism in Roman law, Helmut Coing, 'Klassizismus in der Geschichte des römischen Rechts', in G. E. von Grunebaum, W. Hartner, *Klassizismus und Kulturverfall*, Frankfurt am Main 1960, 69–74.
151 Kaser 1955, 2: 'Das römische Privatrecht hat seine zeitlose Größe erst unter den "klassischen" Juristen der ersten zweieinhalb Jahrhunderte unserer Zeitrechnung erreicht.'
152 Kaser 1955, 1–4.
153 Bretone 2004, 219–225.

elaborate constructions and added needless modifications. The task of Roman law scholars was essentially to remove these later layers. The interpolation critique which took up this task was most influential in the first half of the twentieth century. Both the interpolation critique and the disdain of Late Antiquity were attempts to rescue the *Vorbildlichkeit* of Roman law from the unco-operative historical details. It should be noted that it was the unexpected results of historical research that provoked the need for cleaning the classical heritage in the first place. As the hunt for interpolations later collapsed, due to the impossibility of the task, historians of Roman law have been wondering whether there is a way of constructing an operating model for classical Roman law that is not wholly based on conjecture or adaptation from later schemes. Frier has doubted the possibility of such a model, as we have little to base our views of the jurists other than the excerpts found in the Digest.[154]

The future of Roman legal history was strongly influenced by two separate developments, the simultaneous rise of modern positive law and scientific historiography. Franz Wieacker has famously claimed that it was only through the division of the Historical School in legal history and legal positivism that the first true legal history in the history of legal science could be written.[155] The attempts at combining these two approaches in the spirit of jurists' law failed, because modern law was as hostile to jurists' law as scientific historiography was to the use of history for normative purposes. This led to a rift in the Romanistic scholarship because historical accuracy was incompatible with normative legitimation in the long run.

The finest example of the use of the classicism of Roman law were the lectures given by Schulz in Berlin, in which the magnificence and glory of Roman law were extolled as pure and isolated examples. It is now difficult to appreciate how radical Schulz's lectures at the University of Berlin in 1933 were in their anti-nazism, and in their praises of the Roman virtues of *humanitas, libertas* and *fides*. Due to the reduction of Roman law in the law school curricula and the advent of the anti-Romanist Third Reich, Schulz wrote most of his works at the time of a great crisis of Roman law. The BGB had liberated Roman law from the bounds of applied law, but it also meant that the emphasis in legal education irreversibly moved towards the new

---

[154] Bruce W. Frier, 'Why Did the Jurists Change Roman Law? Bees and Lawyers revisited', *Index* 22 (1994), 135, 144–145; Hoetink 1955, 9. Interpolation critique did not come to a sudden end but rather petered out slowly, with signs of it periodically reappearing. Cf. J. H. A. Lokin, 'The End of an Epoch: Epilegomena to a century of interpolation criticism', in R. Feenstra et al. (eds.), *Collatio Iuris Romani: Études dédiées à Hans Ankum I*, Amsterdam 1995, 261–263.
[155] Wieacker 1988, 46–48.

codification.[156] The repeated attacks on Roman law that are manifest, for example, in the works of Spengler gained new momentum as the NSDAP adopted the eradication of Roman law as part of its party programme.[157] To leftist and Jewish scholars like Schulz and Pringsheim, the latter also meant physical danger and escape to Britain. It is no wonder that their works demonstrate a narrative of Roman law as impartial and equitable.

Schulz's contemporaries wished to germanify Roman jurists in an attempt at relevance and continuity, because the NSDAP took over many of the arguments of the Germanists in their attack on Roman law.[158] To Wieacker, who aspired to but never reached NSDAP membership, the crisis of Roman law was nothing more than a side effect of the final historification of Roman law, more welcomed than feared.[159] Other contemporaries tried to adapt to new circumstances both before and after the Second World War by trying to reinvent Roman legal history so as to continue its relevance. Without even mentioning the most extreme examples, it is perhaps telling to observe how a relative moderate like Max Kaser wished to prove the national socialist credentials of Romans and Roman law by portraying them according to the language and ideals of the age.[160]

* * *

156 Wolfgang Ernst, 'Fritz Schulz', in J. Beatson, R. Zimmermann (eds.), *Jurists Uprooted*, Oxford 2004, 105-104, 124-125; Arnaldo Momigliano, 'The consequences of new trends in the history of ancient law', in *Studies in Historiography*, London 1966b, 250-251: 'Fritz Schulz, with whom I was lucky enough to become friends in the years we shared at Oxford, would lose his habitual mildness if one quoted to him the *Summum ius summa injuria* of J. Stroux. The idea that ancient rhetoric could have contaminated the purity of juristic thought made him physically ill.'
157 Cf. Richard Gamauf, 'Die Kritik am Römischen Recht im 19. und 20. Jahrhundert', *Orbis Iuris Romani* 2 (1996), 48-60.
158 Bender 1979, 107.
159 Elmar Bund, 'Fritz Pringsheim', in H. Heinrichs et al. (eds.), *Deutsche Juristen jüdischer Herkunft*, München 1993, 733-740; Joseph G. Wolf, 'Die Gedenkrede', in J. Wolf (ed.), *In memoriam Franz Wieacker*, Göttingen 1995, 23, 37; Rolf Kohlhepp, 'Franz Wieacker und die NS-Zeit', ZRG 122 (2005), 210, 223: 'Seine Anpassung an das Naziregime und seine Beteiligung an der Rechtserneuerung sind nicht zu rechtfertigen'.
160 Max Kaser, *Römisches Recht als Gemeinschaftsordnung*, Tübingen 1939, 8-9: 'Das stolze Bild, das Schönbauer hier von echtem Römertum entworfen hat, erinnert in manchen Zügen stark an die ältere deutsche Rechtsgeschichte, sind es doch die gleichen Tugenden, "männliche Selbstzucht, nationaler Instinkt, starkes Sendungsbewußtsein, Größe im Unglück und Opferbereitschaft für das Gemeinwesen", die den Character beider Völker bestimmen.' There are also notable references to Nazi scholars like Carl Schmitt (p. 4).

Salvatore Settis, in his famous essay *Futuro del 'classico'*, described how nearly every generation of European thinkers have formulated their own idea of the classics. He claimed that the concept of classic is not simply a figment of the past but presents also a vision of the future.[161]

It is no coincidence that with the rise of modern law and the decline of the practical applications of Roman law, ancient Roman law was reinvented as classical. The juxtaposition of classic ancient and modern is as old as the scholastic debate between the *modernus* Occam and the *antiquus* Aristotle. In terms of language purity, authors like Lorenzo Valla (1407–1457) lauded the classical purity of the *antiqui* and derided the medieval *moderni*.[162] Of the many definitions of classics[163] advanced by Settis, Roman law has been given both the aesthetic argument of purity and beauty, and the continuity argument of tradition and Europe.

According to Gadamer, the concept of classic was originally meant to be a simple description of style without overhistorical value. However, the very concept had an implicit normative element that made it immune to all historical criticism by raising it beyond and above it. It was the conviction of a timeless idea of progress, which every neohumanistic movement claimed as their ideal. This very notion of it as timeless and unreachable is its mode of historical being.[164] This was the role of classical Roman law from the late nineteenth century onwards.

The old idea of classical Roman law as the practical and reusable roots of modern law in the form advocated by the Historical School of jurisprudence and Pandectism were mostly a German phenomenon. The lack of alternative methods of legal development that enabled jurists' law and Roman law to gain such prestige was possible only in a situation such as that found in Germany in the early nineteenth century. Elsewhere, the use of Roman law has been dominated by classicism in the aesthetic and historical sense. For example Henry Sumner Maine, who was strongly influenced by the Historical School, saw Roman law both as the roots of continental legal tradition and a historical source of antiquity.[165]

---

161 Salvatore Settis, *Futuro del 'classico'*, Torino 2004.
162 Settis 2004, 62–63.
163 Settis 2004, 19–22, 72 offers some definitions of classic: 1) as the best and most perfect, also beyond what is now called classical antiquity, 2) classical antiquity, 3) linked to modernity as pre-modern, preceding modern, and 4) as an aesthetic category, harmonious, equilibrious.
164 Gadamer 1965, 270–274.
165 Kelley 1990, 266. Michael Lobban, 'Nineteenth Century English Jurisprudence', *Journal of Legal History* 16 (1995), 49 stressed that while Austin was influenced by Hugo, only Maine introduced the highly advanced German legal

In France, the state had traditionally been strong and the reception of Roman law minimal, confined mostly to learned scholarly law. At the same time Roman law was gaining its new influence in Germany, the legislature in France was extremely active, and the five Napoleonic codes were promulgated during the first decade of the nineteenth century. Despite the fact that 'France was invaded by the Historical School of law during the 1820s' as described by Kelley,[166] the codifications led to a positivistic approach to law in legal scholarship, which concentrated on the punctual and strict exegesis of laws. This has been reflected in scholarship on Roman legal history, regarding the three cases dealt with here. The lack of original French contributions to the discussion on jurists' law is evident, whereas in the questions linked with making and interpretating statutory law, such as the *edictum perpetuum*, French scholars have been active.[167] However, both the legal and historical scholarship of the Historical School and Pandectism were circulated as their works were translated into French and other languages.[168]

The new interpretation of Roman law as classic was to be far more important to the future of the discipline. This was the European narrative, which was first presented by Paul Koschaker in his seminal book *Europa und das römische Recht* (1947), in which he outlined the effect of the ideal of Rome and Roman law in European history and consequently, for the unity of Europe. Equally as important for the European narrative was Wieacker's book *Privatrechtsgeschichte der Neuzeit* (1952), which, despite its enormous scope, describes largely the influence of Roman law on European legal thinking. Both books advanced the idea that Roman law has been a fundamental factor in the development of Europe and constitutes, to quote the title

---

studies to Britain. Henry Sumner Maine, *Ancient Law*, London 1917 [1861], 210–215. See also, Carl Landauer, 'Henry Sumner Maine's Grand Tour: Roman Law in Ancient Law', *Current Legal Issues* 6 (2003), 135–157.

166 Donald Kelley, *Historians and the Law in Postrevolutionary France*, Princeton 1984, 85.

167 Jean Gaudemet, *Les naissances du droit*, Paris 1997, 350–354 wrote that the nature of the *École de l'Exégèse* demanded absolute faithfulness to the Code, its order, articles, and terminology. Gaudemet noted how much the few French studies in Roman law during the nineteenth century were influenced by the Pandectistic scholarship, whereas the dogmatic study of law was in effect unhistorical and positivistic. On the relatively small effect of the Historical School in France because of the different roles of Roman law and positive law, see Jean Gaudemet, 'Histoire et système dans la méthode de Savigny', in *Hommage à René Dekkers*, Bruxelles 1982, 132–133. See also, P.-F. Girard, 'L'enseignement du droit romain en 1912', RHDFE 36 (1912), 559–560.

168 On translations to Italian and the spread of the Historical Schools scholarship, see Crifò 1995, 562–573.

of Bellomo's recent book that continues the same genre, the common legal past of Europe.[169]

The roots and culture approach of Roman law as a fundamental part of a common European culture was continued by Coing as the *ius commune* narrative. The example of European political integration provided a stimulus for the Neopandectistic movement. According to its chief evangelist, Reinhard Zimmermann, this 'new Historical School' strives for the reunification of European private law, beginning from the common roots of Roman law.[170] When Wieacker referred to Pandectists in 1952 as the last generation of jurists who used Roman sources to answer contemporary questions, he probably did not expect Neopandectists such as Zimmermann.[171] Settis's claim that the definition of classic is both a definition of the past and a vision for the future has become strangely accurate. The European narrative of Roman law has provoked much criticism. For example, Monateri wonders how much one can expect Roman law to renew modern law:

> According to this theory of the 'renewal of the old,' Roman Law displays a peculiar capacity to survive and renew itself through the ages as the cement of

[169] Paul Koschaker, 'Die Krise des römischen Rechts und die romanistische Rechtswissenschaft', *Schriften der Akademie für Deutsches Recht: Gruppe Römisches Recht und fremde Rechte* 1 (1938), 1–86. Of Koschaker, see Tomasz Giaro, *Aktualisierung Europas: Gespräche mit Paul Koschaker*, Genova 2000. On the influence of Wieacker, cf. the foreword by R. Zimmermann in Wieacker 1995, vi–xiii; Wolf 1995, 37. The fundamental outline of the European narrative was continued by Helmut Coing, 'European common law: Historical foundations', in M. Cappelletti (ed.), *New Perspectives for a Common Law of Europe*, Leiden etc. 1978, 31–44. Cf. also Charles P. Sherman, *Roman Law in the Modern World I*, (2nd ed.), New Haven 1922, 1: 'Moreover it was the majestic and beneficent Roman law which more than any other single element brought civilization back to Europe following the barbaric deluge of the Dark Ages.' Manlio Bellomo, *The Common Legal Past of Europe, 1000–1800*, Washington 1995.

[170] Reinhard Zimmermann, 'Roman and Comparative Law: The European Perspective', *Journal of Legal History* 16 (1995), 25. See also, Jean Carbonnier, 'Usus hodiernus pandectarum', in R. H. Graveson et al. (eds.), *Festschrift für Imre Zajtay*, Tübingen 1982, 107–116; Aldo Mazzacane, '"Il leone fuggito dal circo": pandettistica e diritto comune europeo', *Index* 29 (2001), 97–111; Massimo Vari, 'Diritto romano "ius commune" europeo?', *Index* 30 (2002), 183–185; Johannes E. Spruit, 'Lebendig und inspirierend. Das "Corpus iuris civilis" als Grundlage der europäischen Rechtssysteme', *Index* 32 (2004), 221–225; Antonio Mantello, 'Di certe smanie "romanistiche" attuali', *Diritto romano attuale* 4 (2000), 37–60; Franco Casavola, 'Diritto romano e diritto europeo', *Labeo* 40 (1994), 161–169; David Johnston, 'The Renewal of the Old', *The Cambridge Law Journal* 56 (1997), 80–95.

[171] Wieacker 1952, 248, 250; Wieacker 1995, 333, 336; Pugliese 1985, 457.

Western legal history. Such a theory is to be intertwined with the restatement of the project to use Roman Law as the common glue with which to build up a newer law for European countries – a project with quite practical implications in the unfolding of Europe as a cultural alternative to the United States.[172]

The search for a new relevance for Roman law has led to Roman law and Roman legal history being divided into different sub-disciplines. The Neopandectistic Roman law shies away from historical contextualisation and concentrates on the rules of Roman law outlined in the Digest. Roman law and modern law are equal players in the dogmatic field of law in the construction of the new European *ius commune*. But the Roman law which the Neopandectists are interested in is contract law, law of obligations, trust law, and other aspects of transnational, mostly private, law.[173]

Conversely, the historical scholarship on Roman law has become more historicised. The Marxist approach to slavery and other forms of dependence in the grand narrative of class struggle has given way to more contemporary subjects like human rights, ethnicity and gender studies. The tendency to idealise the classical era at the expense of Late Antiquity has shown signs of reversal only in the last three decades.[174]

The division of Roman legal history only mirrors that of legal history itself. Legal history has two sides: the narrative historical side and the normative legal side. Both of these sides affect interpretation. The separation of positive law and legal history, or the normative and contemplative sides of law has been amplified by the fact that both traditions have been dismissive

---

172 Monateri 2000, 488.
173 Zimmermann 2000, 107–110; Mario Bretone, 'La "coscienza ironica" della romanistica', *Labeo* 43 (1997), 197; Crifò 1999, 14, 16, 23–25; Dirk Heirbaut, 'Comparative Law and Zimmermann's *ius commune*: A life line or a death sentence for legal history', in R. van den Bergh (ed.), *Ex iusta causa traditum. Essays in honour of Eric H. Pool*, (Fundamina, Editio specialis), Pretoria 2005, 136–153. For the difficulties of defining Neopandectists and Neohistorians, cf. Gerardo Broggini, 'Significato della conoscenza storica del diritto per il giurista vivente', in P. Caroni, G. Dilcher (eds.), *Norm und Tradition*, Köln 1998, 63. For how Eastern Europe was forgotten from the European tradition, see Giaro 2005, 131–143, and dire prediction of the end of the neopandectistic project, 143–156.
174 Bruce W. Frier, 'Roman law's descent into history', *Journal of Roman Archaeology* 13 [2000], 446–448; Elizabeth A. Meyer, *Legitimacy and law in the Roman world: tabulae in Roman belief and practice*, Cambridge 2004, 3; for discussions, cf. J. H. W. G. Liebeschuetz, 'The uses and abuses of the concept of "decline" in later Roman history or Was Gibbon politically incorrect', in *Recent research in Late Antique Urbanism, Journal of Roman Archaeology, Supp.* 42 (2001), 233–238, with comments from A. Cameron, B. Ward-Perkins, M. Whittow, and L. Lavan.

of narratives. In their insistence on being scientific, scholars of modern history have denied narrative characteristics of their discipline.[175] Scholars of positive law have claimed that law is simply the product of legislation, which is interpreted using scientifically rational methods. Both traditions claim to be the highest level of rationality, which has no need for narratives or the whole concept of narratives. This combination of the positivistic characterisation of science and the methodical conceptions of historicism has, ever since the 1970s, formed the basic foundations of legal history.[176]

On a more analytical level, it seems that the insistence of being rational and free of myths, stories, and other irrational matters is another narrative. In a similar way to Hayden White, who has claimed that freedom from narratives is in itself one of the founding narratives of the scientific historiography, Paolo Grossi has claimed that freedom from myths and narratives is an essential part of the self-understanding of modern positive law. The roots of this view go back to the Enlightenment idea of science as the antithesis of backward, medieval myths. Myth and modernity are contradictions in terms.[177]

Zimmermann saw the division of Romanistic tradition as a divide between classical historical Romanists of the type of Kaser and the new Historical School that studies the second life of Roman law for the future legal unification of Europe.[178] According to Giaro, the distinction between tradition and historiography coincides with the internal and external viewpoints of the legal phenomena. The first is by a participant of the system that accepts its rules, the second by an impartial observer.[179] My interpretation would be that both the classicism of Kaser and the classicism of the Neopandectists are expressions of the same legal classicism. The real division is between the normatively oriented Roman lawyers and historically oriented ancient historians. This is important because the legal historian should be intimately acquainted with both the legal and historical traditions,[180] not simply as facts but also as narratives.

Emilio Betti has described the legal historian as a scholar moving between two modes of interpretation: legal and historical. On the one hand the legal historian uses the methods of history, while on the other, he or she is a lawyer who should understand the functioning and inner rules of the legal system. The preconceptions of the legal historian are based on these dual positions,

---

175 The tradition of antinarrativity was initiated already by Thucydides 1,20.
176 Senn 1982, 177.
177 Paolo Grossi, *Mitologie giuridiche della modernità*, Milano 2001, 43–46.
178 Zimmermann 1995, 26–27. 21–33.
179 Giaro 2005, 78.
180 Momigliano 1966b, 240.

which define the associations and concepts used in the interpretative process.[181]

Betti was uncomfortable with the concept of anachronism used by Hoetink and chose instead to see the legal historian as a scholar able to grasp different meanings in the legal material through his intimate knowledge of law. In this sense, legal history is superior to regular history, as are all specialised histories such as the histories of art and literature. The risk of using modern concepts and categories is evident, as has been proven by the Pandectists, but is not confined to legal history: even historians of religion are prone to use modern theology in their understanding of ancient texts. The only way legal history can retain its historical credentials is to acknowledge the autonomy and totality of its object. The interpretation of the legal historian is both legal and historical, but these two must be kept separate while supporting each other.[182]

If Roman law and Roman legal history are completely separated and the narrative tradition created before this separation is neglected, there is a distinct danger in repeating the same narratives without knowing their provenance.

Conclusions

The introduction and influence of the different theories of codification to the history of Roman law were investigated using the case of *edictum perpetuum* supposedly compiled during the reign of Hadrian. Although the conventional wisdom is that the Romans never produced a real systematic codification, the main theories on the Perpetual Edict describe it either as a systematic codification, or a simple compilation.

If based solely on the Roman sources, the history of the *edictum perpetuum* would be rather vague. There are several sources that seem to attest to a

---

181 Emilio Betti, 'Jurisprudenz und Rechtsgeschichte vor dem Problem der Auslegung', *Archiv für Rechts- und Sozialphilosophie* 40 (1952), 354–374.

182 Emilio Betti, 'Storia e dogmatica del diritto', in *La storia del diritto nel quadro delle scienze storiche: Atti del primo Congresso internazionale della Società Italiana di Storia del Diritto*, Firenze 1966, 106, 110–112, 114; Emilio Betti, 'La dogmatica moderna nella storiografia del diritto e della cultura', in G. Crifò (ed.), *Diritto Metodo Ermeneutica*, Milano 1991, 515: 'I contemporanei spesso non dicono ciò che potrebbero dire, poiché sarebbe superfluo per i loro lettori, i quali hanno quotidianamente sott'occhio i rapporti in questione.' A classical critique of Betti, see Gadamer 1965, 482–483. Cf. also Wieacker 1995, 336–340. Of legal history and law, see Jörn Eckert (ed.), *Der praktische Nutzen der Rechtsgeschichte: H. Hattenhauer zum 8. September 2001*, Heidelberg 2003.

compilation of the edict by Julian, such as the fourth century historians Eutropius and Aurelius Victor and the emperor Justinian. However, there are a considerable number of literary and epigraphic evidence on Julian, none of which mentions the *edictum perpetuum*. The nature of the *edictum perpetuum* is likewise not clarified by the sources. There are also serious questions about the vast lacunae in the evidence, as well as the lateness of the sources in relation to the events. Finally, there is the important issue of the different layers of sources. As contemporary sources are lacking, do the sources from Late Antiquity shed any light to the actual events or just the contemporary understanding of, for instance, Justinian's compilers? This puzzle of late Roman filter is of vital importance to the recent attempts at finding a solution to the question of competing historical reconstructions.

The combination of limited historical sources and important legal themes such as codification have made the history of scholarship on the *edictum perpetuum* an interesting display of how the legal ideals of different times projected onto the historiography. In particular, the development of the ideals of codification can be followed from the seventeenth century to the present. The Humanist writers of the sixteenth century separated themselves from medieval scholarship by emphasising the Justinianic evidence. The status of the Perpetual Edict as the precursor of the *Corpus Juris Civilis* extended the glorification usually reserved to the *Corpus* to the Edict. The Perpetual Edict was found to be an expression of correct law, both legally sound and ethically faultless. This line of reasoning was modified by the Natural lawyers of the Enlightenment, who made it a systematic codification produced by the beneficial union of scientific reason and sovereign power.

A more radical transformation followed at the beginning of the nineteenth century, as the emergence of a self-describedly scientific history led to doubts as to the very existence of the Edict. The supposed objectivity of historical science did not hinder the inclusion of contemporary anti-codificationalist themes in the reconstruction of events. Neither did it refrain scholars from resurrecting the old idea of a systematic codification during the codification debate in Germany during the second half of the nineteenth century.

The Neohumanistic turn in Roman law scholarship at the turn of the twentieth century led to new discoveries and an increase in the number of sources. Epigraphical evidence brought new visibility to the issue but did not lead to universally accepted conclusions. A new feature was also the discovery of the political context of the Hadrianic reforms, which were viewed in the context of the centralisation of power and bureaucratisation.

In the current discussion there are three main theories, which all trace their roots to at least the beginning of the nineteenth century: the post-classical legend theory; the compilation theory; and the codification theory. The first and youngest of them, the post-classical legend theory, is based on the ambiguous nature of the historical evidence. Its proponents claim that the whole tradition of codification is based on the intentional misunderstanding by Romans of the Late Empire who wanted to demonstrate that their codification projects had historical precedents. The theory is based on a combination of historical doubt and source criticism and is directly antithetical to the other theories. More interesting is the relationship between the two other theories. The codification theory is an example of the influence of the idea of systematic codification that was first developed by the Humanists and later developed by the Natural law scholars. The historical reasoning behind it was that, as in other areas, Hadrian would have made sweeping changes in law based on the systematic thought of his beloved Greeks. The compilation theory was a modern extension of Justinian's claim that the Perpetual Edict was a predecessor of the *Corpus Juris Civilis* and like it an unsystematic collection of legal norms. The supporters of this theory claim that the low visibility of the Edict is based on the fact that it was similar to earlier annual edicts of the praetor and the compilation did not change the substance of law.

It was a fascinating coincidence that the two theories of codification and compilation found modern resonance during the late nineteenth century in the debate over legal positivism in legal theory. The theory of codification was supported by the followers of scientific legal positivism, who argued for the leading role of legal science in the construction of a legal system. The theory of compilation was supported by textual legal positivists, who maintained that law was whatever was decreed by the legislator and the task of jurisprudence was to examine that.

Both of the theories have used the Perpetual Edict as a phantom modernity to serve as a canvas for the projection of modern ideals onto the history of Roman law. The codificationalists still support the idea of a codification as an expression of systematic legal science. The compilationalists for their part use Hadrian as a mirror image of a modern sovereign legislator, who builds something resembling a proto-modern state. Within the framework of contemporary Roman legal history Emperor Hadrian and jurist Julian stand as symbols of state centralism and the growth of imperial power. Hadrian initiated the bureaucratic process, in which salaried imperial officials supplanted the old republican magistrates. An important part of that process was the creation of the Perpetual Edict, which accomplished two things. First, the powers of the republican office of the praetor were greatly reduced. Secondly, the emperor achieved a monopoly of legislative power. This monopoly also meant the monopoly of professional jurists, as lay praetors were excluded from developing the law.

In conclusion, the importance of Hadrian's Perpetual Edict today is the product of three converging narrative traditions: the narrative of the centralisation of power in Imperial Rome; the narrative of modernity and codification of law; and the narrative of the Golden Age. These three traditions have together created an image of phantom modernity, in which the Hadrianic Roman state is presented as an anachronistic reflection of the modern constitutional state.

Chapter 5

Conclusions: Ancient Roman Lawyers and Modern Legal Ideals

During this study the influence of modern legal phenomena on the history of ancient Roman law was studied through three cases, with a comparison of Roman sources and the historical presentations or reconstructions from the sixteenth century Humanists to the present. The three cases presented are good examples of fecund dead ends in scholarship. Very little is known of them in the light of the Roman sources, but they nevertheless occupy a central position in the history of Roman law and attract continuous interest. Because they are unresolved puzzles, their treatment is a useful indicator of the effects of contemporary ideals in the writing of Roman legal history. The three cases represent three ideals significant to modern law. The simultaneous occurrence of science, autonomy and codification is typical to many classical reconstructions or descriptions of modern continental law.[1] In the most rudimentary fashion the three ideals can be said to form parts of the basic developmental process of modern law: autonomous legal science produces a codification.

In the course of scholarship from the Humanists of the sixteenth century to the present, Roman legal history has taken on narrative qualities in its presentation of Roman history. Despite the claims of radical narrativist historians, these narrative qualities do not change the fundamental nature of historiography into something else than the description and analysis of the past. History is not fiction, but the writing of history has some characteristics of creative writing.

There were three main questions associated with this pattern of interpretation: how the Roman jurists were modernised by giving them thoughts and attributes of contemporary significance; how stories of Roman jurists were used as instructive narratives, and how Roman jurists were elevated as stereotypical ideal characters. The great narratives of Roman law can be understood as constructions of a legal world-view, of legal identities, as well as observations of the relevance of Roman law then and now. The development of narratives in legal history is complicated due to the interplay between

---

[1] The group is heterogeneous and consists of works as different as Weber's *Rechtssoziologie* (in English translation by Max Rheinstein, in Weber 1978, 641–900) and Kelsen's *Reine Rechtslehre*, Wien 1934.

the narrative historical elements and normative legal elements in the making of legal history. Roman legal history has been influenced by its common trajectory with legal science in general, of which the latter half of the nineteenth century is of vital interest, since it was a time of fervent activity in both fields.

The basic premise in all the three cases of this study has been that even in the current historicised Roman legal history there are still visible remnants and traces of centuries old traditions and disputes. The value of *Wissenschaftsgeschichte* in legal history is that it provides us with tools to explain the existence of these oddities in the current research literature. The purpose of this method of presentation is to distinguish different narratives of the historical tradition and the ideological currents within, so as to discern the Roman and Romanistic layers of our historical understanding of Roman law.

The impact of the ideal of science was examined through the case of Quintus Mucius as the supposed founder of legal science. He has been the center of a lively tradition that has proposed him as the founding father of Roman and even Western legal tradition. How this science should be defined has not been answered clearly, but the attempts reveal more about the definition of legal science employed by legal scholars than of the Romans.

The Roman sources have not been helpful either. The tradition is based on a very narrow selection of Roman sources isolated from their context, and even their reading is ambivalent and subject to dispute.

The historical tradition surrounding Quintus Mucius can be interpreted as an invented tradition intended to provide historical precedents for the Historical School of jurisprudence. The tradition of Quintus Mucius as the founding father was formulated during the latter part of the nineteenth century in the writings of legal historians, initiated by Puchta.

There had been a tradition extending to the sixteenth century that described legal science in the model provided by Cicero and arriving at his conclusions. The birth of the story of Quintus Mucius as the founding father coincided with the development of the systematic legal science by the Historical School, especially Puchta, the same man who formulated the Quintus Mucius tradition. The coalescence of the two traditions meant that in the last decades of the nineteenth century, Quintus Mucius was seen as developing a closed system in the manner advocated by contemporary German jurists of the *Begriffsjurisprudenz* or jurisprudence of concepts.

The tradition of Quintus Mucius is not the only foundational narrative of legal science. Some medievalists have their own, claiming that legal science, or even science itself, was only created by Gratian and his colleagues during the eleventh century with the combination of the Digest and the learning of Plato and Aristotle. The Romanists on the other hand have tried very hard to prove that there was a link between Greek theory and Roman law. Both of the foundational narratives are exercises in presentism, the evaluation of the past according the standards of the present.

The preoccupation of the Historical School with a system and the systematisation of law was a result of a continuation and deepening of the systematising tradition introduced into the history of Roman law by Puchta. The legal system was their main concern, history was only a method of finding and legitimating it.

The ideal of the autonomy of law was studied in the context of the *ius respondendi* and the relationship between the emperors and lawyers in the early Principate. The traditional division of the scholarship revolved around the question of whether the jurists retained the freedom of jurisprudence by preventing the emperor from taking control of their profession or whether Augustus managed to create a superior class of jurists under his control and facilitating his domination over the development of jurists' law.

The Roman sources on the matter are inconsistent, as there are a number of sources such as Pomponius, Gaius, and the Institutes of Justinian that, when combined, provide a strong case for the *ius respondendi*. However, it is strange that a change of this magnitude is not mentioned in any other sources, not in the general literature or the epigraphic sources. Lately, a view that stresses the evolution of our sources has been gaining popularity. According to its supporters, the Institutes of Justinian, a later Roman source that confirms the existence of the institution and forms much of its current interpretation, may in fact only be a Late Antique interpretation or misinterpretation of the classical sources.

As the sources are ambiguous, there has been considerable leeway in the interpretations. From the sixteenth century on, the interpretation has promoted two stereotypes: the benevolent and the malevolent emperor. The benevolent supported jurists, while the malevolent one used and controlled them. Different themes were raised as the debate developed. In the early sixteenth century, it centred around the issues of the freedom of opinion, while in the seventeenth century the issue was imperial control over the law. From the eighteenth to the nineteenth centuries the debate further evolved as scholars became more interested in the question of the authority of the lawyers and the emperors' will to control it.

In the twentieth century debates, these tendencies were condensed into two opposing positions, the idealists and the realists. The idealists claimed that the *ius respondendi* never existed because it does not fit with what is generally known of the jurists and because the sources are so few. The realists said that Augustus created a superior class of jurists, who accepted his authority in return for their added influence. As Jhering had observed earlier, lawyers could not oppose the emperor, as jurists' law demanded the existence of a central power.

The idealists and realists both reflect and repeat a patriotic narrative of the jurists' profession. In the idealistic version, the emperor was not capable of interfering with the law, whereas in the realistic version he collaborated with the jurists but was not interested in the content of the law.

The patriotic narrative functions as a means by which to construct continuity between the ancient Roman past and the present. The stereotypical story of Labeo and Capito has been used for that purpose from the sixteenth century onwards. That story is basically a moral portrayal of the virtues of the independent jurist. The good lawyer, represented by Labeo and Bulgarus in these stories, relies only on his skills and good reputation among his peers, whereas those who become sycophants of the powerful do it because they have no other way to achieve recognition.

The effect of the ideal of codification was analysed through the discussion on the Hadrianic *edictum perpetuum*. The *edictum perpetuum* has been the only possibility to claim that the Romans made something resembling a modern systematic codification. In contrast to the XII Tables and the *Corpus Iuris*, the *edictum perpetuum* was compiled during the height of both the Roman state and Roman jurisprudence. In the current debate three main options for the understanding of the *edictum perpetuum* have been presented: that it was a true systematic codification, or that it was a compilation of rules not different from the previous yearly edicts, or that it did not exist at all as the two preceding theories claim. These options are all derived from long traditions and important disagreements over the principle of codification. The idealisation of Hadrianic Rome and the tendency to see it as a mirror image of the modern world have also been influential.

The Roman sources are unclear and the interpretation of sources has been a subject of fierce debate. The Late Roman historians mentioned briefly Julian as the organiser of the Perpetual Edict, while Justinian saw him as an important predecessor to his own compilation. However, contemporary literature and epigraphic sources do not mention Julian as a codifier, and the use of the term *edictum perpetuum* does not give any hint regarding its nature. There are some sources to back up the claim that Julian compiled the *edictum perpetuum*, but very few inform us of what it really meant.

The three contemporary theories on the *edictum perpetuum* all trace their roots back to the early Roman legal history. The notion of a systematic codification is the oldest. This began with the Humanistic legal scholarship, when the edict was presented as a perfect law. The rationalist natural lawyers emphasised the wisdom and learning involved, which led to the conclusion that the edict would have been a scientific and rational codification that combined scholarly wisdom and sovereign power for the beneficial renewal of law. The compilation theory can also be traced to the Humanists, as they also asserted that the edict was compiled from previous edicts. The claim of its non-existence was created during the rise of historical scholarship by Hugo on the grounds that the lack of contemporary evidence on the *edictum perpetuum* means that it was a later invention. The late nineteenth century saw the debate over the *edictum perpetuum* as a struggle over legal positivism. The scientific legal positivists envisioned the edict as a systematic codification that would have reflected the inner order of the legal system. The textual legal positivists argued that the *edictum perpetuum* was simply a tool for the praetor and the system of law had nothing to do with it. Those who denied its existence were representing the old preference of the Historical School for jurists' law and the influence of lawyers over statutory law.

There are many modern characteristics in the discussion over the *edictum perpetuum*, such as the different traditions of codification and their allusions to positivism, and the centralisation of power along bureaucratic lines. These quasi-modern tendencies were complemented by the glorification of Hadrian as the ideal monarch. The combined modernisation of Hadrian's Rome can be called a phantom of modernity, with the idealisation of the Roman state and its leader and the belief that it represented the rule of law.

The goal of all of these inquiries was to remind us of the genealogy of Roman legal history, and of the fact that interpretations made in a bygone era often continue into the present in the work of modern scholars.

* * *

During the development of Roman legal history in the nineteenth century, there was a profound change in the way Roman law was seen. Before the nineteenth century, the practical value of the classical heritage was pre-eminent, but by mid-century it began to fade. If there was scant interest in historical accuracy as a value in itself previously, this was reversed during the latter part of the century. Historians were not the only ones preoccupied with accuracy; an artist like Lawrence Alma-Tadema, who spent days drawing houses in Pompei, also took it seriously in his work. As the usable classical antiquity began to be replaced by the aesthetic classical ideal, the classical past was left to its own devices as antiquity in itself.[2]

In a recent book, Simon Goldhill, a professor of Greek at Cambridge, discussed the extent to which classics form a part of our imagination as a

2   Rosemary J. Barrow, *Lawrence Alma-Tadema*, London 2001, 6–7, 28–41, 99; A. Wilton, I. Bignamni (eds.), *Grand Tour: The Lure of Italy in the Eighteenth Century*, London 1996.

living cultural heritage and 'why learning about classics makes a fundamental difference to understanding the major concerns of modern Western life – a fundamental difference to our self-understanding.'[3] One of the most acute observations of Goldhill's book is that the modern significance of classics is not primarily due to the fact that many aspects of Western civilisation have their roots in the classics, but rather that classics are seen and imagined as the roots of Western civilisation.

> Generations of European and American writers, politicians and artists have repeatedly found one fundamental, idealistic answer to the question 'Where do you think you come from?' – the classical past. The very distance of the classical past allows for an ideal picture to be developed and utilized, and the ideal image of Greece in particular has again and again fuelled the most stirring cultural and political revolutions of Western society. Greece is seen as the fountainhead of Western values. It has been a banner to march under, a spur to revolutionaries, an inspiration and aspiration.[4]

Roman law and Roman legal history as part of classical civilisation and the entity known collectively as Classics have drawn from the same source: imagination. The reception and reuse of Roman law from Late Antiquity onwards is hard to imagine without the influence of the cultural idea of Rome in Western civilisation. The reception and the cultural idea contributed both to the use of Roman legal history as a surrogate stage on which to present contemporary themes. Like art, literature, music, and historiography, legal history took storylines and narratives from the ancient sources and adapted them to current fashion and contemporary needs. Some of these adaptations proved to be so captivating that they began to live a life of their own like Shakespeare's reading of Plutarch in *Coriolanus*. Some are pure fictions of the imagination, wholly detached from Antiquity. Roman legal history has been as much a question of the imagination as other stories from Antiquity, hence every period tended to write a Roman legal history in its own image and to suit its own needs. These versions of Roman narratives have then made their own way into the historiography as they in turn have been used for novel purposes.

A fascinating example of this revision of history can be found in the transformation of the image of St. Jerome. Erasmus, one of the most famous of all Renaissance scholars who began to study the correctness of the Vulgata against the Greek and Hebrew originals, rewrote the description of St. Jerome while editing his writings. In the Middle Ages St. Jerome had been turned into a fasting and flagellating, ascetic hermit in the mold of medieval saints, but

---

3   Simon Goldhill, *Love, Sex & Tragedy: Why Classics Matter*, London 2005, 3.
4   Goldhill 2005, 256.

Erasmus made him into an enlightened scholar and a civilised gentleman with a wide knowledge of antiquity and history. As Goldhill writes, 'As Erasmus tries to paint a correct portrait of his hero, his hero starts to look increasingly like himself.'[5]

It is somehow natural that every tendency should find a history matching its persuasions. For instance, Sparta served as an ideal model for thinkers from Plato to Mill and to Rousseau, ending up as the idealised antiquity of Nazi Germany. Similarly Socrates has been the hero and martyr of liberal political thinkers: model of a heroic individual who dares to dissent and question the conventions of society.[6]

The way the history of Roman law has been written has always been linked to and influenced by the later use of Roman law. Either Roman law has been seen through a modernising lens and given the attributes of modern law, or themes from the history of Roman law have been used as arguments and examples. The first is a symptom of the use of Roman law as a practical source of law, the second an example of the use of Classical Antiquity and Roman law as an ideal cultural model. These two uses of Roman law were and are inseparably linked where one has been used to justify the other.

Jacques Godefroy described how Roman Republican jurisprudence goes through three phases, anomia, isonomia, and eunomia, in which the uncertainty of the early Republic gradually turns into legal clarity and certainty through the actions of jurists, who create a *scientia* of law. As the Republic was changed into the Empire, the jurists maintained their authority, which was further augmented by the *ius respondendi*. Finally, the great jurists surround the emperor while he sits in judgement, advising him.[7] This teleological path to greatness was the foundation of the view of Roman law as innately fair and balanced.[8]

Gravina, one of the so-called pioneers of legal history of the early eighteenth century, spent his scholarly life in constant battle with other schools of law, the casuists, scholastics and legists. He saw historical method as the only way of studying law that would equal scholastics and dialectics in intellectual gravity. Gravina's work is characterised by a glorification of classical Roman law, his ideal was the sublime learned law, which would rise far above the cheap practical casuism that was dominant in his day. The positive presenta-

---

5   Goldhill 2005, 146, 149–150.
6   Goldhill 2005, 201, 206: 'Sparta was the first volkisch state – a state where the purity of the people, the Volk, strengthened by obedience and military training, led to a perfection of social order.' (p. 201).
7   Gothofredus 1766, 15–25 [ch. 1–3].
8   Schröder 2001, 7–8 et passim.

tion he gives of Roman jurists is derived from the Humanist legal historiography. He used this to promote his idea of returning to the pure science of studying the noble Roman legal texts.[9] The idealising tendencies can be recognised in a multitude of places. Heineccius' views of the *edictum perpetuum* as an enterprise dominated by scientific reason and his portrayal of Hadrian as the ideal emperor and the protector of jurists are both efforts to bestow validity and relevance upon the Romans and their law. Similarly the theme of scientific truthfulness deriving from the good use of Greek philosophy presented by Maiansius and Gibbon was based on the idea that the correctness and rationality of the content of law was a decisive factor in its validity.

Classical Antiquity, especially Rome, formed a practical and malleable precedent in law, which gained its legitimacy from the idealised standing of classical civilisation. What parts of it were used and how, was a question for the author to decide. History was an auxiliary to jurisprudence and classical precedents were also regularly cited as arguments in works that were not historical in nature. For example, the works of Hugo Grotius, who is counted as the initiator of the natural law movement, are filled with references to classical literature, which he used as arguments for the existence of a rule.[10] The sections of Pomponius' *Enchiridion* that were examined above in this study were simply not of interest to some authors. For instance, Grotius' commentary on Justinian skips every one of them and makes no mention of anything linked to those discussions.[11]

The eighteenth century was marked by rising classicism and a general enthusiasm for ancient culture. Partially because the language of science was still Latin, there was still an affinity to Rome and Roman jurists that was difficult to understand later.[12] What is also noteworthy is that the works of the eighteenth century have a different approach to authorship than what was later thought appropriate. Thomasius might copy pages and pages of Huber, and Heineccius might in turn copy long passages from Thomasius, and everybody would copy the Roman authors at length, which naturally represented a different idea of scientific progression and creativity than what

---

[9] Carlo Ghisalberti, *Gian Vincenzo Gravina: Giurista e storico* (Ius nostrum 8), Varese 1962, 52, 58–59, 61, 179.

[10] The most famous of his works, *De iure belli ac pacis* (1625), demonstrates through its voluminous references to ancient sources how the classics were a matter of common reference.

[11] Hugo Grotius, *Florum sparsio ad ius Iustinianeum*, Halle 1729, 83–88.

[12] J. W. Burrow, *Gibbon*, Oxford 1985, 38 described how for Gibbon and his contemporaries, Rome was a 'shrine' as well as 'history's greatest lesson and warning'.

is expected of science currently. There is a sense of timelessness in Roman legal history, of which the writings of Maiansius are a good example. In describing his own predecessors, he made no distinction between near contemporary authors and those predating him by several centuries. Alciatus, Cujas, Balduinus, Connanus, Donellus, Faber, and others are all equal.[13]

The appearance of critical historiography and the self-proclaimed juxtaposition of old and new scholarship brought only a partial change in the timelessness of scholarship, though both the practical and aesthetic portrayals of Roman law remained the same. Hugo clearly doubted the traditional presentations of both the *ius respondendi* and the *edictum perpetuum*, and was puzzled by the fact that the classical jurists did not devote a single line to what a judge should do in the case of contradictory *responsa*.[14] A similar tendency for historical accuracy can be seen in the works of Puchta, whose historical criticism of established interpretations coexisted with his use of Roman legal history as an authoritative precedent. For instance, Puchta used *ius respondendi* as a representative of the eternal juxtaposition of lawyers and sovereigns on the right to create new law. Both Hugo and Puchta embody the first seeds of the emerging distinction between dogmatic acceptance of the norm and historical knowledge of it.[15]

The identification with Antiquity is impossible to understand without an appreciation of the nineteenth century context and how classicism permeated the lives of the educated classes. In both Germany and Britain, classics were taught in schools to the extent that roughly two thirds of the curriculum could consist of Greek and Roman texts. This gave students such a familiarity with the ancient civilisation that the classics became a part of their very way of being. Classics, as the foundation of a gentleman's education, created both the unity of the elite and a distinction between them and the lower classes.[16]

Despite the claims of scientific historiography and modern positive law, stories or narratives have proven to be remarkably resilient. Despite the attempts to ignore them, stories have been perpetuated within the historiographic tradition. A good example is the glorifying patriotic narrative, which has always been adapted to new circumstances.

---

13   Maiansius 1764, v–vii. His native Spain is only present in only a few references to his lesser known compatriots.
14   Hugo 1806, 337.
15   Giaro 2005, 79.
16   Hingley 2000, 9–10; Gilbert Highet, *The Classical Tradition*, Oxford 1967, 490–498 et passim; T. P. Wiseman, *The Myths of Rome*, Exeter 2004, 296–303: 'For Macaulay as for Machiavelli, the Romans were a living presense.' (p. 296).

This has by no means signified that individual authors have no choice but to perpetuate the stories of the tradition. On the contrary, authors like Fritz Schulz, Franz Wieacker, Antonio Guarino, and many others have made their own versions of Roman legal history, emphasising their own ideas and preferences. Theirs are the narratives that keep the tradition in a state of constant change, as their competing grand narratives are extended to the details and marketed in innumerable publications.

In the cases presented during this study, there have emerged several competing metanarratives. In the case of Quintus Mucius, the dispute has been about science and the possibility of Roman precedents. In the case of the *ius respondendi* the question has been the freedom of jurisprudence, while in the case of the *edictum perpetuum*, bureaucracy and codification. As was demonstrated, in all three cases, the different interpretations formed their own competing narratives.

Modernity in history and law was supposed to remove all meaning from traditional narratives: only scientifically proven knowledge was valued. The trouble seems to have been that narratives formed by the Pandectist interpretation and its predecessors were proficient in creating models and structures for interpretation, which were presented with persuasive clarity. The contemplative mode of critical historiography is, by its nature, ill-adapted to forming authoritative interpretations as its way of functioning is the presentation of criticism and doubt. The models of Pandectism were persuasive precisely because they offered explanations, even if they were based at times solely on semi-fictitious constructions. Some of the narratives dealt with in this study are of such long duration that both the Pandectistic period and the advent of modern historiography have only affected the way the narratives were written. The differences they introduced are mostly in the conventions of writing, the notations and the use of sources, the explanatory narrative they adopt is largely the same as that adopted earlier.

One of the purposes of this inquiry has been to demonstrate that even though legal dogmatics and legal history were largely separated over a century ago, there are still remains from the centuries of coexistence to be found in the present history of Roman law. The most obvious Pandectistic hyperboles have been eradicated by scholarly criticism, but small details and emphases in interpretations endure. In scholarly matters the preservation and continuation of all things is based on repetition and duplication. Consequently, there must be something in these persistent narratives that appeals to the modern reader in order to make their preservation seem reasonable.

Because modern continental law is to some extent a descendant of the Historical School and the jurisprudence of concepts, the reconstructions of Roman law made by representatives of those schools are familiar to modern jurists. The crucial question, then, is whether the lineage of modern law should be traced to Roman law at all, or simply to the later Romanistic tradition that combined the material of Roman law with the systematic tradition and the natural law influences that began in the sixteenth century. Are the common parts Roman or just Romanistic?

It is sometimes tempting to adopt a mental image from anthropology and see research in the light of some kind of anthropology of science, in which the scientific community is seen as a tribe of sorts, whose customs bind the researcher. The dead Germans of the distant past would be its venerated ancestral spirits and the professors of law its priests. The tradition would have an authoritative and binding presence in the present and the social nature of science would be paramount. The existence of roots and traditions can be both conscious and unconscious. If the former are constructed by knowingly seeking parallels and precedents from history, the latter are repetitions caused by simply following precedents and models laid out by predecessors. The latter is a traditionalistic model of science, based on academic ancestry, a genealogy of teachers and students in which influences are transferred all the way to the Academic Grandsons.[17] If the teachings of masters are largely accepted and perpetuated by the pupils and then passed on to their pupils, the permanence of narratives reaches new levels through scientific socialisation.

The purpose of the self-reflection in legal history is to remind us where we come from. The most blatant examples of literature where this has been forgotten are the ones that supposedly explore different legal traditions of the world but serve mainly as the descriptions of the writer's own presuppositions and culture of origin.[18] In not knowing one's own tradition there is the distinct possibility of confusing the object and subject of historical inquiry.

One of the most crucial dangers associated with not knowing the roots of your own tradition is that roots and traditions have been created and will be created for many non-historical purposes. Roots, in the form of myths and traditions, are also dogmatic elements and are present in every history of law. The significance of Roman law in the development of modern European law is an historical peculiarity that could have been conjured up only on the basis of another historical peculiarity: Pandectism.

Narratives and myths are essential in the construction of an identity. A myth can be understood as a narrative that tells the members of a community

---

17   The concept of Academic Grandson or *Enkelschüler* is used earnestly by Zimmermann 2000, 31 and ridiculed by Osler 2000.
18   Cf. for instance H. Patrick Glenn, *Legal Traditions of the World*, Oxford 2000; Uwe Wesel, *Geschichte des Rechts*, München 1997.

where they come from. Knowing myths is vital to belonging to a community. Roman legal history in its many forms is a foundational story of where lawyers and law come from. The stories exist and make a fundamental contribution to their respective cultural spheres. As Goldhill writes: 'Myth and history construct the past for us and in us. Our sense of the here and now is formed through the stories we tell of where we come from.'[19] The stories of Roman legal history are not only the stories of Romans, they are also the classical stories and the foundational myths of the scholars of Roman law.

Roman legal history has been a wonderful canvas onto which to project a desired image, because so little is known about it. The scholarship before the nineteenth century used this possibility to the full. The systematic historical scholarship that began to delve more deeply into the ancient culture during the nineteenth century tremendously enriched the view of classical civilisation. The contrasts that appeared between the detailed results of the historical scholarship and the idealised traditional image of the classics were not in any way limited to legal history. In Roman legal history these contrasts were between the idealised image of Roman jurisprudence and the law of the Romanistic tradition and what the new historical sources revealed of them.[20]

The tension between the idealisation of antiquity and the modern historical scholarship defines the development of the nineteenth century scholarship in Roman legal history. Scholars studying ancient law had little difficulty in explaining their research topics to their contemporaries, who cultivated their own affinities for the classics. The British upper classes were rereading Greek classics in Greek and striking classical poses at dinner-parties. French revolutionaries studied classics for inspiration, American founding fathers used Roman pseudonyms and sculpted George Washington repeatedly as a Roman, and the Germans were completely swept away by their Graeco-mania.[21]

The usefulness of Roman legal history has often been simply to provide stories of who we modern lawyers are. The culture that produced Roman law has disappeared but the narrative tradition has remained. To dismiss the narratives as myths and stories, and to say that scientific history is the only

---

19 Goldhill 2005, 255.
20 Goldhill 2005, 78: 'Since so little is actually known about the real Sappho, she is a wonderful canvas on to which to project an image of desire.', p. 88: 'For the Victorians who wanted their Greeks to be pure and white, and who wanted to criminalize homosexuality at any age, the tensions between the idealized image of the past and what that past produced by way of art, philosophy, literature and, simply, behaviour was hard to deal with. At one level, the most common and proper level, the tension was actively and awkwardly silenced.'
21 Goldhill 2005, 257–288.

real route to the past, is to be blind to their continuing cultural significance and the way they are still a part of our imagination. As Goldhill maintains, 'The categories of "myth" and "history" mutually define each other. But, more importantly, a cultural imagination will always use its repeated and accepted stories, however much it believes in analysis or critical enquiry.'[22] Refusing to analyse and read the narratives does not mean that they do not exist.

In addition to myth breaking, scientific history also contains a generous amount of myth making. Despite its long tradition of self-understanding, which stated that scientific history deals only with the verified facts and discards myths as unverifiable matters of belief, it is increasingly recognised how important it is for historians to understand their own myths.[23] The narratives of Roman legal history contain many mythical elements: Quintus Mucius as a founding father; Labeo as a martyr; and Hadrian and Julian as creators of a new order. The purposes of these myths have changed constantly.

The peculiar feature of all three narratives is that they have continued strongly into the present history of Roman law, though the position of Roman law and the Roman law tradition itself has undergone a tremendous change from Puchta to Wieacker. Puchta's Roman law was a rational system that would spread and bloom under the guiding light of science. Quintus Mucius was a building stone in the foundation myth of a growing and developing scientific law. In Schulz's time, the political significance of Roman law was rapidly disappearing and it was necessary to defend its continuing value. Furthermore, Roman law as a discipline was facing a major crisis in terms of its academic relevance because of modern codifications. Quintus Mucius was needed again, this time as a stone in the defensive wall of the fortress of Roman law under a barbarian siege. In the later days of Wieacker, the modern world had lost the need for Roman law for anything other than educational purposes.

Sources, interpretations and narratives all contribute to the formation of history, which has been shaped and reworked by the grand narrators, whose mastery of the interrelations between past and present augmented their credibility above the rest. The grand narrators weave together historical agents and contemporary questions in a manner that their contemporaries can relate to. Because facts are elusive in the light of the historical sources, all that remains are stories. But does the actualisation of legal history necessarily mean a distortion of history?

22 Goldhill 2005, 316.
23 McNeill 1986, 9.

If we imprint our ideals on the Romans, are we in fact any more talking about the Romans or ourselves? Because narration creates a story that gives meaning to fragmentary sources, is a story meaningful only when we can relate to it? Are the Romans of Roman legal history simply us, assembled in a historical togaparty?

Abbreviations

The abbreviations of ancient authors and their works follow the system used in the *Thesaurus Linguae Latinae*.

AE	L'Année épigraphique
ANRW	Aufstieg und Niedergang der römischen Welt
BGB	Bürgerliches Gesetzbuch
BIDR	Bullettino dell'Istituto di diritto romano 'Vittorio Scialoja'
CIL	Corpus Inscriptionum Latinarum
ILS	Inscriptiones Latinae Selectae
NSDAP	Nationalsozialistische Deutsche Arbeiterpartei
RHDFE	Revue historique de droit français et étranger
RIDA	Revue internationale des droits de l'antiquité
RISG	Rivista Italiana per le Scienze Giuridiche
SDHI	Studia et Documenta Historiae et Iuris
TR	Tijdschrift voor Rechtsgeschiedenis
ZRG	Zeitschrift der Savigny-Stiftung für Rechtsgeschichte, Rom. Abt. Known in 1861–1880 as Zeitschrift für Rechtsgeschichte.

Bibliography

The location of old books (printed between 1500–1800) consulted has been indicated with the following abbreviations: BAV = Biblioteca Apostolica Vaticana, EFR = École Française de Rome, HYK = Helsinki University Library, IDR = Istituto di Diritto Romano e dei Diritti dell'Oriente Mediterraneo, Università degli studi di Roma 'La Sapienza', MPI = Max-Planck-Institut für europäische Rechtsgeschichte.

References to certain books that have numerous editions with different pagination have also been marked with a reference to chapters or some other system of division.

Albanese, Bernardo, 'Volonta negoziale e forma in una testimonianza di Q. Mucio Scaevola', in Manfred Harder, Georg Thielmann (eds.), *De iustitia et iure, Festschrift für U. von Lübtow*, Berlin 1980, 155–161.
Ankersmit, Frank, *History and Tropology*, Berkeley 1994.
Amarelli, Francesco, 'Giuristi e principe. Conflitti compromessi collaborazioni', in D. Mantovani (ed.), *Per la storia del pensiero giuridico Romano da Augusto agli Antonini*, Torino 1996, 183–197.
Anderson, Benedict, *Imagined communities: reflections on the origin and spread of nationalism*, London 1991.
Ankum, J.A., 'Utilitas causa receptum. On the pragmatical methods of the Roman lawyers', in J.A. Ankum et al., *Symbolae iuridicae et historicae Martino David dedicatae I*, Leiden 1968, 1–29.
Arangio-Ruiz, Vincenzo, *Storia del diritto romano*, (7th ed.), Napoli 1985.

Bach, Johannes Augustus, *Historia Jurisprudentiae Romanae*, Lucca 1762. EFR
Balduinus, Franciscus, *Commentarius de iurisprudentia muciana*, Basel 1558. BAV
Balduinus, Franciscus, *De institutione historiae universae et eius cum iurisprudentiae coniunctione prologomenon ... vol. II*, Halle, 1726. MPI
Barnes, Timothy D., 'A senator from Hadrumentum, and three others', in A. Alföldi (ed.), *Bonner Historia-Augusta Colloquium 1968/1969*, Antiquitas 4.7, Bonn 1970, 45–51.
Baron, Equinarius, 'Ad omnes partes Digestorum seu Pandectarum iuris enucleati Manualium', in *Opera*, Paris 1562. BAV
Barrow, Rosemary J., *Lawrence Alma-Tadema*, London 2001.
Bauman, Richard A., *Lawyers and Politics in the Early Roman Empire*, München 1989.
Bauman, Richard A., *Lawyers in Roman Republican Politics*, München 1983.
Bederman, David J., *Classical Canons: Rhetoric, classicism and treaty interpretation*, Aldershot 2001.
Behrends, Okko, 'Die Wissenschaftslehre im Zivilrecht des Q. Mucius Scaevola pontifex', *Nachrichten der Akademie der Wissenschaften in Göttingen, Philologisch-historische Klasse* 7 (1976), 263–304.
Behrends, Okko, 'Otto Lenel', in O. Behrends, F. d'Ippolito (eds.), *Otto Lenel, Gesammelte Schriften I*, Napoli 1990, xix–xxxiii.
Behrends, Okko, 'Das Werk Otto Lenels und die Kontinuität der romanistischen Fragestellungen', *Index* 19 (1991), 169–213.

Behrends, Okko, et al., *Corpus Iuris Civilis: Text und Übersetzung II*, Heidelberg 1995.
Behrends, Okko, 'Gustav Hugo: Der Skeptiker als Wegbereiter der vom Geist der Romantik geprägten Historischen Rechtsschule', in E. Gibbon, *Historische Übersicht des Römischen Rechts, übersetzt, eingeleitet und kommentiert von Gustav Hugo*, Göttingen 1996, 159–226.
Bellomo, Manlio, *The Common Legal Past of Europe, 1000–1800*, Washington 1995.
Bender, Peter, *Die Rezeption des römischen Rechts im Urteil der deutschen Rechtswissenschft*, Frankfurt am Main 1979.
Berger, [Adolf], 'Iurisprudentia', *Pauly-Wissowas Real-Encyclopädie* 10 (1919), 1159–1200.
Berger, Adolf, 'Due note su Salvio Giuliano', in V. Arangio-Ruiz (ed.), *Studi in memoria di Emilio Albertario I*, Milano 1953, 605–621.
Berman, Harold J., *Law and Revolution*, Cambridge 1983.
Bernal, Martin, *Black Athena: The Afroasiatic Roots of Classical Civilization I–II*, London 1987.
Berriat-Saint-Prix, M., *Histoire de droit romain*, Paris 1821.
Bertrand, Jean, *Bioi nomikon, sive de jurisperitis libri duo*, Toulouse 1617. BAV, MPI
Betti, Emilio, 'Jurisprudenz und Rechtsgeschichte vor dem Problem der Auslegung', *Archiv für Rechts- und Sozialphilosophie* 40 (1952), 354–374.
Betti, Emilio, 'Storia e dogmatica del diritto', in *La storia del diritto nel quadro delle scienze storiche: Atti del primo Congresso internazionale della Società Italiana di Storia del Diritto*, Firenze 1966, 105–115.
Betti, Emilio, 'La dogmatica moderna nella storiografia del diritto e della cultura', in G. Crifò (ed.), *Diritto Metodo Ermeneutica*, Milano 1991, 495–521.
Beuchot, A., 'Mayans y Siscar, Grégoire', in *Biographie universelle, ancienne et moderne XXVII*, Paris 1820, 610–612.
Biondo, Flavio, *De militia et iurisprudentia* (ed. Otto Lobeck), Dresden 1892.
Bird, H. W., *The breviarium ab urbe condita of Eutropius*, Liverpool 1993.
Birley, Anthony R., *Hadrian: The restless emperor*, London and New York 1997.
Björne, Lars, *Deutsche Rechtssysteme im 18. und 19. Jahrhundert*, Ebelsbach 1984.
Bohnert, Joachim, *Über die Rechtslehre Georg Friedrich Puchtas (1798–1846)*, Karlsruhe 1975.
Boissonade, J. F., *Eunapii vitae sophistarum*, Paris 1849.
Bona, Ferdinando, 'L'ideale retorico ciceroniano ed il "ius civile in artem redigere"', SDHI 46 (1980), 282–382.
Borkowski, Andrew, *Textbook on Roman Law*, (2nd ed.), London 1997.
Boulard, Louis, *L. Salvius Julianus: Son œuvre, ses doctrines sur la personalité juridique*, Paris 1903.
Bremer, F. P., *Die Rechtslehrer und Rechtsschulen im Römischen Kaiserreich*, Berlin 1868.
Bremer, F. P., *Iurisprudentiae Antehadrianae quae supersunt I*, Lipsiae 1896.
Bretone, Mario, 'La logica dei giuristi di Roma', *Labeo* 1 (1955), 74–78.
Bretone, Mario, 'La tecnica del responso serviano', *Labeo* 16 (1970), 7–16.
Bretone, Mario, 'Pomponio lettore di Cicerone', *Labeo* 16 (1970), 177–182.
Bretone, Mario, 'Cicerone e i giuristi del suo tempo', *Ciceroniana* 3 (1978), 69–77.
Bretone, Mario, *Techniche e ideologie dei giuristi romani*, (2nd ed.), Napoli 1982, 241–254.
Bretone, Mario, 'La "coscienza ironica" della romanistica', *Labeo* 43 (1997), 187–201.
Bretone, Mario, *Diritto e tempo nella tradizione europea*, Bari 2004.

Breuilly, John, 'Historians and the Nation', in P. Burke (ed.), *History and Historians in the Twentieth Century*, Oxford 2002, 55–87.
Broggini, Gerardo, 'Significato della conoscenza storica del diritto per il giurista vivente', in P. Caroni, G. Dilcher (eds.), *Norm und Tradition*, Köln 1998, 59–73.
Brown, Michael F., 'Can Culture be Copyrighted?', *Current Anthropology* 39 (1998), 193–222.
Budaeus, Gulielmus, *Opera tomus III, annotationes in pandectas*, Basel 1557 [reprinted 1969].
Buhl, Heinrich, *Salvius Julianus*, Heidelberg 1886.
Bund, Elmar, 'Salvius Iulianus, Leben und Werk', ANRW II. 15, (1976), 408–454.
Bund, Elmar, 'Fritz Pringsheim', in H. Heinrichs et al. (eds.), *Deutsche Juristen jüdischer Herkunft*, München 1993, 733–740.
Bund, Elmar, 'Rahmenerwägungen zu einem Nachweis stoischer Gedanken in der römischen Jurisprudenz', in Manfred Harder, Georg Thielmann (eds.), *De iustitia et iure: Festschrift für U. von Lübtow*, Berlin 1980, 127–145.
Burke, Peter, *The Fabrication of Louis XIV*, New Haven 1992.
Burke, Peter, *Varieties of Cultural History*, Cambridge 1997.
Burke, Peter, 'Western Historical Thinking in a Global Perspective – 10 Theses', in J. Rüsen (ed.), *Western Historical Thinking: An intercultural debate*, New York 2002, 15–32.
Burmeister, Karl-Heinz, 'Ulrich Zasius', in P. G. Schmidt (ed.), *Humanismus im Deutschen Südwesten*, Sigmaringen 1993, 105–124.
Burrow, J. W., *Gibbon*, Oxford 1985.
Bynkershoek, Cornelius van, *Observationes Juris Romani I*, Leiden 1735. BAV

Cancelli, Filippo, 'Il presunto "ius respondendi" istituito da Augusto', BIDR 90 (1987), 543–568.
Cappellini, Paolo, *Systema Iuris I*, Milano 1984.
Carbonnier, Jean, 'Usus hodiernus pandectarum', in R. H. Graveson et al. (eds.), *Festschrift für Imre Zajtay*, Tübingen 1982, 107–116.
Carcaterra, Antonio, *Le definizioni dei giuristi romani*, Napoli 1966.
Caroni, Pio, 'La storia della codificazione e quella del codice', *Index* 29 (2001), 55–81.
Carr, David, 'Narrative and the Real World: An Argument for Continuity', in B. Fay et al. (eds.), *History and Theory: Contemporary Readings*, Oxford 1998, 137–152.
Carroll, Noël, 'Interpretation, history and narrative', in G. Roberts (ed.), *The History and Narrative Reader*, London 2001, 246–265. Originally appeared in *The Monist* 73.
Cary, E., *Dio's Roman history*, London 1924.
Casavola, Franco, 'Diritto romano e diritto europeo', *Labeo* 40 (1994), 161–169.
Casavola, Francesco Paolo, 'Verso la codificazione traverso la compilazione', in L. De Giovanni, A. Mazzacane (eds.), *La codificazione del diritto dall'antico al moderno*, Napoli 1998, 303–311.
Caunce, Stephen, *Oral History and the Local Historian*, London 1994.
Christ, Karl, 'Aspekte der Antike-Rezeption in der deutschen Altertumswissenschaft des 19. Jahrhunderts', in K. Christ, A. Momigliano (eds.), *L'Antichita nell'Ottocento in Italia e Germania*, Bologna 1988, 21–37.
Clark, J. C. D., 'National identity, state formation and patriotism: the role of history in the public mind', *History Workshop Journal* 29 (1990), 95–102.
Coing, Helmut, 'Zum Einfluß der Philosophie des Aristoteles auf die Entwicklung des römischen Rechts', ZRG 69 (1952), 24–59.

Coing, Helmut, 'Klassizismus in der Geschichte des römischen Rechts', in G. E. von Grunebaum, W. Hartner, *Klassizismus und Kulturverfall*, Frankfurt am Main 1960, 69–74.
Coing, Helmut, 'Der juristische Systembegriff bei Rudolf von Ihering', in J. Blühdorn, J. Ritter (eds.), *Philosophie und Rechtswissenschaft*, Frankfurt am Main 1969, 149–171.
Coing, Helmut, 'European common law: Historical foundations', in M. Cappelletti (ed.), *New Perspectives for a Common Law of Europe*, Leiden etc. 1978, 31–44.
Costa, Emilio, *Storia delle fonti del diritto romano*, Milano 1909.
Craddock, Patricia, *Edward Gibbon, luminous historian 1772–1794*, Baltimore and London 1989.
Crifò, Giuliano, 'Contributo dei giuristi allo studio del mondo antico', in *Soggetti individuali e soggetti collettivi*, Milano 1995, 543–545.
Crifò, Giuliano, *Materiali di storiografia romanistica*, Torino 1998.
Crifò, Giuliano, 'Pandettisti e storicisti nel diritto romano oggi', *Diritto romano attuale* 1 (1999), 11–28.
Cuiacius, Iacobus, *Opera quae de iure fecit I*, Frankfurt 1623. HYK, BAV
Cuiacius, Iacobus, 'De origine iuris et iuris auctoribus ex Enchiridio Pomponii cum commentario', in *Opera II*, Frankfurt 1623. HYK
Cuq, Edouard, *Les institutions juridiques des Romains II*, Paris 1908.

Daube, David, 'Hadrian's rescript to some ex-praetors', ZRG 67 (1950), 511–518.
David, Jean-Michel, *Le patronat judiciare au dernier siècle de la république Romaine*, (B.E.F.A.R. 277), École Française de Rome 1992.
De Francisi, Pietro, 'Per la storia dell'editto perpetuo nel periodo postclassico', RIDA 4 (1950), Mel. F. de Visscher III, 319–360.
De Giovanni, Lucio, 'Giuristi e principe. Aspetti e problemi', in Mantovani, Dario (ed.), *Per la storia del pensiero giuridico Romano da Augusto agli Antonini*, Torino 1996, 199–214.
Dilcher, Gerhard, 'Von der Geschichtlichen Rechtswissenschaft zur Geschichte des Rechts', in P. Caroni, G. Dilcher (eds.), *Norm und Tradition*, Köln 1998, 109–141.
Di Marzo, Salvatore, *Saggi critici sui Libri di Pomponio 'Ad Quintum Mucium'*, Palermo 1899.
Diplovatatius, Thomas, *De claris iuris consultis*, (ed. F. Schulz), Berlin und Leipzig 1919.
D'Ippolito, Federico, 'Cicerone e i maestri di Servio', in F. Cancelli (ed.), *La giustizia tra i popoli nell'opera e nel pensiero di Cicerone, Atti del convegno*, Roma (1993).
Ducos, Michèle, *Les Romains et la loi. Recherches sur les rapports de la philosophie grecque et la tradition romaine à la fin de la République*, Paris 1984.
Du Rivail, Aymar, *Civilis historiae iuris*, Lyon 1551. BAV

Earl, Donald, *The Moral and Political Traditions of Rome*, London 1967.
Ebrard, Friedrich, 'Das zeitliche Rangverhältnis der Konstitutionen De confirmatione Digestorum 'Tanta' und *'Dedoken'*, ZRG 40 (1919), 113–135.
Eckert, Jörn (ed.), *Der praktische Nutzen der Rechtsgeschichte: H. Hattenhauer zum 8. September 2001*, Heidelberg 2003.
Eco, Umberto, *Serendipities*, London 1998.
Ernst, Wolfgang, 'Fritz Schulz', in J. Beatson, R. Zimmermann (eds.), *Jurists Uprooted*, Oxford 2004, 105–204.

Falchi, Gian Luigi, 'Interpretazione "tipica" nella "Causa Curiana"', SDHI 46 (1980), 383–430.
Falchi, Gian Luigi, *Le controversie tra Sabiniani e Proculiani*, Milano 1981.
Falk, Ulrich, *Ein Gelehrter wie Windscheid*, Frankfurt am Main 1989.
Feltmannus, Gerhardus, *Commentarius ad Digestorum seu Pandectarum lib. I et II.*, Leipzig 1678. BAV
Ferrary, Jean-Louis, 'Naissance d'un aspect de la recherche antiquaire. Les premiers travaux sur les lois romaines: de l'*Epistula ad Cornelium* de Filelfo à *Historia iuris civilis* d'Aymar du Rivail', in M. H. Crawford, C. R. Ligota (eds.), *Ancient History and the Antiquarian*, London 1995, 33–72.
Ferro, Marc, *The use and abuse of history or how the past is taught*, London 1984.
Finley, Moses I., *Ancient Slavery and Modern Ideology*, New York 1980.
Finley, Moses I., *Ancient History: Evidence and Models*, London 1985.
Finley, Moses I., *Democracy Ancient and Modern*, (2nd ed.), London 1985.
Finley, Moses I., *The use and abuse of history*, London 1986.
Finnis, John, 'The Truth in Legal Positivism' in R. P. George (ed.), *The Autonomy of Law: Essays on Legal Positivism*, Oxford 1996, 195–214.
Fioravanti, Maurizio, *Giuristi e costituzione politica nell'ottocento tedesco*, Milano 1979.
Flaig, Egon, *Den Kaiser herausfordern*, Frankfurt am Main 1992.
Fögen, Marie Theres, *Römische Rechtsgeschichten*, Göttingen 2002.
Forster, Valentinus, *De historia iuris romani*, Helmstedt 1609. HYK
Franklin, Julian H., *Jean Bodin and the sixteenth-century revolution in the methodology of law and history*, New York 1963.
Frier, Bruce W., *The Rise of the Roman Jurists: Studies in Cicero's pro Caecina*, Princeton 1985
Frier, Bruce W., 'Why Did the Jurists Change Roman Law? Bees and Lawyers revisited', *Index* 22 (1994), 135–145.
Frier, Bruce W., 'Roman law's descent into history', *Journal of Roman Archaeology* 13 (2000), 446–448.
Frier, Bruce W., 'Law, Roman, sociology of', in *The Oxford Classical Dictionary*, (3rd, rev. ed.), Oxford 2003, 823–825.
Fuhrmann, Manfred, *Das systematische Lehrbuch*, Göttingen 1960.

Gadamer, Hans-Georg, *Wahrheit und Methode*, (2nd ed.), Tübingen 1965.
Gamauf, Richard, 'Die Kritik am Römischen Recht im 19. und 20. Jahrhundert', *Orbis Iuris Romani* 2 (1996), 48–60.
Gaudemet, Jean, 'Organicisme et évolution dans la conception de l'histoire du droit chez Jhering', in F. Wieacker, C. Wollschläger (eds.), *Jherings Erbe*, Göttingen 1970, 29–39.
Gaudemet, Jean, 'Histoire et système dans la méthode de Savigny', in *Hommage à René Dekkers*, Bruxelles 1982, 117–133.
Gaudemet, Jean, 'La Codification. Ses formes et ses fins', in J. Roset Esteve (ed.), *Estudios en homenaje al Profesor Juan Iglesias I*, Madrid 1988, 309–327.
Gaudemet, Jean, *Les naissances du droit*, Paris 1997.
Ghisalberti, Carlo, *Gian Vincenzo Gravina: Giurista e storico*, (Ius nostrum 8), Varese 1962.
Ghisalberti, Carlo, 'Il commentario dello Zasio al Dig. 1.2.2', *La Parola del passato* 21 (1966), 81–110.
Giardina, Andrea, Vauchez, André, *Il mito di Roma: Da Carlo Magno a Mussolini*, Roma 2000.
Giaro, Tomasz, 'Romanistische Constructionsplaudereien: Auf den Spuren eines anachronistischen Begriffes', *Rechtshistorisches Journal* 10 (1991), 209–232.

Giaro, Tomasz, 'Von der Genealogie der Begriffe zur Genealogie der Juristen. De Sabinianis et Proculianis fabulae', *Rechtshistorisches Journal* 11 (1992), 508–554.
Giaro, Tomasz, 'Die Illusion der Wissenschaftlichkeit', *Index* 22 (1994), 107–134.
Giaro, Tomasz, 'Geltung und Fortgeltung des römischen Juristenrechts', ZRG 111 (1994b), 66–94.
Giaro, Tomasz, 'Römisches Recht, Romanistik und Rechtsraum Europa', *Ius commune* 22 (1995), 1–16.
Giaro, Tomasz, 'Max Kaser 1906–1997', *Rechtshistorisches Journal* 16 (1997), 231–357.
Giaro, Tomasz, *Aktualisierung Europas: Gespräche mit Paul Koschaker*, Genova 2000.
Giaro, Tomasz, 'Diritto romano attuale. Mappe mentali e strumenti concettuali', in P. G. Monateri, T. Giaro, A Somma, *Le radici comuni del diritto europeo: Un cambiamento di prospettiva*, Roma 2005, 77–168.
Gibbon, Edward, *The Decline and Fall of the Roman Empire IV*, London 1977 [1788].
Gibbon, Edward, *The Decline and Fall of the Roman Empire I*, London 1980 [1788].
Gibbon, Edward, *Historische Übersicht des Römischen Rechts, übersetzt, eingeleitet und kommentiert von Gustav Hugo*, Göttingen 1996 [1789].
Gilmore, Myron P., *Argument from Roman Law in Political Thought 1200–1600*, Cambridge 1941.
Giphanius, Hubertus, *Oeconomia juris sive dispositio methodica*, Strasbourg 1612. BAV
Girard, P.-F., 'L'Edit perpetuel', RHDFE 29 (1904), 117–164.
Girard, P.-F., 'La date de l'édit de Salvius Julianus', RHDFE 34 (1910), 5–40.
Girard, Paul, *Manuel élémentaire de droit romain*, Paris 1911.
Girard, P.-F., 'L'enseignement du droit romain en 1912', RHDFE 36 (1912), 557–572.
Giuffrè, Vincenzo, *La traccia di Quinto Mucio*, Napoli 1993.
Gleitman, Henry et al., *Psychology*, (6th ed.), New York 2004.
Glenn, H. Patrick, *Legal Traditions of the World*, Oxford 2000.
Glück, Christian F., *Ausführliche Erläuterung der Pandekten I*, (2nd ed.), Erlangen 1797.
Goldhill, Simon, *Love, Sex & Tragedy: Why Classics Matter*, London 2005.
Gordon, W. M. and Robinson, O. F., *The Institutes of Gaius*, New York 1988.
Gothofredus, Jacobus, *Fontes quatuor iuris civilis in unum collecti*, Geneve 1653. BAV
Gothofredus, Jacobus, *Codex Theodosianus cum perpetuis commentariis*, Lyon 1665. MPI
Gothofredus, Jacobus, *Manuale juris seu parva juris mysteria*, Napoli 1766. BAV
Goudy, Henry, *Trichotomy in Roman Law*, Oxford 1910.
Gradenwitz, Otto, *Interpolationen in den Pandekten: Kritische Studien*, Berlin 1887.
Gravina, Gian V., *De ortu et progressu juris civilis*, Leipzig 1704. HYK
Gregorovius, Ferdinand, *Geschichte des römischen Kaisers Hadrian und seiner Zeit*, Königsberg 1851.
Grossi, Paolo, *Mitologie giuridiche della modernità*, Milano 2001.
Grosso, Giuseppe, *Problemi sistematici nel diritto romano, cose – contratti*, Torino 1974.
Grosso, Giuseppe, 'Labeone e Capitone: tradizionalismo e conformismo nei giuristi [1947]', in *Scritti storici giuridici*, Torino 2000, 144–150.

Grotius, Hugo, *De Iure belli ac pacis Libri tres in quibus Ius Naturae et Gentium item iuris publici praecipua explicantur*, (eds. B. J. A. De Kanter et al.), Aalen 1993 [1625].

Grotius, Hugo, *Florum sparsio ad ius Iustinianeum*, Halle 1729. MPI

Grotius, Wilhelm, *Vitae Jurisconsultorum*, Leiden 1690. MPI

Guarino, Antonio, 'Salvius Iulianus: Profilo biobibliografico', *Labeo* 10 (1964), (reprint of the original printed in Catania by Crisafulli 1945), 364-426.

Guarino, Antonio, 'Il "ius publice respondendi"', RIDA 1.2 (1949), 401-419.

Guarino, Antonio, 'La leggenda sulla codificazione dell'editto e la sua genesi', in *Atti del congresso internazionale di diritto romano e di storia del diritto, Verona 27.-29.9.1948, II*, Milano 1951, 169-182.

Guarino, Antonio, 'La pretesa codificazione dell'editto', in V. Arangio-Ruiz (ed.), *Studi in memoria di Emilio Albertario I*, Milano 1953, reprinted in *Le ragioni del giurista*, Napoli 1983, 265-288.

Guarino, Antonio, 'Alla ricerca di Salvio Giuliano', *Labeo* 5 (1959), 67-78.

Guarino, Antonio, 'Spunti sul metodo di Giuliano', *Labeo* 12 (1966), 393-395.

Guarino, Antonio, 'La pista dell'"avunculus"', *Index* 3 (1972), 421-426.

Guarino, Antonio, 'La formazione dell'editto perpetuo', ANRW II. 13, (1980), 62-102.

Guarino, Antonio, 'L'editto in casa Cupiello', *Labeo* 36 (1990), 50-57.

Guarino, Antonio, 'Inter amicos', *Labeo* 40 (1994), 349-352.

Haferkamp, Hans-Peter, 'Recht als System bei Georg Friedrich Puchta', *Forum historiae iuris* 19.11.2003.

Haferkamp, Hans-Peter, *Georg Friedrich Puchta und die 'Begriffsjurisprudenz'*, Frankfurt am Main 2004.

Hägerström, Axel, *Der römische Obligationsbegriff I*, Uppsala 1927.

Hahn, Otto, 'Das Kaisertum', *Das Erbe der Alten VI*, Leipzig 1913.

Hardwick, Lorna, *Reception Studies*, Oxford 2003.

Harries, Jill, *Law and Empire in Late Antiquity*, Cambridge 1999.

Harrison, Robert, Jones, Aled and Lambert, Peter, 'The institutionalisation and organisation of history', in P. Lambert, P. Schofield (eds.), *Making history: an introduction to the history and practices of a discipline*, London 2004, 9-25.

Haubold, C. G., *Institutionum iuris romani privati historico dogmaticarum lineamenta*, Leipzig 1826.

Heineccius, Johann Gottlieb, *Elementa iuris civilis secundum ordinem Pandectarum*, Amsterdam 1728. HYK

Heineccius, Johann Gottlieb, 'Salvio Iuliano iurisconsultorum sua aetate coryphaeo, seu exercitatio XXIV', in *Opera II*, Geneva 1746, 798-818. BAV

Heineccius, Johann Gottlieb, *Antiquitatum Romanarum Iurisprudentiam Illustrantium Syntagma secundum ordinem Institutionum*, Geneva 1747. BAV

Heineccius, Johann Gottlieb, *Historia Iuris Civilis Romani et Germanici*, Strasbourg 1751. HYK

Heineccius, Johann Gottlieb, 'Historia edictorum edictique perpetui', in *Opera XI*, Napoli 1777, 3-194. BAV

Heineccius, Johann Gottlieb, 'Edicti perpetui, ordini et integritati suae restituti', in *Opera XI*, Napoli 1777b, 195-340. BAV

Heirbaut, Dirk, 'Comparative Law and Zimmermann's *ius commune*: A life line or a death sentence for legal history', in R. van den Bergh (ed.), *Ex iusta causa traditum. Essays in honour of Eric H. Pool*, (Fundamina, Editio specialis), Pretoria 2005, 136-153.

Helssig, R., 'Die römische Rechtswissenschaft im Zeitalter des Augustus', in V. Gardthausen (ed.), *Augustus und seine Zeit 1.1*, Leipzig 1891, 1318-1333.
Henderson, B.W., *The Life and Principate of the Emperor Hadrian*, London 1923.
Henel, Nicolaus, *De veteribus jure consultis commentarius*, Leipzig 1654. BAV
Heuss, Alfred, *Theodor Mommsen und das 19. Jahrhundert*, Kiel 1956.
Highet, Gilbert, *The Classical Tradition*, Oxford 1967.
Hingley, Richard, *Roman Officers and English Gentlemen*, London 2000.
Hobsbawm, Eric, 'Introduction: Inventing Traditions', in E. Hobsbawm, T. Ranger (eds.), *The Invention of Tradition*, Cambridge 1983, 1-14.
Hoetink, H.R., 'Les notions anachroniques dans l'historiographie du droit', TR 23 (1955), 1-20.
Hondius, Ewould, 'The supremacy of Western law', in L. De Ligt et al. (eds.), *Viva vox iuris romani*, Amsterdam 2002, 337-342.
Honoré, A.M., *Gaius*, Oxford 1962.
Honoré, Tony, *Emperors and Lawyers*, (2nd ed.), Oxford 1994.
Honoré, Tony, *Ulpian: Pioneer of Human Rights*, Oxford 2002.
Horak, Franz, *Rationes decidendi*, Innsbruck 1969.
Horak, Franz, 'Die römischen Juristen und der "Glanz der Logik"', in D. Medicus, H.H. Seiler (eds.), *Festschrift für Max Kaser zum 70. Geburtstag*, München 1976, 29-56.
Horvat, Marijan, 'Note intorno allo "ius respondendi"', in A. Guarino, L. Labruna (eds.), *Synteleia Vincenzo Arangio-Ruiz 2*, Napoli 1964, 710-716.
Hotomannus, Franciscus, *De iurisconsultorum vitis*, Frankfurt 1587. MPI
Huber, Ulrich, 'Oratio inauguralis habita Franekerae ... exhibens historiam juris Romani', *Opera minora et rariora I*, Utrecht 1746, 101-123. BAV
Hugo, Gustav, *Lehrbuch der Geschichte des Römischen Rechts*, (Lehrbuch eines civilistischen Cursus 3, 3rd ed.), Berlin 1806.
Hugo, Gustav, *Lehrbuch der Geschichte des Römischen Rechts*, (Lehrbuch eines civilistischen Cursus 3, 8th ed.), Berlin 1822.
Hugo, Gustav, 'Vorrede', in E. Gibbon, *Historische Übersicht des Römischen Rechts, übersetzt, eingeleitet und kommentiert von Gustav Hugo*, Göttingen 1996 [1789].
Huschke, D., 'Ueber den Gregorianus und Hermogenianus Codex', ZRG 6 (1867), 279-331.
Hylland Eriksen, Thomas, *Ethnicity and Nationalism*, London 1993.

Iggers, Georg, *Historiography in the Twentieth century*, Hanover 1997.

Jackson, John, *Tacitus: the histories*, London 1962.
Jakobs, Horst H., *Die Begründung der geschichtlichen Rechtswissenschaft*, Paderborn 1992.
Jhering, Rudolf von, *Der Kampf um's Recht*, (6th ed.), Wien 1880.
Jhering, Rudolf von, *Der Besitzwille: Zugleich eine Kritik der herrschenden juristischen Methode*, Aalen 1968 [1889].
Jhering, Rudolf von, *Scherz und Ernst in der Jurisprudenz*, Leipzig 1892.
Jhering, Rudolf von, *Geist des römischen Rechts I, III*, (vol. I, 11th ed. [1907], vol. III, 10th ed. [1906]), Aalen 1993.
Jhering, Rudolf von, *Law as Means to an End*, (translated by I. Husik), New York 1968.
Jhering, Rudolf von, *Ist die Jurisprudenz eine Wissenschaft? Jhering's Wiener Antrittsvorlesung vom 16. Oktober 1868*, Göttingen 1998.
Johnston, David, 'The Renewal of the Old', *The Cambridge Law Journal* 56 (1997), 80-95.

Johnston, David, *Roman Law in Context*, Cambridge 1999.
Jörs, Paul, *Römische Rechtswissenschaft zur Zeit der Republik I: Bis auf die Catonen*, Berlin 1888.
Jörs, Paul, 'Geschichte und System des römischen Privatrechts', in Kohlrausch, Kaskel (eds.), *Enzyklopädie des Rechts- und Staatswissenschaft, Abteilung Rechtswissenschaft II*, Berlin 1927.
Jousserandot, Louis, *L'édit perpétuel*, Paris 1883.

Kalman, Laura, *The Strange Career of Legal Liberalism*, New Haven 1996.
Karlowa, Otto, *Römische Rechtsgeschichte I*, Leipzig 1885.
Kaser, Max, *Römisches Recht als Gemeinschaftsordnung*, Tübingen 1939.
Kaser, Max, *Das römische Privatrecht I*, München 1955.
Kaser, Max, *Zur Methode der römischen Rechtsfindung*, Göttingen 1962.
Kaser, Max, *Römische Rechtsgeschichte*, Göttingen 1965.
Kaser, Max, *Römische Rechtsquellen und angewandte Juristenmethode*, Wien 1986.
Kelley, Donald, *Foundations of Modern Historical Scholarship: Language, Law, and History in the French Renaissance*, New York and London 1970.
Kelley, Donald, *Historians and the Law in Postrevolutionary France*, Princeton 1984.
Kelley, Donald, *The Human Measure: Social Thought in the Western Legal Tradition*, Cambridge 1990.
Kelley, Donald, *The Descent of Ideas*, Aldershot 2002.
Kelly, J. M., *Roman Litigation*, Oxford 1966.
Kelsen, Hans, *Reine Rechtslehre*, Wien 1934.
Kipp, Theodor, *Geschichte der Quellen des Römischen Rechts*, Leipzig 1909.
Kisch, Guido, 'Die humanistische Jurisprudenz', in *La storia del diritto nel quadro delle scienze storiche: Atti del primo Congresso internazionale della Società Italiana di Storia del Diritto*, Firenze 1966, 469-490.
Kohlhepp, Rolf, 'Franz Wieacker und die NS-Zeit', ZRG 122 (2005), 203-223.
Kornemann, E., 'Der Jurist Salvius Julianus und Kaiser Didius Julianus', *Klio* 6 (1906), 178-184.
Koschaker, Paul, 'Die Krise des römischen Rechts und die romanistische Rechtswissenschaft', *Schriften der Akademie für Deutsches Recht: Gruppe Römisches Recht und fremde Rechte* 1 (1938), 1-86.
Koschaker, Paul, *Europa und das römische Recht*, (2nd ed.), München 1953.
Koschaker, Paul, *Europa und das römische Recht*, (4th ed.), München 1966.
Kriechbaum, Maximiliane, 'Römisches Recht und neuere Privatrechtsgeschichte in Savignys Auffassung von Rechtsgeschichte und Rechtswissenschaft', in R. Zimmermann (ed.), *Rechtsgeschichte und Privatrechtsdogmatik*, Heidelberg 1999, 41-63.
Krüger, Paul, *Geschichte der Quellen und Litteratur des Römischen Rechts*, Leipzig 1888.
Krüger, Paul, *Geschichte der Quellen und Litteratur des Römischen Rechts*, (2nd ed.), München und Leipzig 1912.
Kübler, Bernhard, *Geschichte des Römischen Rechts*, Leipzig 1925.
Kunkel, Wolfgang, 'Das Wesen des ius respondendi', ZRG 66 (1948), 423-457.
Kunkel, Wolfgang, 'Über Lebenszeit und Laufbahn des Juristen Julians', *IURA* 1 (1950), 192-203.
Kunkel, Wolfgang, *Die Römischen Juristen: Herkunft und soziale Stellung*, (reprint of 2nd edition 1967), Köln 2001.
Kunkel, Wolfgang, *An Introduction to Roman Legal and Constitutional History* (translated by J. M. Kelly), Oxford 1972.
Kunkel, Wolfgang, 'Theodor Mommsen als Jurist', *Chiron* 14 (1984), 369-380.

Kuntze, Johannes Emil, *Das Jus respondendi in unserer Zeit: Ideen über die moderne Rechtsfortbildung*, Leipzig 1858.
Kuttner, Stephan, 'The Scientific Investigation of Medieval Canon Law: The Need and the Opportunity', *Speculum* 24 (1949), now in *Gratian and the schools of law, 1140–1234*, London 1983, vol. I, 493–501.

Laetus, Pomponius, *De magistratibus et sacerdotiis, praeterea de diversis legibus Romanorum*, Basel 1535. BAV
Landauer, Carl, 'Henry Sumner Maine's Grand Tour: Roman Law in Ancient Law', *Current Legal Issues* 6 (2003), 135–157.
Lantella, Lelio, *Le opere della giurisprudenza romana nella storiografia*, Torino 1979.
La Pira, Giorgio, 'La genesi del sistema nella giurisprudenza romana: 1. Problemi generali', in *Studi in onore di F. Virgili*, Siena 1935.
La Pira, Giorgio, 'La genesi del sistema nella giurisprudenza romana: 2. L'arte sistematrice', *Bullettino dell'Istituto di diritto romano 'Vittorio Scialoja'* 42 (1934), 336–355.
La Pira, Giorgio, 'La genesi del sistema nella giurisprudenza romana: 3. Il metodo', *Studia et Documenta Historiae Iuris* 1 (1935), 319–348.
La Pira, Giorgio, 'La genesi del sistema nella giurisprudenza romana: 4. Il concetto di scienza', *Bullettino dell'Istituto di diritto romano 'Vittorio Scialoja'* 44 (1936–37), 131–159.
Leibnitz, Gothofredus Guillelmus, 'Methodus nova discendae docendaeque iurisprudentiae', in *Opera omnia IV*, Geneve 1768, 169–230. BAV
Lenel, Otto, *Palingenesia juris civilis*, Leipzig 1889.
Lenel, Otto, *Das Edictum Perpetuum: Ein Versuch zu seiner Wiederherstellung*, (3rd ed.), Aalen 1956 [1927].
Lepointe, Gabriel, *Quintus Mucius Scaevola: Sa vie et son œuvre juridique: Ses doctrines sur le Droit pontifical*, Paris 1926.
Levine, Joseph, *The autonomy of history: truth and method from Erasmus to Gibbon*, Chicago 1999.
Lewis, Bernard, *History: Remembered, Recovered, Invented*, Princeton 1975.
Liebeschuetz, J. H. W. G., 'The uses and abuses of the concept of "decline" in later Roman history or Was Gibbon politically incorrect', in *Recent research in Late Antique Urbanism, Journal of Roman Archaeology, Supp.* 42 (2001), 233–238.
Lind, L. R., 'Roman moral conservatism', in C. Deroux (ed.), *Studies in Latin Literature and Roman History I*, Bruxelles 1979, 7–58.
Lobban, Michael, 'Nineteenth Century English Jurisprudence', *Journal of Legal History* 16 (1995), 34–62.
Lokin, J. H. A., 'The End of an Epoch: Epilegomena to a century of interpolation criticism', in R. Feenstra et al. (eds.), *Collatio Iuris Romani: Études dédiées à Hans Ankum I*, Amsterdam 1995, 261–273.
Lorich, Johann, *Iureconsulti. Catalogus iureconsultorum veterum, quotquod aut vita, aut scriptis celebres sunt, succinto Carmine descripti*, Basel 1545. BAV
Lübtow, Ulrich von, 'Cicero und die Methode der römischen Jurisprudenz', in P. Koschaker (ed.), *Festschrift für Leopold Wenger zu seinem 70. Geburtstag*, München 1944, 224–235
Lübtow, Ulrich von, 'De iustitia et iure', ZRG 66 (1948), 458–565.
Lübtow, Ulrich von, 'Miscellanea', in M. Lauria (ed.), *Studi in onore di Vincenzo Arangio-Ruiz II*, Napoli 1953, 377–378.
Luig, Klaus, 'Römische und germanische Rechtsanschauung, individualistische und soziale Ordnung', in J. Rückert, D. Willoweit (eds.), *Die Deutsche Rechtsgeschichte in der NS-Zeit*, Tübingen 1995, 95–137.

Luig, Klaus, 'Johann Gottlieb Heineccius als Kritiker des Naturrechts von Hugo Grotius', in E. Donnert (ed.), *Europa in der Früher Neuzeit: Festschrift für Günter Mühlpfordt* 2, Weimar 1997.

Maffei, Domenico, *Gli inizi dell'umanesimo giuridico*, Milano 1956.
Magdelain, Andre, 'Ius respondendi', RHDFE 29 (1950), 1–22.
Maiansius, Gregorius, *Ad triginta jurisconsultorum omnia fragmenta quae exstant in juris civilis corpore commentarii*, Geneva 1764. BAV
Maine, Henry Sumner, *Ancient Law*, London 1917 [1861].
Mantello, Antonio, *Per una storia della giurisprudenza romana: Il problema dei 'Miscelliones'*, Milano 1984.
Mantello, Antonio, 'Di certe smanie "romanistiche" attuali', *Diritto romano attuale* 4 (2000), 37–60.
Mantovani, Dario, 'Iuris scientia e honores', in S. Romano (ed.), *Nozione formazione e interpretazione del diritto: Ricerche dedicate al F. Gallo I*, Napoli 1997.
Mantovani, Dario, 'L'editto come codice e da altri punti di vista', in L. De Giovanni, A. Mazzacane (eds.), *La codificazione del diritto dall'antico al moderno*, Napoli 1998, 129–178.
Mantovani, Dario, 'L'édit comme code', in E. Lévy (ed.), *La codification des lois dans l'antiquité*, Paris 2000, 257–272.
Marshall, B. A., 'The Date of Q. Mucius Scaevola's Governorship of Asia', *Athenaeum* 54 (1976), 117–130.
Martini, Remo, *Le definizioni dei giuristi romani*, Milano 1966.
Martino, Armando de, 'Illuminismo e codificazione', in L. De Giovanni, A. Mazzacane (eds.), *La codificazione del diritto dall'antico al moderno*, Napoli 1998, 339–376.
Mascovius, Gotfrid, *De sectis Sabinianorum et Proculianorum in jure civili diatriba*, Leipzig 1728. BAV
Mayer-Maly, Theo, *Römisches Recht*, (2nd ed.), Wien 1999.
Mazzacane, Aldo, *Savigny e la storiografia giuridica tra storia e sistema*, Napoli 1974.
Mazzacane, Aldo, '"Il leone fuggito dal circo": pandettistica e diritto comune europeo', *Index* 29 (2001), 97–111.
McNeill, William H., 'Mythistory, or Truth, Myth, History, and Historians', *The American Historical Review* 91 (1986), 1–10.
Menagius, Egidius, *Juris civilis amoenitate*, (3rd ed.), Frankfurt & Leipzig 1680. HYK
Merlin, Alfred, 'Le jurisconsulte Salvius Julianus proconsul d'Afrique', *Mémoires de l'Académie des inscriptions et belles-lettres* 43.2 (1941), 93–122.
Mette, Hans J., *Ius civile in artem redactum*, Göttingen 1954.
Meyer, Elizabeth A., *Legitimacy and law in the Roman world: tabulae in Roman belief and practice*, Cambridge 2004.
Minkkinen, Panu, *Thinking Without Desire: A First Philosophy of Law*, Oxford 1999.
Miquel, Juan, 'Stoische Logik und römische Jurisprudenz', ZRG 87 (1970), 85–122.
Momigliano, Arnaldo, 'Ancient History and the Antiquarian', in *Studies in Historiography*, London 1966a, 1–39.
Momigliano, Arnaldo, 'The consequences of new trends in the history of ancient law', in *Studies in Historiography*, London 1966b, 239–256.
Mommsen, Theodor, 'Die Bedeutung des römischen Rechts', in *Gesammelte Schriften III: Juristische Schriften III*, Berlin 1907, 591–600.
Mommsen, Theodor, *Römisches Staatsrecht*, Basel 1952 [1887].
Mommsen, Theodor, 'Salvius Julianus', ZRG 23 (1902), 54–60.

Mommsen-Krüger-Watson (eds.), *The Digest of Justinian*, Philadelphia 1985.
Monateri, Pier G., 'Black Gaius: A Quest for the Multicultural Origins of the "Western Legal Tradition"', *Hastings Law Journal* 51 (2000), 479–555.
Monateri, Pier G., 'Gaio nero', in P. G. Monateri, T. Giaro, A Somma, *Le radici comuni del diritto europeo: Un cambiamento di prospettiva*, Roma 2005, 19–76.
Moyle, J. B., *The Institutes of Justinian*, (5th ed.), Oxford 1955.
Münzer, Friedrich and Kübler, Bernhard, 'Quintus Mucius', *Pauly-Wissowas Real-Encyclopädie* 16 (1933), 437–446.

Nietzsche, Friedrich, 'Vom Nutzen und Nachteil der Historie für das Leben', in *Unzeitgemässe Betrachtungen*, Leipzig 1930, 95–195.
Noodt, Gerard, 'Commentarius ad Digesta seu Pandectas', *Opera omnia III*, Napoli 1786. BAV
Nora, Pierre, 'Between Memory and History', in *Realms of Memory: Rethinking the French Past*, New York 1996, 1–20.
Norman, Andrew, 'Telling It Like It Was: Historical Narratives On Their Own Terms', in B. Fay et al. (eds.), *History and Theory: Contemporary Readings*, Oxford 1998, 153–171.
Nörr, Dieter, 'Spruchregel und Generalisierung', ZRG 89 (1972), 18–93.
Nörr, Dieter, *Divisio und partitio. Bemerkungen zur römischen Rechtsquellenlehre und zur antiken Wissenschaftstheorie*, Berlin 1972.
Nörr, Dieter, 'Drei Miszellen zur Lebensgeschichte des Juristen Salvius Julianus', in Alan Watson (ed.), *Daube Noster: Essays in Legal History for David Daube*, Edinburgh and London 1974, 233–252.
Nörr, Dieter, 'Pomponius oder zum Geschichtsverständnis der römischen Juristen', ANRW II. 15 (1976), 497–604.
Nörr, Dieter, 'I giuristi romani: Tradizionalismo o progresso?', BIDR 84 (1981), 9–33.
Nörr, Dieter, 'Romanistische Phantasien', *Rechtshistorisches Journal* 11 (1992), 163–165.
Nörr, Dieter, 'Innovare', *Index* 22 (1994), 61–86.

Oexle, Otto G., 'Das Mittelalter als Waffe', in O. G. Oexle (ed.), *Geschichtswissenschaft im Zeichen des Historismus*, Göttingen 1996, 163–215.
Ong, Walter J., *Orality and Literacy*, London 1982.
Orestano, Riccardo, 'Diritto romano, tradizione romanistica e studio storico del diritto', RISG 87 (1950), 156–264.
Orestano, Riccardo, 'Diritto e storia nel pensiero giuridico del secolo XVI', in *La storia del diritto nel quadro delle scienze storiche: Atti del primo Congresso internazionale della Società Italiana di Storia del Diritto*, Firenze 1966, 389–415.
Orestano, Riccardo, *Introduzione allo studio del diritto romano*, Bologna 1987.
Orgeval, Bernard d', 'La carrière de Salvius Julianus e la codification de l'édit', RHDFE 26 (1948) 301–311.
Orgeval, Bernard d', *L'Empereur Hadrien: Œuvre législative et administrative*, Paris 1950.
Ors, Alvaro d', 'La signification de l'œuvre d'Hadrien dans l'histoire du droit romain', in Piganiol et al. (eds.), *Les empereurs romains d'Espagne*, Paris 1965, 147–158.
Osler, Douglas J., 'The myth of European Legal History', *Rechtshistorisches Journal* 16 (1997), 393–410.

Osler, Douglas J., 'Preface', in *Bibliographica iuridica* 2, Ius Commune Sonderheft 131, Frankfurt am Main 2000, vii–xxv.

Osler, Douglas J., 'Teramo and the *ius commune*', in P. Campanella, R. Viola (eds.), *Le Cinquecentine della Facoltà di giurisprudenza*, Pescara 2004, xiv–xix.

Palazzolo, Nicola, 'Il princeps, i giuristi, l'editto. Mutamento istituzionale e strumenti di trasformazione del diritto privato da Augusto ad Adriano', in F. Milazzo (ed.), *Res publica e princeps*, Napoli 1996, 289–322.

Palonen, Kari, *Quentin Skinner: History, Politics, Rhetoric*, Cambridge 2003.

Panziroli, Guido, *De claris legum interpretibus*, Leipzig 1721. IDR

Paradisi, Bruno, 'La storia del diritto della storiografia contemporanea', in *La storia del diritto nel quadro delle scienze storiche: Atti del primo Congresso internazionale della Società Italiana di Storia del Diritto*, Firenze 1966, vii–xlvii.

Paricio, Javier, 'El *ius publice respondendi ex auctoritate principis*', in J. Paricio (ed.), *Poder político y derecho en la Roma Clásica*, Madrid 1996, 85–105.

Paricio, Javier, 'La vocación de Servio Sulpicio Rufo', in M. Schermaier (ed), *Iurisprudentia universalis: Festschrift für Theo Mayer-Maly zum 70. Geburtstag*, Köln 2002, 549–561.

Parrow, Kathleen A., 'Prudence or Jurisprudence? Etienne Pasquier and the *Responsa Prudentium* as a Source of Law', in A. T. Grafton and J. H. M. Salmon (eds.), *Historians and Ideologues*, Rochester 2001, 49–70.

Pasini, Dino, *Saggio sul Jhering*, Milano 1959.

Peltonen, Matti, 'After the Linguistic Turn? Hayden White's Tropology and History Theory in the 1990s', in Castrén et al. (eds.), *Between Sociology and History*, Helsinki 2004, 87–101.

Pernice, Alfred, *Marcus Antistius Labeo*, Halle 1873.

Perowne, S., *Hadrian*, London 1960.

Piano Mortari, Vinzenzo, 'La sistematica come ideale umanistico dell'opera di Francesco Connano', in *La storia del diritto nel quadro delle scienze storiche: Atti del primo Congresso internazionale della Società Italiana di Storia del Diritto*, Firenze 1966, 521–531.

Piano Mortari, Vincenzo, 'L'idea di codificazione nel rinascimento', in L. De Giovanni, A. Mazzacane (eds.), *La codificazione del diritto dall'antico al moderno*, Napoli 1998, 325–336.

Postema, Gerald J., 'Law's autonomy and public practical reason', in R. P. George (ed.), *The Autonomy of Law: Essays on Legal Positivism*, Oxford 1996, 79–118.

Premerstein, Anton von, 'Vom Werden und Wesen des Prinzipats', *Abhandlungen der Bayerischen Akademie der Wissenschaften; Philosophisch-historische Abteilung Neue Folge*, Heft 15 (1937).

Pringsheim, Fritz, 'The Legal Policy and Reforms of Hadrian', *Journal of Roman Studies* 24 (1934), 144–149.

Pringsheim, Fritz, 'Zur Bezeichnung des Hadrianischen Edictes als edictum perpetuum', in *Symbolae Friburgensis in Honorem Ottonis Lenel*, Leipzig 1934b, 1–39.

Pringsheim, Fritz, 'Höhe und Ende der römischen Jurisprudenz', in *Gesammelte Abhandlungen I*, Heidelberg 1961, 53–62.

Provera, Giuseppe, 'Ancora sul "ius respondendi"', SDHI 28 (1962), 342–360.

Puchta, Georg F., 'Betrachtungen über alte und neue Rechtssysteme' [1829], in *Kleine zivilistische Schriften*, Aalen 1970 [1851], 221–239.

Puchta, Georg F., 'Nachträgliches über das Ius respondendi', in *Kleine zivilistische Schriften*, Aalen 1970b [1851], 297–303.

Puchta, Georg F., 'Die Quellen des römischen Rechts', in *Kleine zivilistische Schriften*, Aalen 1970c [1851], 611–650.
Puchta, Georg F., 'Geschichte des Rechts bei dem römischen Volk', in *Cursus der Institutionen*, (8th ed.), Leipzig 1875.
Puchta, Georg F., *Pandekten*, (12th ed.), Leipzig 1877.
Pugliese, Giovanni, 'I pandettisti fra tradizione romanistica e moderna scienza del diritto', in *Scritti giuridici scelti III: Diritto romano*, Napoli 1985, 446–447. First published in RISG 17 (1973) 89–132.
Pugliese, Giovanni, 'L'autonomia del diritto rispetto agli altri fenomeni e valori sociali nella giurisprudenza romana', in *La storia del diritto nel quadro delle scienze storiche: Atti del primo Congresso internazionale della Società Italiana di Storia del Diritto*, Firenze 1966.

Quadrato, Renato, 'Iuris conditor', *Index* 22 (1994), 87–106.

Raevardus, Iacobus, 'Ad titulum de diversis Regulis Juris antiqui Commentarius anno 1568' in *Opera omnia I*, Napoli 1779, 146–150. BAV
Ranchinius, Guilelmius, *Edictum perpetuum Adrianeum*, Parma 1721 [1597]. IDR
Ranke, Leopold von, *Geschichte der romanischen und germanischen Völker von 1494 bis 1514*, (2nd ed.), Leipzig 1874.
Reimann, Mathias, 'Rechtsgeschichte im Common Law', in P. Caroni, G. Dilcher (eds.), *Norm und Tradition*, Köln 1998, 209–229.
Rhodes, P.J., *Ancient Democracy and Modern Ideology*, London 2003.
Roberts, Geoffrey, 'Introduction: the history and narrative debate, 1960–2000', in G. Roberts (ed.), *The History and Narrative Reader*, London 2001, 1–21.
Robinson, Olivia F., *The Sources of Roman Law*, London 1997.
Rotondi, Giovanni, *Leges publicae populi romani*, Hildesheim 1962 [1912].
Rousso, Henry, *The Vichy syndrome: History and Memory in France since 1944*, Cambridge 1991.
Rowan, Steven, *Ulrich Zasius: A Jurist in the German Renaissance 1461–1535*, Frankfurt am Main 1987.
Rudorff, A.F., 'Ueber die Julianische Edictsredaktion', ZRG 3 (1864), 1–89.
Rudorff, A.F., *Edicti perpetui quae reliqua sunt*, Leipzig 1869.
Russo, Daniel, 'Religion civique et art monumental à Florence au XIVe siècle. La décoration peinte de la salle capitulaire à Sainte-Marie-Nouvelle', in A. Vauchez (ed.), *La religion civique à l'époque médiévale et moderne (chrétienté et islam)*, Roma 1995, 279–296.
Rutilius, Bernard, *Iurisconsultorum vitae, veterum quidem*, Basel s.a. [1537]. BAV

Salomies, Olli, *Die römischen Vornamen*, Helsinki 1987.
Samuel, Raphael, *Theatres of memory 1: Past and present in contemporary culture*, London 1999.
Sandberg, Kaj, *Magistrates and Assemblies: A Study of Legislative Practice in Republican Rome*, Acta Instituti Romani Finlandiae 24, Rome 2001.
Sanio, Friedrich D., *De Antiquis Regulis Iuris*, Königsberg 1833.
Sanio, Friedrich D., 'Beiträge zur Geschichte der Regulae Juris', in *Rechtshistorische Abhandlungen und Studien*, Königsberg 1845, 136–152.
Sanio, Friedrich D., *Zur Geschichte der römischen Rechtswissenschaft*, Napoli 1981 [1858].
Sarsila, Juhani, *Some aspects of the concept of virtus in Roman literature until Livy*, Jyväskylä 1982.

Savigny, Friedrich C. von, 'Einleitung zu den Pandekten 1811–1842', in A. Mazzacane (ed.), *Friedrich Carl von Savigny, Vorlesungen über juristische Methodologie 1802–1842*, Frankfurt am Main 1993, 174–216.
Savigny, Friedrich C. von, *Vom Beruf unserer Zeit für Gesetzgebung und Rechtswisseschaft*, Heidelberg 1814. Reprinted in H. Akamatsu, J. Rückert (eds.), *F. C. von Savigny, Politik und Neuere Legislationen*, Frankfurt am Main 2000.
Savigny, Friedrich C. von, *Pandektenvorlesung 1824/25*, Frankfurt am Main 1993.
Savigny, Friedrich C. von, *Geschichte des römischen Rechts im Mittelalter IV*, Darmstadt 1956 [1826].
Savigny, Friedrich C. von, *Geschichte des römischen Rechts im Mittelalter VI*, Bad Homburg 1950 [1831].
Savigny, Friedrich C. von, *System des heutigen Römischen Rechts I*, Berlin 1849.
Scarano Ussani, Vincenzo, *L'utilità e la certezza. Compiti e modelli del sapere giuridico in Salvio Giuliano*, Milano 1987.
Schiavone, Aldo, 'Quinto Mucio teologo', *Labeo* 20 (1974), 315–361.
Schiavone, Aldo, *Nascita della giurisprudenza*, (2nd ed.), Bari 1976.
Schiavone, Aldo, *Giuristi e nobili nella Roma repubblicana*, Bari 1987.
Schiavone, Aldo, 'Forme normative e generi letterari. La cristallizzazione del *ius civile* e dell'editto fra tarda repubblica e primo principato', in L. De Giovanni, A. Mazzacane (eds.), *La codificazione del diritto dall'antico al moderno*, Napoli 1998, 51–72.
Schiavone, Aldo, *The End of the Past: Ancient Rome and the Modern West*, Harvard 2002.
Schiller, Arthur A., 'Jurist's Law', in *An American Experience in Roman Law*, Göttingen 1971, 148–160, reprinted from 58 *Columbia Law Review* (1958), 1226–1238.
Schmidlin, Bruno, 'Horoi, pithana und regulae', in ANRW II. 15 (1976), 91–109.
Schmidlin, Bruno, *Die römischen Rechtsregeln*, Köln 1970.
Schneider, A., *Die drei Scaevola Ciceros*, München 1879.
Schneider, R., *Questionum de Servio Sulpicio Rufo*, Leipzig 1834.
Schröder, Jan, *Christian Thomasius und die Reform der juristischen Methode*, Leipzig 1997.
Schröder, Jan, *Recht als Wissenschaft: Geschichte der juristischen Methode vom Humanismus bis zur historischen Schule (1500–1850)*, München 2001.
Schulz, Fritz, *Prinzipien des Römischen Rechts*, Berlin 1934.
Schulz, Fritz, *History of Roman Legal Science*, Oxford 1946.
Schwarz, Andreas B., 'Zur Entstehung des modernen Pandectensystems', ZRG 42 (1921), 578–610.
Schönbauer, Ernst, 'Die Entwicklung des "ius publice respondendi"', *IURA* 1 (1950), 288.
Schönbauer, Ernst, 'Zur Entwicklung des "ius publice respondendi"', *IURA* 4 (1953), 224–227.
Segrè, Gino, *Di alcune pericolose tendenze nello studio sistematico del diritto romano*, Cagliari 1892.
Seidl, Erwin, 'Wege zu Julian', W. Becker (ed.), *Sein und Werden im Recht: Festgabe für Ulrich von Lübtow zum 70. Geburtstag*, Berlin 1970, 215–222.
Senn, Félix, *Les origines de la notion de jurisprudence*, Paris 1926.
Senn, Marcel, *Rechtshistorisches Selbstverständnis im Wandel*, Zürich 1982.
Serangeli, Sandro, *'Abstenti', 'beneficium competentiae' e 'codificazione' dell'editto*, Ancona 1989.
Serangeli, Sandro, 'Ancora su Dio 36,40,1 e la codificazione dell'editto', in S. Romano (ed.), *Nozione formazione e interpretazione del diritto: Ricerche dedicate al F. Gallo II*, Napoli 1997, 267–278.

Serrao, Feliciano, 'Il giurista Salvio Giuliano nell'iscrizione di "Thuburbo Maius"', in *Atti del III Congresso Internazionale di Epigrafia Greca e Latina*, Roma 1959, 395–413.
Settis, Salvatore, *Futuro del 'classico'*, Torino 2004.
Sherman, Charles P., *Roman Law in the Modern World I*, (2nd ed.), New Haven 1922.
Siber, Heinrich, 'Der Ausgangspunkt des "ius respondendi"', ZRG 61 (1941), 397–402.
Skinner, Quentin, 'Meaning and understanding in the history of ideas', in *Visions of Politics I*, Cambridge 2002, 67–79.
Sohm, Rudolf, *Institutionen: Geschichte und System des römischen Privatrechts*, (14th ed.), Leipzig 1911.
Sokolowski, Paul, *Die Philosophie im Privatrecht I*, Halle 1907.
Solazzi, Siro, 'Glosse a Gaio', in *Studi in onore di Salvatore Riccobono*, Palermo 1936, 70–191.
Spruit, Jop E., *Enchiridium*, Deventer 1994.
Spruit, Johannes E., 'Lebendig und inspirierend. Das "Corpus iuris civilis" als Grundlage der europäischen Rechtssysteme', *Index* 32 (2004), 221–225.
Stahlmann, Ines, 'Vom Despoten zum Kaiser. Zum deutschen Augustusbild im 19. Jahrhundert', in K. Christ, A. Momigliano (eds.), *L'Antichità nell'Ottocento in Italia e Germania*, Bologna 1988, 303–319.
Starr, June, 'The "Invention" of Early Legal Ideas: Sir Henry Maine and the Perpetual Tutelage of Women', in J. Starr, J. Collier (eds.), *History and Power in the Study of Law*, Ithaca 1989, 345–368.
Steedman, C., 'Battlegrounds: History in primary Schools', *History Workshop Journal* 17 (1984), 102–112.
Stein, Peter, *Regulae Iuris: From Juristic Rules to Legal Maxims*, Edinburgh 1966.
Stein, Peter, 'The place of Servius Sulpicius Rufus in the development of Roman legal science', in O. Behrends et al. (eds.), *Festschrift für Franz Wieacker zum 70. Geburtstag*, Göttingen 1978, 175–184.
Stein, Peter, 'Le scuole', in D. Mantovani (ed.), *Per la storia del pensiero giuridico Romano da Augusto agli Antonini*, Torino 1996, 1–13.
Stein, Peter, *Roman law in European History*, Cambridge 1999.
Steinwenter, Artur, 'Römisches Recht und Begriffsjurisprudenz', in *Recht und Kultur. Aufsätze und Vorträge eines österreichischen Rechtshistorikers*, Graz 1958, 52–56.
Stephanitz, Dieter von, *Exakte Wissenschaft und Recht: der Einfluß von Naturwissenschaft und Mathematik auf Rechtsdenken und Rechtswissenschaft in zweieinhalb Jahrtausenden; ein historischer Grundriß*, Berlin 1970.
Stinzing, Roderich, *Geschichte der Deutschen Rechtswissenschaft*, München und Leipzig 1880.
Stolfi, Emanuele, *Studi sui 'libri ad edictum' di Pomponio I*, Napoli 2002.
Stolzenberg, Nomi Maya, 'A book of laughter and forgetting: Kalman's "Strange career" and the marketing of civic Republicanism', *Harvard Law Review* 111 (1998), 1024–1084.
Stroux, Johannes, *Römische Rechtswissenschaft und Rhetorik*, Potsdam 1949.
Stryk, Samuel, *Specimen usus moderni pandectarum I*, Halle 1713. HYK
Syme, Ronald, *The Roman revolution*, Oxford 1939.

Talamanca, Mario, 'Lo Schema "Genus–Species" nelle sistematiche dei giuristi romani', *La Filosofia Greca e il Diritto Romano II*, Roma 1977.
Talamanca, Mario, 'Développements socio-économiques et jurisprudence romaine à la fin de la république', in *Studi in onore di Cesare Sanfilippo 7*, Milano 1987.

Tellegen, Jan W., 'Oratores, Iurisprudentes and the "Causa Curiana"', RIDA 30 (1983).
Tellegen, Jan W., and Tellegen-Couperus, Olga E., 'Law and Rhetoric in the causa Curiana', *Orbis Iuris Romani* 6 (2000), 171–202.
Terrasson, Antoine, *Histoire de la jurisprudence romaine*, Paris 1750. BAV
Teubner, Gunther, *Recht als autopoietisches System*, Frankfurt am Main 1989.
Thieme, Hans, 'L'œuvre juridique de Zasius', in P. Mesnard (ed.), *Pédagogues et juristes*, Paris 1963, 31–38
Thomas, Philip J., '*Usus modernus Pandectarum*; a spurious transplant', RIDA 47 (2000), 483–496.
Thomas, Yan, 'La romanistique allemande et l'état depuis les pandectistes', in H. Bruhns et al. (eds.), *Die späte römische Republik*, Paris 1997, 113–126.
Thomasius, Christian, *Naevorum jurisprudentiae romanae antejustinianae libri duo*, (2nd ed.), Magdeburg 1707. HYK
Torrent, Armando, 'La *ordinatio edicti* en la politica juridica de Adriano', *Anuario de Historia del Derecho Español* 53 (1983), 17–44.
Torrent, Armando, *Salvius Iulianus liber singularis de ambiguitatibus*, Salamanca 1971.
Tosi, Renzo, *Dizionario delle sentenze latice e greche*, (4th ed.), Milano 1992.
Troje, Hans Erich, 'Wissenschaftlichkeit und System in der Jurisprudenz des 16. Jahrhunderts', in J. Blühdorn, J. Ritter (eds.), *Philosophie und Rechtswissenschaft*, Frankfurt am Main 1969, 63–88.
Tuori, Kaius, 'Weber and the Ideal of Roman law', *Current Legal Issues* 6 (2003), 201–214.

Ubaldis, Baldus de, *In primam Digesti Veteris partem Commentaria*, Venezia 1586. BAV
Urban, Greg, *Metaculture: How Culture Moves through the World*, Minneapolis 2001.

Vacca, Letizia, 'La "svolta adrianea" e l'interpretazione analogica', in S. Romano (ed.), *Nozione formazione e interpretazione del diritto: Ricerche dedicate al F. Gallo II*, Napoli 1997, 441–479.
Vano, Cristina, *'Il nostro autentico Gaio': Strategie della scuola storica alle origini della romanistica moderna*, Napoli 2000.
Vansina, Jan, *Oral Tradition as History*, London 1985.
Vari, Massimo, 'Diritto romano "ius commune" europeo?', *Index* 30 (2002), 183–185.
Vernant, Jean-Pierre, 'Greek Tragedy: Problems of Interpretation', in E. Macksey, E. Donato (eds.), *The Structuralist Controversy*, Baltimore 1970, 273–289.
Viehweg, Theodor, *Topik und Jurisprudenz*, München 1965 [1953].
Villey, Michel, 'Logique d'Aristote et droit romain', RHDFE 29 (1951), 309–328.
Visscher, Ferdinand de, 'Le "ius publice respondendi"', RHDFE 15 (1936), 615–650.
Vogt, Heinrich, 'Hadrians Justizpolitik im Spiegel der römischen Reichsmünzen', in *Festschrift Fritz Schulz II*, Weimar 1951, 193–200.
Voigt, Moritz, 'Über das Aelius- und Sabinus-System, wie über einige verwandte Rechts-Systeme', *Abhandlungen der Philologisch-historischen Klasse der Königlich sächsischen Gesellschaft der Wissenschaften* 7.4 (1879).
Voppel, Reinhard, *Der Einfluß des Naturrechts auf den Usus modernus*, Köln 1996.

Waldstein, Wolfgang, 'Konsequenz als Argument klassischer Juristen', ZRG 92 (1975), 26–68.

Waldstein, Wolfgang, 'Cicero, Servius und die "Neue Jurisprudenz"', *IURA* 44 (1993), 85–147.
Walker, Bryan, *The fragments of the Perpetual Edict of Salvius Julianus*, Cambridge 1877.
Wallinga, Tammo, *Tanta / Dedoken: Two introductory constitutions to Justinian's Digest*, Groningen 1989.
Watson, Alan, *Law-making in the later Roman republic*, Oxford 1974.
Watson, Alan, *The Evolution of Law*, Oxford 1985.
Weber, Max, *Economy and Society, an outline of interpretative sociology II*, Berkeley 1978.
Wenger, Leopold, *Institutionen des Römischen Zivilprozessrechts*, München 1925.
Wenger, Leopold, 'Ueber Stempel und Siegel', ZRG 42 (1921), 611–638.
Wenger, Leopold, 'Praetor und Formel', in *Sitzungsberichte der Bayerischen Akademie der Wissenschaften; Philosophisch-philologische und historische Klasse*, Jahrgang 1926, 3. Abhandlung, 1–122.
Wesel, Uwe, *Geschichte des Rechts*, München 1997.
White, Hayden, *Tropics of discourse: Essays in cultural criticism*, Baltimore 1978.
White, Hayden, *Metahistory: The Historical Imagination in Nineteenth-Century Europe*, Baltimore 1990 [1973].
Whitman, James Q., *The Legacy of Roman Law in the German Romantic Era*, Princeton 1990.
Whitman, James Q., 'Long Live the Hatred of Roman Law!', *Rechtsgeschichte* 3 (2003), 40–57.
Wieacker, Franz, 'Studien zur Hadrianischen Justizpolitik', in A. Ehrhardt et al. (eds.), *Romanistische Studien: Freiburger Rechtsgeschichtliche Abhandlungen* 5 (1935), 43–81.
Wieacker, Franz, *Privatrechtsgeschichte der Neuzeit*, Göttingen 1952.
Wieacker, Franz, 'Griechische Wurzeln des Institutionen-Systems', ZRG 70 (1953), 93–126.
Wieacker, Franz, 'Aufstieg, Blüte und Krisis der Kodifikationsidee', in *Festschrift für Gustav Boehmer*, Bonn 1954, 34–50.
Wieacker, Franz, *Gründer und Bewahrer*, Göttingen 1959.
Wieacker, Franz, *Vom römischen Recht*, (2nd ed.), Stuttgart 1961.
Wieacker, Franz, 'Eclipse et permanence du droit romain', in P. Mesnard (ed.), *Pédagogues et juristes*, Paris 1963, 59–72.
Wieacker, Franz, 'The Causa Curiana and contemporary Roman Jurisprudence', *Irish Jurist* 2 (1967).
Wieacker, Franz, 'Über das Verhältnis der römischen Fachjurisprudenz zur griechisch-hellenistischen Theorie', *IURA* 20 (1969), 448–477.
Wieacker, Franz, 'Augustus und die Juristen seiner Zeit', TR 37 (1969b), 331–349.
Wieacker, Franz, 'Cicero und die Fachjurisprudenz seiner Zeit', *Ciceroniana* 3 (1978).
Wieacker, Franz, 'Respondere ex auctoritate principis', in J. A. Ankum et al. (eds.), *Satura Roberto Feenstra oblata*, Fribourg 1985, 71–94.
Wieacker, Franz, *Römische Rechtsgeschichte I*, München 1988.
Wieacker, Franz, *A history of private law in Europe*, (translation by T. Weir), Oxford 1995.
Wilhelm, Walter, *Zur juristischen Methodenlehre im 19. Jahrhundert*, Frankfurt am Main 1958.
Winkel, Laurens, 'Le droit romain et la philosophie grecque', in TR 65 (1997), 373–384.

Winkel, Laurens, 'Quintus Mucius Scaevola once again', in R. van den Bergh (ed.), *Ex iusta causa traditum. Essays in honour of Eric H. Pool*, (Fundamina, Editio specialis), Pretoria 2005, 425–433.
Wilton, A. and Bignamni, I. (eds.), *Grand Tour: The Lure of Italy in the Eighteenth Century*, London 1996.
Wiseman, Timothy P., *The Myths of Rome*, Exeter 2004.
Wolf, Erik, *Große Rechtsdenker der Deutschen Geistesgeschichte*, Tübingen 1951.
Wolf, Erik, 'Ulrich Zasius (1461–1535): Monument historique ou exemple actuel?', in *Mélanges en l'honneur de Jean Dabin I*, Paris 1963, 373–396.
Wolf, Joseph G., 'Die Gedenkrede', in *In memoriam Franz Wieacker*, Göttingen 1995, 17–42.
Wright, W. C., *Philostratus and Eunapius: the lives of the sophists*, London 1912.
Wyke, Maria, *Projecting the Past: Ancient Rome, Cinema, and History*, New York 1997.

Zachariä, C. E., *Ius Graeco-Romanum 2*, Leipzig 1856.
Zanker, Paul, *The Power of Images in the Age of Augustus*, Ann Arbor 1990.
Zasius, Ulrich, 'In iuris civilis originem scholia, quibus l. II. ff. de orig. iuris elucidatur', in *Singularia responsa sive intellectus juris singulares*, Basel 1541, 207–290. BAV, HYK.
Zimmermann, Reinhard, 'Roman and Comparative Law: The European Perspective', *Journal of Legal History* 16 (1995), 21–33.
Zimmermann, Reinhard, *Roman law, contemporary law, European law*, Oxford 2000.
Zwalve, Willem J., 'Einige Bemerkungen zur Constitutio *Tanta/Dedoken* § 18', TR 51 (1983), 135–149.

Index locorum

☞ Literary sources

Amm. 27,9,5   98
Aristides Or. 48,9   141
Aristides Or. 26,90–109   161
Ascon.
   Pis. 62   32
   Corn. 67,20–23   32
   Corn. 59   142
Aug. civ. 4,27   32
R. Gest. div. Aug. 34,2   94
Marcus Aurelius *Ta eis heauton* 4,50   141
Aur. Vict. Caes. 19,1–2   139
Cic.
   Att. 6,1,15   27
   Att. 8,3,5–6   30
   Brut. 30,115   30
   Brut. 39,145   30
   Brut. 40,147   28
   Brut. 41,152   26, 31
   Brut. 43,161   28
   Brut. 64,229   28
   Caecin. 18,53   28, 30
   Caecin. 24,69   29
   fam. 7,10   29
   fam. 7,22   29
   Lael. 1,1   27, 28
   leg. 1,15,42–16,43   29
   leg. 2,19,47   28, 29
   Mur. 28   101
   nat. deor. 3,32,80   31
   off. 1,6,19   31
   off. 1,32,116   27
   off. 2,16,57   28
   off. 2,65   103
   off. 3,11,47   28, 32
   off. 3,15,62   28
   off. 3,17,70   29, 44
   de orat. 1,11,45   31
   de orat. 1,39,180   29, 30
   de orat. 1,42,190   31
   de orat. 1,53,229   30
   Rab. perd. 7,21,100   28
   top. 29   29, 44
   top. 31   23, 31
   Verr. 2,10,27   28

Verr. 2,13,34   28
Verr. 2,21,51   28
Verr. 2,49,122   28
Verr. 3,90,209   28
Verr. 4,59,133   28
Colum. 1,4,6   32
Dio Cassius 36,40   142, 155
Dio Cassius 57,17   114
Diodorus Siculus
   37,5–6   32
   37,29   32
   38/39,17   32
Eunapius Vitae sophistarum 23,3   80
Eutr. 8,17   138
Fronto p. 54–55 v. d. H.   141
Gell.
   3,2,12   33
   4,1,17   44
   5,19,6   33
   6,15,2   33
   13,10   80
   17,7   33, 44
Hier. chron. a. Abr. 131 p. Chr.   138
Hist. Aug.
   Did. 1,1   139
   Hadr. 18   82, 141
   Pius 12,1   141
Isid. orig. 5,14   85
Lact. inst. 5,11,18   85
Liv. perioch. 70   32
Liv. perioch. 86   32
Lucan. 2,126–130   32
Plin. nat. 18,32   32
Plin. epist. 6,1,5,3   80
Quint. inst. 12,3,7   85
Sen. apocol. 12,2   109
Sen. epist. 94,27   85
Suet.
   gramm. 10,2   82
   gramm. 22   114
   Cal. 34   85, 91, 94, 109
   Nero 37,1   82, 109
Tac. ann. 3,75   113
Tac. ann. 16,9   109
Thucydides 1,20   175

Val. Max.
   4,1,11 32
   6,4,4 32
   8,15–16 32
Varro
   ling. 6,4,30 32
   ling. 5,15,83 32
   ling. 7, 105 44
Vell. 2,26,2 32
Vitr. 1,1,3 84

☞ Legal sources

Cod. Iust.
   1,14,12,4 81
   1,17,2,20 81
   2,1,3 142
   2,2,2 142
   2,4,13pr 142
   2,11,15 142
   2,11,18 142
   2,12,5 142
   2,12,13 142
   2,19,3 142
   2,19,4 142
   2,25,1 142
   2,32,1 142
   2,54,1 142
   3,42,5 82
   4,5,10,1 140
   4,5,11pr 81
   4,18,2,1a 81
   4,26,12 142
   4,29,19 142
   5,21,2 142
   5,71,11,1 142
   6,2,18 142
   6,9,6 142
   6,10,1 142
   6,20,9 142
   6,20,11 142
   6,26,10pr 81
   6,37,26pr 81
   7,1,1 81
   7,7,1pr 81
   7,16,21 142
   7,18,1,1 81
   7,50,2 142
   7,75,6 142
   8,6,1 142
   8,30,3 142
   8,37,4 82
   8,46,9 142
   8,47,10,5 81
   9,35,8 142
Cod. Theod.
   4,4,3,3 82
   4,4,7pr 139
   11,36,26 139
Dig.
   1,1,1pr 23
   1,1,10,17 23
   1,2,2,38 42
   1,2,2,41 26, 33
   1,2,2,43 34
   1,2,2,47 113
   1,2,2,48–50 74
   1,2,2,48–49 88
   1,2,2,49 103
   1,2,2,52 109
   1,3,11 162, 166
   1,5,2 142
   3,1,1,3 80
   7,8,4,1 34
   8,2,7pr 34
   8,3,15 34
   9,1,1,11 34
   9,2,31pr 34
   9,2,31 44
   9,2,39pr 34
   12,1,40pr 81
   13,6,5,3 34
   17,1,48pr 34
   17,2,11 34
   17,2,30pr 34
   17,2,30 44
   18,1,59 34, 44
   18,1,66,2 34, 44
   18,2,13pr 34
   19,1,40 34
   20,2,9 81
   21,2,75pr 44
   21,2,75 34
   22,1,32pr 81
   24,1,51pr 34
   26,1,3pr 34
   27,1,30pr 81, 82
   28,5,35,3 34, 44
   31,77,29 142
   32,29,1 34
   32,55pr 34, 35
   33,1,7pr 34
   33,5,9,2 34
   33,9,3pr 34, 35
   33,9,3,6 34, 35
   33,9,3,9 34, 35, 44

34,2,10   34, 35
34,2,19,9   34, 35, 44
34,2,27pr   34, 35, 44
34,2,33pr   34, 35, 45
34,2,34pr   34
34,2,34,1   34, 45
34,2,34,2   34, 45
34,7   42
37,14,17pr   81, 82
39,3,1,3   34
39,3,1,4   34
40,7,29,1   34
40,7,39pr   34
40,12,23pr   34
41,2,3,23   26, 34, 35, 44
41,2,25,2   34
43,24,1,5   34, 35
43,24,5,8   34, 45
43,24,5,9   34
44,4,4,14   81
44,7,52,6   142
45,1,4,1   42
45,1,91,3   23
45,1,115,2   34
46,3,81,1   34
47,2,77,1   34
47,11,5   142
49,5,7,1   142
49,14,1,1   142
49,15,4   35
50,7,18   34
50,13,5,2   142
50,16,25,1   34, 35
50,16,98,1   34
50,17,73   25, 33, 36
50,17,73,4   45

Gaius
    Inst. 1,7   77, 78, 105, 111
    Inst. 1,188   26, 33, 44
    Inst. 3,149   33, 44
Inst. Iust. 1,2,8   78, 80, 81, 88, 105

☞ Inscriptions

AE
    1903, 319   84
    1904, 58   84
    1904, 81   84
    1908, 35   84
    1916, 20bis   83
    1916, 87   83
    1916, 88   83
    1926, 29   84
    1963, 73   83
    1975, 793   83
    1980, 35   84
    1988, 1051   83
Corpus de Inscripciones latinas de Andalucia, IV: Granada, 131   84
CIL
    III, 2936   84
    III, 141882   84
    V, 714   141
    V, 1026add.   84
    VI, 375   141
    VI, 855   141
    VI, 1422   82, 83
    VI, 1534   82, 83
    VI, 1602   84
    VI, 1621   84
    VI, 1628   82, 83
    VI, 1853   84
    VI, 9487   84
    VI, 10229   82, 83
    VI, 10525   82, 83
    VI, 12133   82, 83
    VI, 30865   141
    VI, 33865   82, 83
    VI, 33867   84
    VI, 33868   84
    VI, 38585   84
    VI, 41294   82, 83
    VI, 41307   84
    VIII, 1640   84
    VIII, 2220   82, 83
    VIII, 7059   82, 83
    VIII, 7060   182, 83
    VIII, 7061   82, 83
    VIII, 8489a   84
    VIII, 10490   82, 83
    VIII, 10899   84
    VIII, 11045   82, 83
    VIII, 12418   84
    VIII, 15876   84
    VIII, 17614   82, 83
    VIII, 17714   82, 83
    VIII, 18348   84
    VIII, 20164   84
    VIII, 24094   81, 140
    VIII, 27505   84
    X, 569   84
    X, 3163   84
    X, 4919   82, 83
    X, 6662   84
    X, 7457   141

X, 8387   84
XII, 3339   84
XII, 5900   84
XIV, 175add.   82, 83
XIV, 2916   84
XIV, 5348   83
XV, 7240   141
XVI, 95   141

ILS
  1067   82, 83
  1455   84
  1456   82, 83
  7742   84
  7742c   84
  7743   84
  7748   84
  7750   82, 83
  7776   141
  8365   82, 83

Inscr. Aq. 705   84
ILA 244   141
ILAlg.
  1, 1362   84
  1, 3064   84
  1, 3071   84
  2, 645   82, 83
  2, 646   82, 83
  2, 647   82, 83

ILAfr. 273   83
ILPBardo 357   83
Inscr. Ital. XIII. 1 (Fasti Ostienses)
  28,148   141
IRT 647   84